New Waves in

New Waves in Philosophy

Series Editors: **Vincent F. Hendricks** and **Duncan Pritchard**

Titles include:

Otavio Bueno and Oystein Linnebo (*editors*)
NEW WAVES IN PHILOSOPHY OF MATHEMATICS

Boudewijn DeBruin and Christopher F. Zurn (*editors*)
NEW WAVES IN POLITICAL PHILOSOPHY

Allan Hazlett (*editor*)
NEW WAVES IN METAPHYSICS

Vincent F. Hendricks and Duncan Pritchard (*editors*)
NEW WAVES IN EPISTEMOLOGY

P.D. Magnus and Jacob Busch (*editors*)
NEW WAVES IN PHILOSOPHY OF SCIENCE

Yujin Nagasawa and Erik J. Wielenberg (*editors*)
NEW WAVES IN PHILOSOPHY OF RELIGION

Jan Kyrre Berg Olsen, Evan Selinger and Søren Riis (*editors*)
NEW WAVES IN PHILOSOPHY OF TECHNOLOGY

Thomas S. Petersen, Jesper Ryberg and Clark Wolf (*editors*)
NEW WAVES IN APPLIED ETHICS

Sarah Sawyer (*editor*)
NEW WAVES IN PHILOSOPHY OF LANGUAGE

Kathleen Stock and Katherine Thomson-Jones (*editors*)
NEW WAVES IN AESTHETICS

Forthcoming:

Jesús Aguilar, Andrei A. Buckareff and Keith Frankish (*editors*)
NEW WAVES IN PHILOSOPHY OF ACTION

Thom Brooks (*editor*)   1006064971 ⌐
NEW WAVES IN ETHICS

Nikolaj Pedersen and Cory Wright (*editors*)
NEW WAVES IN TRUTH

Future Volumes

New Waves in Philosophy of Mind
New Waves in Meta-Ethics
New Waves in Formal Philosophy
New Waves in Philosophy of Law

New Waves in Philosophy

Series Standing Order ISBN 978–0–230–53797–2 (hardcover)
Series Standing Order ISBN 978–0–230–53798–9 (paperback)
(outside North America only)

You can receive future titles in this series as they are published by placing a standing order. Please contact your bookseller or, in case of difficulty, write to us at the address below with your name and address, the title of the series and one of the ISBNs quoted above.

Customer Services Department, Macmillan Distribution Ltd, Houndmills, Basingstoke, Hampshire RG21 6XS, England

---

New Waves in Metaphysics

Edited By

Allan Hazlett
Fordham University, New York, USA

First published 2010 by
PALGRAVE MACMILLAN

Palgrave Macmillan in the UK is an imprint of Macmillan Publishers Limited,
registered in England, company number 785998, of Houndmills, Basingstoke,
Hampshire RG21 6XS.

Palgrave Macmillan in the US is a division of St Martin's Press LLC,
175 Fifth Avenue, New York, NY 10010.

Palgrave Macmillan is the global academic imprint of the above companies
and has companies and representatives throughout the world.

Palgrave® and Macmillan® are registered trademarks in the United States,
the United Kingdom, Europe and other countries.

ISBN: 978–0–230–22232–8 hardback
ISBN: 978–0–230–22233–5 paperback

This book is printed on paper suitable for recycling and made from fully
managed and sustained forest sources. Logging, pulping and manufacturing
processes are expected to conform to the environmental regulations of the
country of origin.

A catalogue record for this book is available from the British Library.

A catalog record for this book is available from the Library of Congress.

10 9 8 7 6 5 4 3 2 1
19 18 17 16 15 14 13 12 11 10

Printed and bound in Great Britain by
CPI Antony Rowe, Chippenham and Eastbourne

Contents

Figures

Chapter 11

Chapter 12

Foreword to *The New Waves in Philosophy* Series

The aim of this series is to gather the young and up-and-coming scholars in philosophy to give their view of the subject now and in the years to come, and to serve a documentary purpose, that is, "this is what they said then, and this is what happened". It will also provide a snap-shot of cutting-edge research that will be of vital interested to researchers and students working in all subject areas of philosophy.

The goal of the series is to have a *New Waves* volume in every one of the main areas of philosophy. We would like to thank Palgrave Macmillan for taking on the entire *New Waves in Philosophy* series.

VINCENT F. HENDRICKS
DUNCAN PRITCHARD
(Series editors)

Contributors

Ross P. Cameron is a lecturer in philosophy at the University of Leeds. His main interests are in metaphysics. Recently he has published on presentism, the open future, monism, modality, and why there are no musical works.

Sara Rachel Chant is assistant professor in philosophy at the University of Missouri-Columbia. Much of her work is concerned with issues at the intersection of philosophy of mind and metaphysics. She is the author of a number of recent articles on collective intention and action. She and her co-author, Zachary Ernst, are currently preparing a book on collective action. She can be reached at chants@missouri.edu.

Joshua Glasgow works on a variety of topics in moral and political philosophy, including issues that intersect with metaphysics and the philosophy of language.

Allan Hazlett teaches in the philosophy department at Fordham University in New York City. His main research interests are in epistemology, metaphysics, and aesthetics. He can be reached at allanhazlett@gmail.com.

Neal Judisch is assistant professor of philosophy at the University of Oklahoma. His mean areas of research are in metaphysics, philosophy of mind, and philosophical theology.

Uriah Kriegel is a professor of philosophy and cognitive science (and Associate Director of the Center for Consciousness Studies) at the University of Arizona.

Douglas Kutach teaches at Brown University in the philosophy department. His primary research interests are in philosophy of physics and metaphysics. A forthcoming series of books on fundamentalism presents his own empirical analysis of causation.

Rae Langton is professor of philosophy at the Massachusetts Institute of Technology, and works in the history of philosophy, moral and political philosophy, feminist philosophy, and metaphysics. Born and raised in India, she studied at Sydney and Princeton, and has taught at Monash University (Melbourne), the Australian National University, Sheffield University and the University of Edinburgh. She is author of *Kantian Humility: Our Ignorance of Things in Themselves* (Oxford: Oxford

University Press, 1998) and *Sexual Solipsism: Philosophical Essays on Pornography and Objectification* (Oxford: Oxford University Press, 2009).

Mari Mikkola is a lecturer in philosophy at Lancaster University, U.K. Her work is mainly on feminist philosophy and metaphysics. In feminism, Mari's latest work has been on pornography and speech acts; in metaphysics, her interests are mainly on anti-realism/realism debates and everyday metaphysics.

Kristie Miller is a research fellow at the University of Sydney, Australia. She works primarily in metaphysics, particularly in the areas of composition and persistence. Her book, *Issues in Theoretical Diversity: Persistence, Composition and Time* (Springer, 2006), is concerned primarily with these issues. On a purely personal note she would quite like Platonism to be true, and would most like to meet the number 2 should that ever prove feasible.

Alyssa Ney is assistant professor of philosophy at the University of Rochester in Rochester, New York. She received her B.S. in physics and philosophy from Tulane University in 1999, and her Ph.D. in philosophy from Brown University in 2005. She works primarily in metaphysics, the philosophy of mind, and the philosophy of physics.

Jay Odenbaugh is a member of the Department of Philosophy and the Environmental Studies Program at Lewis and Clark College. His main areas of research are in the philosophy of the environmental sciences (especially ecology) and environmental ethics.

Christopher Robichaud is an instructor in public policy at the Harvard Kennedy School of Government and is finishing his doctorate in philosophy at the Massachusetts Institute of Technology. His main research interests are in metaphysics, epistemology, and ethics. He can be reached at cjrobichaud@gmail.com.

Carolina Sartorio is associate professor of philosophy at the University of Arizona (before that she taught at the University of Wisconsin – Madison). Her main research interests are in metaphysics, ethics, and their intersection.

Introduction

Allan Hazlett

This book contains 13 new essays by more-or-less young metaphysicians, on a wide range of metaphysical issues: free will, mathematical objects, the reality of race, the nature of ontology, causation, the existence and nature of fundamental intrinsic properties, and many others. This diversity of topics reflects the diversity of contemporary metaphysics; the field is vast, and this book presents a taste of metaphysics from the 13 young philosophers working within it.

1 Metaphysics and its discontents

A curious feature of metaphysics, at least since the Early Modern period, is that the very enterprise of metaphysical speculation is perennially called into question. Not only is there little agreement about basic metaphysical questions (something hardly unique to metaphysics in particular), there also regularly arise challenges to the legitimacy of metaphysics itself. Reasons for scepticism about metaphysics are and continue to be diverse: Hume and Kant's worries are largely epistemological, those of ordinary language philosophers primarily methological, and those of the logical positivists (by their own lights, anyway) semantic. For whatever reasons, we philosophers continue to find ourselves uneasy with metaphysics, and we often find ourselves in the process of trying to move beyond it, or to give it up, or to reform it, or to replace it with something else.

Metaphysics is still around, of course, and its survival plays a central role in a gloss on the history of metaphysics in the twentieth century that you sometimes hear. It goes like this: the logical positivists rejected metaphysics, but positivism failed and died (i.e., was killed by Quine), and old-fashioned metaphysics was resurrected (e.g., by Lewis, Kripke, and Van Inwagen). This gets its wrong in at least two ways, and each illustrates a helpful lesson.

First, the idea that the positivists rejected metaphysics. Sure enough, A. J. Ayer's classic exposition of positivism, *Language, Truth, and Logic* (1946), begins with a chapter on 'The Elimination of Metaphysics.' But what Ayer attacks is 'the metaphysical thesis that philosophy affords us knowledge of a reality transcending the world of science and common sense' (p. 33), or later 'the phenomenal world' (Ibid.). Ayer's principle of verification requires of any meaningful sentence that some 'observations be relevant to the determination of its truth or falsehood' (p. 38), that a meaningful hypothesis must 'provide a rule for the anticipation of experience' (p. 41). What is going on here is not the elimination of metaphysics; it is the elimination of various metaphysical views in favour of Ayer's own preferred one: an austere phenomenalistic ontology of sense-data. To denounce the metaphysician who posits a reality 'transcending the world of science and common sense' is, presumably, to embrace as metaphysically real the world of science and common sense; to reject a reality beyond 'the phenomenal world' is to endorse the existence of the phenomenal alone. An austere metaphysic – one that makes ineliminable reference only to 'observations' or 'experiences' – is no less a metaphysic for being austere. This is not to say that Ayer was up to anything illegitimate; it is just to say that what he was up to was metaphysics.

This leads to a general point. Philosophers who describe themselves as opponents of metaphysics are, in general, actually opponents of some particular metaphysical view or views. Take, as another example, the conceptual relativism of Hilary Putnam, according to which 'the notions of object and existence…have a multitide of different uses rather than one absolute "meaning"' (1987, p. 19). This kind of view is offered, at least by some, as a critique of metaphysical disputes: metaphysicians argue about whether these simples compose a table, or are just a plurality of simples arranged in the shape of a table, and (so the critique goes) this is all a big mistake, since the logical notions involved in the dispute don't have one fixed meaning. Rather, on one use of those notions, it is true to say that the simples compose a table, and on another use of those notions, it is true to say that they don't. The idea of an objective answer to the metaphysical question of composition rests on a linguistic mistake.

I don't mean to challenge the correctness of this Putnam-inspired critique of metaphysics. What I want to point out, rather, is just that this critique itself rests on some substantial metaphysics. Putnam maintains that there are no objective answers to questions about existence (fair enough), but when asked to say what this means in terms of a picture of the world, he can't resist a metaphor: 'the mind and the world jointly make up the mind and the world' (1981, p. xi), as opposed to the mind simply making up the world (idealism) or the world existing independently from the mind (realism). But the literal content of this metaphor has to be something like this: there are no objective facts about what there is. And that is substantial metaphysics; it is to say that the world is *not* the way that metaphysical realists claim it is, 'ready-made' with joints, carved up into the things that there really are.[1]

The fashionable metaphysicians of the last half of the twentieth century had richer, more profligate ontologies than the fashionable empiricist metaphysicians of the first half. But that doesn't mean that metaphysics was dead and then resurrected; at best, it was hibernating.

The second problem with the toy story of metaphysics that I sketched here is the idea that we returned to 'old-fashioned' metaphysics, upon the total demise of logical positivism. What is right is that a verificationist criterion of meaning was a centrepiece of positivistic philosophy, and that very few philosophers today would accept such a view. But this obscures the fact that many even more fundamental doctrines of the positivists have been inherited, in various ways, by contemporary 'analytic' metaphysicians. I have in mind, in particular, the positivist's conviction that philosophy should be scientific. This was the source of the idea that philosophy's scope was limited, and the motivation for the verificationist criterion of meaning. But this idea – the idea of naturalized philosophy – didn't die as people abandoned verificationism; rather, its appeal has grown throughout the twentieth century and beyond, so that at present it is deeply embedded in our practice. Naturalism is our inheritance from the positivists, and this is manifest in the fact that the 'analytic' philosophy of the twenty-first century is largely a secular, naturalized affair (although its practitioners are by no means exclusively secularists or naturalists). There are critics of naturalism and secularism within contemporary 'analytic' philosophy. What I am suggesting is that 'analytic' metaphysics, at least partly in virtue of its history, enjoys a bias towards secularism and naturalism.

2   Physics or metaphysics?

All this means that our philosophical theorizing can, for us, be criticized on the grounds that it is not sufficiently scientific or naturalistic, and this is especially true of metaphysical theorizing. Without attempting a definition of metaphysics, we can agree that it concerns, in some central way, questions about what most fundamentally exists. But, given our openness to scientific and naturalistic challenges, are metaphysicians not open to a more basic objection, based on the fact that the science of *physics* treats of the question of what most fundamentally exists? Metaphysics – at least the metaphysics of what fundamentally exists – can never be 'sufficiently scientific' (so the charge goes), since we already have a scientific field that addresses the question of fundamental existence. It would be as if there were a philosophical discipline devoted to the classification of animal species. The existence of zoology, which includes the scientific classification of animal species, would pose an existential problem for any philosophical work on the same.

Several recent criticisms of metaphysics – at least 'traditional' metaphysics – take aim at its lack of naturalistic or scientific credentials.[2] One basic question we are faced with, in considering this kind of criticism, is the proper relationship between physics and metaphysics. One extreme answer would be that the relationship between physics and metaphysics (at least the metaphysics of fundamental existence) should be identity; that metaphysics (at least the metaphysics of fundamental existence) should be eliminated in favour of physics – or perhaps in favour of a radically stripped-down kind of metaphysics, closer to what the logical positivists imagined, in which the metaphysician's role is to articulate and interpret the work of physicists.

On the other extreme, consider an argument for the metaphysical irrelevance of physics: metaphysical questions are by their nature answerable a priori, if answerable at all; empirical science has no bearing on them. What sort of scientific inquiry *could* there be into the reality of universals or the special composition question? Philosophers and scientists who maintain that science will or could answer such questions either badly misunderstand the questions or badly misunderstand the methods of science. (It is important to distinguish here between scientific inquiry into human cognition, which might reveal something about how we think about composition, and scientific inquiry into the question of composition itself. Compare the 'scientific study of morality,' which is the scientific study of moral thinking.)

Between these extremes lie more moderate, if less exciting, positions. One might insist that metaphysical theories be *consistent* with our current best science. This is a weak condition, but one violated by more than a few contemporary metaphysical theories. Or one could ask for something stronger, say a *coherence* with science, where this goes beyond mere consistency. One might spell out a moderate view in terms of logical or epistemic priority: science must be prior to metaphysics, and not the other way around. But in any event, such moderate views will all share the idea that metaphysical speculation, uninformed by empirical science, is not credible. This is a widespread assumption in the contemporary metaphysical scene.

3 The scope and 'core' of metaphysics

Richard Taylor's *Metaphysics* (1963) is concerned with the mind-body problem, the existence of God, free will, fatalism, and time. Many of these topics are not central to the work being done by contemporary 'analytic' metaphysicians. In the case of some of these topics, we now have the idea of distinct philosophical 'areas' where their study belongs: in the philosophy of mind, or the philosophy of religion, or philosophical theology, or in action theory. These are not merely distinct 'areas of specialization' but, in some respects, autonomous domains of inquiry. And some issues at the core of contemporary metaphysics are completely different from Taylor's topics; consider questions about material composition, modality, and (ontic) vagueness. (We're still deeply concerned with time, perhaps a tribute to its eternal significance.)

What then is metaphysics, what questions and issues fall under its scope, and what questions and issues constitute the core or center of the discipline? The familiar etymology of the word 'metaphysics' tells us next to nothing about this question. Moreover, 'metaphysics' has suggested different things to different people at different times and places, like most words in philosophy. (Consider all the things that 'logic' has and continues to mean.) Given this, is seems a mistake to suppose that the questions of the scope and core of metaphysics have objective, timeless answers. We might propose a line of inquiry as important or potentially interesting or relevant in some other way, and we might denounce another as backwards or mistaken in its presuppositions or whatever, but we should not think of ourselves as getting at what metaphysics 'really is.'

But there are reasons to prefer a broad conception of metaphysics. First, from a pragmatic point of view, this avoids the embarrassment of excluding issues that historically defined metaphysics, as well as those that will define it in the future. We should therefore include Taylor's issues within the scope, if not the core, of metaphysics, as well as the issues that were central to metaphysics at other times in the history of philosophy. And we should avoid positivistic restrictions on the

legitimate scope of metaphysical inquiry. To properly criticize a philosophical position is to argue that it is false, or not well supported; it is
not to argue that it is 'not really metaphysics,' or even worse, 'not really
philosophy.'

Second, given that the dramatic increase in specialization (throughout academia) in the twentieth century has brought with it increasingly
narrow definitions of our 'areas of specialization,' a broad conception of
metaphysics betrays a respect for the kind of philosophical generalism
that is threatened by these trends. An adequate defence of generalism
would be impossible to mount here, but here are two quick remarks.
First, we are constantly reminded of the value of generalism when we see
ideas developed in connection with one philosophical question applied
fruitfully in connection with another. Consider what insight has come
from the recognition of the similar structure of tense and modality, for
example. Second, the generalist is notable for her ability to see 'the big
picture': to survey the philosophical landscape at a remove from the
presumptions and background commitments embedded in our inquires
into various specific philosophical questions. It is from this perspective
that we are capable of some of our deepest insights, insights that may
move philosophy in significant new directions. Think here of Thomas
Nagel's (1979) identification of a common structure in the problem of
scepticism, the problem of free will, and the mind-body problem.

For a third and final reason to prefer a broad conception of metaphysics, consider some issues that lie, at present, at or beyond the margins
of 'analytic' metaphysics: I have in mind here questions (for example)
about the reality of race and gender, about whether sexuality is a behaviour or a categorical feature of a person, about the environment, about
the metaphysical status of animals, about the distinction between
physical and psychological pain deployed by defenders of torture.[3] It
is easy to dismiss these questions, to relegate them to the margins of
metaphysics, or even to insist that they are not properly metaphysical
issues. The danger of this lies not in getting the objective boundaries of
metaphysics wrong – I suggested earlier that there are none – but rather
in the possibility of letting the tools of 'analytic' metaphysics go to
waste. Questions of social, ethical, and political importance are rarely
the subject matter, at least not the explicit subject matter, of 'analytic'
metaphysics; questions fitting that description, such as some of those
listed here, are ubiquitous elsewhere, and have long been the intellectual
property of ethicists, sociologists, anthropologists, and 'Continental'
philosophers. That such questions belong within the scope of 'analytic'
metaphysics, of course, is not to be determined a priori, but through

experimentation: by trying out the methods of 'analytic' metaphysics on those questions. We should not (from an ethical point of view) let the discussion of them proceed without our input, if there is any chance that our tradition's input will be useful to the ongoing conversation.

It is an embarrassment to the critics of metaphysics that, having been declared dead a thousand times, it keeps showing up alive. As for the future of metaphysics, I have suggested two questions that twenty-first-century metaphysicians face: a question about our relationship with physics, and by implication the natural sciences in general, and a question about the scope of our discipline, which I take as a challenge to those who would conceive of it narrowly. I hope these essays are evidence enough that metaphysics is alive and well, and will be for many centuries to come.

Notes

1. I owe this point to Ted Sider; he makes it in his forthcoming *Writing the Book of the World*.
2. I have in mind Van Fraassen 2004, Maddy 2007, and Ladyman and Ross 2007.
3. This raises the issue of why these questions, some of them obviously metaphysical, have been and continue to be considered outré. I'll leave the investigation of that (largely genealogical) matter for another day.

Bibliography

Ayer, A. J. (1946), *Language, Truth, and Logic* (New York: Dover Publications).

Ladyman, J. and Ross, D. (2007), *Every Thing Must Go: Metaphysics Naturalized* (Oxford, UK: Oxford University Press).

Maddy, P. (2007), *Second Philosophy* (Oxford: Oxford University Press).

Nagel, T. (1979), 'Subjective and Objective,' in his *Mortal Questions* (Cambridge, UK: Cambridge University Press), pp. 196–13.

Putnam, H. (1981), *Reason, Truth, and History* (Cambridge: Cambridge University Press).

—— (1987), *The Many Faces of Realism* (La Salle: Open Court Publishing Company).

Taylor, R. (1963), *Metaphysics* (Englewood Cliffs, NJ: Prentice Hall).

Van Fraassen, B. (2004), *The Empirical Stance* (Oxford , UK: Oxford University Press).

1
Quantification, Naturalness, and Ontology

Ross P. Cameron

Quine (1948) said that the ontological question can be asked in three words, 'What is there?,' and answered in one, 'everything.' He was wrong. We need an extra word to ask the ontological question: it is 'What is there, *really?*'; and it cannot be answered truthfully with 'everything' because there are some things that exist but which don't really exist (and maybe even some things that really exist but which don't exist).

You may doubt both the coherence of, and the motivation for, what I've just said; the purpose of this chapter is to motivate this departure from Quineanism and to show that it is perfectly coherent.

1 Ontology and language

A while back there was the linguistic turn: questions about reality were to be answered by reflection on the way we describe reality. Then, to the delight of some and the chagrin of others, there was the ontological turn: conceptual analysis was frowned upon, and serious ontology made, if not respectable, at least prevalent again. Advocates of the onto-logical turn remained wary of lurking 'linguisticism,' however; and it became a particularly biting criticism of your opponent to catch them in the practice of 'reading their ontology off of their language.'[1]

What is linguisticism? And what does it mean to read one's ontology off of language in an objectionable way? Here are some examples of the (alleged) mistake in action.

1.1 The special composition question[2]

What circumstances are required for the Xs to compose some further object? Merely their existence (as the universalist says)? Their being fas-tened together, or in contact, or some other condition that can be met but is not always met (as the restrictivist says)? Or are there simply no circumstances under which objects will compose some further object (as the nihilist says)?

This is the special composition question. How on Earth are we to answer it? The empirical evidence, on the face of it, won't decide the issue for us: things would look the same if there is a table in front of us than if there are merely some table-arranged simples.

One thing we could appeal to are the general theoretical virtues that we appeal to in science. On these grounds, nihilism seems (at least prima facie) to be a clear winner. If the data to be explained really are equally well explained on each candidate answer to SCQ then surely the most parsimonious answer – nihilism – is, other things being equal, the most preferable.

But nihilism has not proven very popular. Why not? The main cost the nihilist faces is that it is, apparently, in substantial conflict with common sense. The nihilist denies that there are tables, chairs, humans, and so on. Is anything more unbelievable?! Nihilism is in conflict with 'Moorean truths.' 'Here is a hand,' said Moore (1959); and the truth of this was meant to be in such good standing that we'd do better to reject any premise of a philosophical argument whose conclusion ruled this out than to reject it itself. The nihilist says there isn't a hand, so we should reject the argument that took us to nihilism.

The ontological turner, as I conceive of her, objects that this is to read ontology off of language. We are deciding a serious ontological question – what complexity there is in reality – by reflecting on what claims of English we consider inviolable. What is a datum – the Moorean truth – is that the English sentence 'there is a hand' says something true: that is, that it is a true description of reality. But to take this to refute nihilism is to read off features of the world from features of our representations of the world in an objectionable way.

1.2 The statue and the clay[3]

Here is a statue – Statue – composed of some clay – Clay. Statue and Clay are, at least for the moment, occupying exactly the same region of space, and are composed of exactly the same parts. And yet, seemingly, they are distinct, since Clay existed before Statue. Statue is obviously closely related to Clay: when you move one, you move the other, and so on. What is Statue, then? Two options dominate the literature: on the first, the perdurantist option, Statue is a proper part of Clay – a temporal part, existing only during that time when Clay is statue-shaped; on the second, Statue is a distinct object that is constituted from the enduring object Clay at all and only those times at which Clay is statue-shaped. Both theorists are driven to complicating their ontology, then: the perdurantist to admitting temporal parts, the constitutionalist to admitting distinct objects which are in exactly the same place at the same time.

My ontological turner complains that there is simply no puzzle here: that both the admission of temporal parts and constituted entities are solutions to a problem that arises only as a result of confusing features of our representation of the world with features of the world that is thereby represented. What is a datum – a Moorean truth – in this case is that it is true now to say that both Clay and Statue exist, whereas it was the case that Clay but not Statue existed. But to conclude from this that there has occurred some change in being – that our ontology contains some thing, be it a space time worm or a constituted entity, that it didn't contain previously – is to read off features of the world from features of our representations of the world in an objectionable way.

1.3   Abstracta

There are football teams. The number of football teams is greater than 1. The set of football players is a proper subset of the set of all the people that there are. So there are groups (of which football teams are a kind – so there are kinds, too), numbers, and sets. And so our ontology includes the abstract as well as the concrete.

Similarly, van Inwagen (2004) argues that one must be a Platonist concerning properties, because the following is true: 'there are anatomical features that insects have and spiders also have.' This sentence quantifies over anatomical features (properties): so by the Quinean criterion of ontological commitment (which van Inwagen explicitly accepts), we're now ontologically committed to properties, unless we reject this 'simple fact of biology.' So biology entails Platonism about abstracta.

Likewise, Lewis and Lewis's (1970) protagonist Bargle argues for the existence of holes on the grounds that 'there are four holes in my cheese' is obviously true. And various people argue for the existence of possible ways for the world to be by pointing to the truth of, for example, 'there are four ways in which I could win this Chess game.'

'Not so quick,' says the ontological turner. Those are all truths, to be sure; but to conclude from their truth that our ontology includes abstracta such as numbers, sets, groups, holes, properties, ways and the like is to read off features of the world from features of our representations of the world in an objectionable way.

What should one do if they want to resist such easy commitment to complex entities, statues, abstracta, and the like? The traditional answer is: offer a paraphrase of the guilty sentences – sentences that can be uttered in exactly the same circumstances as the target sentences, that will convey the information we wanted them to convey, but which don't quantify over – and hence don't bring a commitment to – the offending entities. And so the ontological debate proceeds by examining the prospects for a successful paraphrase strategy.

The ontological turner sees this paraphrase strategy as mistaken. It's a mistake to think that the ontological question concerning abstracta, for example, has anything at all to do with the availability of a paraphrase of certain *sentences* which talk about abstracta in terms of certain other sentences that don't. That's to let facts about language drive ontology – that's linguisticism. It's also a mistake to think that the literal truth of, for example, 'there are four holes in my cheese' is ontologically committing to things that are holes (or indeed numbers, or cheese) in the first place. What's wrong is the Quinean methodology that says that the way to find out about our ontology is to find out about what true existential claims (even in a regimented language[4]) can be made. The truth of a *sentence* – even one that begins with 'there exists...' – is one thing, ontology another: and to conclude that we are ontologically committed to the Xs just because there is a true sentence in English (or even a regimented English) that proclaims the existence of the Xs is to read off features of the world from features of our representations of the world in an objectionable way.

In each case, then, the (alleged) mistake that so infuriates our ontological turner is to read off ontological conclusions from the truth of sentences in English of the form '...exists.' The mistake is to attempt to answer the ontological question by listing what there is.

2 Quantifiers and naturalness

But how can that be a mistake? How can there be more to finding out about our ontology than finding out what sentences of the form '...exists' are true?

Easily. My claim is simply that in English, 'exists' works such that not everything that exists has being (is an element of ontology). The view to be offered is that 'X exists' can express a truth not because there's some element of our ontology X (not because X *really* exists) but because there's some element of our ontology Y (because Y really exists), and we just happen to use our language in such a way that 'X exists' expresses a truth when Y really exists. It's true that X exists, then, but X *really is* no addition to our ontology over Y. *Really,* all there is is Y – we just happen to use our language in such a way that the sentence 'X exists' truly describes the world when (but perhaps not only when) Y really exists. So, for example, perhaps really all there is are simples; but that the arrangements of certain of those simples suffice for the truth of sentences proclaiming the existence of complex objects like tables and chairs, and so on: the idea here would be that 'the sum of the Xs' is a literally true sentence of English, but that it isn't ontologically committing to any complex entity because it is *made true* simply by the Xs themselves.

Of course, I don't believe we made some conscious decision to let the sentence 'the sum of A, B, and C exists' be made true not by any mereological sum but solely by A, B, and C. How sentences get matched up to ontology is a function of both how we use them and how the world is. Consider as actual a universalist world – a world where there *really is* a complex object composed of the Xs whenever there *really are* the Xs. On the supposition that such a world is actual it's natural to think that in order to express a truth with the sentence 'the sum of A, B, and C exists,' the proposition expressed by that sentence has to be made true by a complex object: namely, that complex object which is the sum of A, B, and C. In that case, we should only take this sentence to be true at some world w (w considered as counterfactual) if w really does contain a complex object that is the sum of A, B, and C.

But on the supposition that a nihilist world – a world where everything that there really is is simple – is actual, the charitable reading of what we say is not that sentences like 'the sum of A, B, and C exists' do not express truths, but that they express truths which are made true simply by A, B, and C. So on the supposition that the universalist world is actual we should describe the nihilist world, considered as *counterfactual,* as being a world where the sentence 'the sum of A, B, and C exists' does not express a truth; but on the supposition that *our* world is the nihilist world, we should consider that sentence to express a truth, but not to require the inclusion of complex objects amongst our fundamental ontology in order to make it true. So if W1 is the nihilist world and W2 the universalist world, the two-dimensional matrix for a proposition such as 'there are complex objects' will be:

	W1	W2
W1	T	T
W2	F	T

Let's add W3: the organicist world. This is a world where everything that really exists is a simple or a living complex object – there are no complex objects that are not alive. The two-dimensional matrix for the proposition 'there is a non-living complex object' will be:

	W1	W2	W3
W1	T	T	T
W2	F	T	F
W3	T	T	T

Whereas the matrix for 'something is the sum of every thing' might be:

	W1	W2	W3
W1	F	T	F
W2	F	T	F
W3	F	T	F

The difference between these two last matrices being that the proposition associated with the former but not the latter is a commitment of our folk ontology, and so we can be sure that it is true, and will be made true, no matter how the world is fundamentally. (Hence, for any world Wn, there will be a 'T' at the intersection of row n and column n in the matrix.) Whereas sentences proclaiming the existence of arbitrary gerrymandered sums are not a commitment of folk ontology, and so it's natural to think that they will only be made true if there really are such gerrymandered sums. (Hence, there's only a 'T' at the intersection of row n and column n when Wn is a world that really contains such sums (such as the universalist world); consider any other world as actual and that is to consider a world as actual where there are no truthmakers for that proposition, in which case the proposition is judged false relative to that same world.)

What are the rules for when sentences about entities that don't *really* exist get to express truths? Basically, I am a neo-Carnapian when it comes to what merely exists, but not when it comes to what *really* exists. I am a neo-Carnapian in saying that the truth of claims about what there is are sensitive simply to how we speak about the world; but I reject the characteristic neo-Carnapian claim that there is no further ontological question to be asked. Questions about what there is, I agree, are not substantial metaphysical questions. But the 'external' question – what is there, *really?* – is not, I think, a defective question.

Neo-Carnapianism, a meta-ontological view championed recently by Eli Hirsch, and historically held (or at least, something close to it was) by Carnap and Putnam,[5] is the view that (at least some) ontological questions are not questions about how the external world is, but rather about our way of conceptualizing or describing this world.

Consider again the debate between the universalist, the nihilist and the restrictivist. *They* think they are arguing about how the world is, but the neo-Carnapian thinks that their debate is at worst defective and at best about not how the world is but about the language, or conceptual scheme, we use to describe the world. According to the neo-Carnapian, the question as to whether there exists something that is the sum of you and I is not a question sensitive to some realm of compositional facts but rather a question as to how the term 'exists' is used. There are, on this view, a range of equally good – meaning, equally *natural*[6] – meanings for the term 'exists,' and whether or not the sentence 'there exists a sum of you and I' expresses a truth depends on which of these equally good meanings is the one that attaches to 'exists.' At worst, then, all but one of the universalist, nihilist and restrictivist are speaking analytic falsehoods; a bit better is that they're simply talking past each other: when the universalist says 'there is something that is the sum of every thing' and the restrictivist and nihilist say 'no, there's not,' when the nihilist says 'every thing there is simple' and the universalist and the restrictivist say 'no, it's not,' they simply mean different things by 'there is,' and so their debate is simply defective: akin to the debate between the Briton and the American as to whether some man is wearing suspenders. At best, their debate is not a debate about the world but a debate about the meaning of 'exists' and 'there is' in English: when the universalist says 'there is something that is the sum of every thing' and the restrictivist and nihilist say 'no, there's not,' the source of their disagreement is (if unbeknownst to them) solely over whether the meaning of 'there is' in English is such that that sentence expresses a truth; this is a substantial question, and so there is a genuine debate here: but it is a semantic one, not a metaphysical one – so at the very least, the way the various parties are trying to resolve their debate is completely on the wrong track.

The neo-Carnapian's claim is there is no quantificational structure to the world. It is exactly analogous to Goodman's claim that there is no predicational structure in the world.[7] For Goodman, the world doesn't come 'pre-carved' into divisions of objects for our predicates to latch onto: *we* do the carving, not the world. One who divides the things into the grue and the non-grue things does *just as good a job* (metaphysically speaking) of describing the world as one who divides them into the things that are green and not green.[8] There's nothing metaphysically better about using the predicate 'green' rather than 'grue': they are just as natural. There are at best pragmatic reasons pointing in favour of using one rather that the other, but there's no metaphysical reason to favour 'green' over 'grue.' Likewise, for the neo-Carnapian, the world doesn't come ready carved into objects for us to quantify over. We carve the world into objects by choosing to mean one thing rather than another by 'exists,' and no carving is any better at revealing the structure of the world than any other. No meaning for the quantifier is any more natural than any other.

I find both the Goodman and the neo-Carnapian position entirely unbelievable. The world comes with both predicational and quantificational structure, I believe. I believe that there *is* a single candidate meaning for the quantifier that is more natural than any other. This is the meaning for the quantifier that carves the world at its quantificational joints. Speakers of a language where 'exists' has this meaning do better at describing the objective structure of the world, other things being equal, than speakers of a language where 'exists' means one of the other candidate meanings, just as speakers of our language do better – we suppose – than speakers of the gruesome language which is just like ours except that it replaces 'green' with 'grue' and 'blue' with 'bleen.' But 'exists' in English does not have this meaning. It has one of the unnatural meanings.

There is no contradiction here. Naturalness is a reference magnet, in that natural meanings are intrinsically more eligible to be meant by our terms than unnatural meanings.[9] But that doesn't mean your expressions can't mean the unnatural meanings: it is no part of the Lewisian theory that naturalness necessarily trumps use. The theory says only that if a natural meaning and an unnatural meaning fit equally well with our usage of a term, we will mean the natural one; it is simply silent as to what happens when an unnatural meaning better fits our usage than a natural one. And the most plausible story here is that naturalness would trump a slightly better fit with our usage but that a *significantly* better fit with our usage would trump naturalness: that there will be some, perhaps vague, point at which it doesn't matter that there's a more natural meaning out there, because it just doesn't fit our usage as well as some of the unnatural candidates to be what we mean.

Consider again the nihilist world as actual. On this assumption, the quantificational structure of the world is best captured by a nihilistic language: so the most natural meaning for the quantifier will be one such that 'there exists an F,' or 'A exists' will only express truths if A, and the thing that is F, are simple. But I don't think we should give up, on this assumption, the claim that our utterances of 'there are tables' or 'there is something complex' are literally true. What we should give up is the claim that our quantifier carves the world at its joints. 'There are tables' is true – and it's not that it *means* the same as 'there are simples arranged table-wise' or anything like that; it truly and literally describes the world, but it doesn't capture the *structure* of the world because the world doesn't come pre-carved into complex objects but only into simples. Nevertheless, the meaning of 'exists' is such that 'there exist tables' is true, because this just fits *so much better* with our usage: it doesn't have us speaking falsely almost all of the time!

Whilst there is a single most natural meaning for the quantifier, and hence it is *metaphysically* better to mean this by 'exists' – in the sense that our existence claims would then be sensitive to the deep ontological structure of the world – it may nevertheless be *pragmatically* better to mean something else, something unnatural, by 'exists.' Even if we knew that our world was the nihilist world, we wouldn't aim to only speak of simples, their properties and the relations that hold between them: that's simply impractical. We would still speak of the existence of tables and chairs, of persons and planets, and so on. That much I think all will agree on; but there has been a tendency for philosophers to think that we would thereby speak *falsely:* that whilst such existence claims might be warrantedly assertable they could not be strictly and literally speaking true.[10] I think that's a mistake: such existence claims would still be true – it's just that our quantifier wouldn't be carving the world at its quantificational joints. To speak truly *and* to carve reality at its joints we would have to restrict ourselves to speaking only of simples, and how those simples are in themselves and in relation to one another. But most of the time we're not concerned with carving reality at its joints, only with speaking truly, and there's no reason at all to deny that we do.

That means that once we *do* want to carve reality at its joints we can't do so by asking what exists, because finding out what exists, given that 'exists' means one of the unnatural candidate meanings, is not to find out about the quantificational structure of reality. But this is no problem; for of course, even though 'exists' in English doesn't carve the world at its quantificational joints, we can still 'get at' the quantificational structure of the world. We can introduce a term[11] – *'really exists'* – which is simply stipulated to take the natural meaning of the quantifier. (Of course, stipulating that doesn't guarantee it does have the natural meaning: the thought is just to introduce a new term that we'll agree isn't to be used without its technical sense, and so the use facts won't trump naturalness and lead to it meaning something unnatural.) The ontological question, then, is: What *really* exists? That is why it is a mistake to read ontological conclusions straightforwardly from true claims in English about what there is. Ontology isn't concerned with what there is – or at least, it shouldn't be, since that's not an ontological issue but a linguistic/conceptual one; ontology should be concerned with what there really is. In my view, what there really is is what *grounds* the true sentences describing the world: that is, the real existents are the *truthmakers* for the true sentences of English.[12] So the ontologist's concern should be: what must the quantificational structure of the world be like to *ground* the true English claims we make?

So, to summarize the view: there is quantificational structure to the world: the world comes 'ready carved' into objects, just as those objects come ready divided into similarity classes. 'x really exists' is true iff the quantificational structure of the world carves an x out of the world. The most natural meaning of 'exists' mirrors this quantificational structure of the world in that if 'exists' means that then an utterance of 'x exists' is true iff x really exists. *It may be* the case that in English 'exists' means the most natural of its candidate meanings, in which case an object exists if and only if it really exists. But we've got no guarantee that that's the case. It will only be the case if our usage of 'exists' doesn't deviate too much from how it should if we were only concerned to describe the quantification structure of the world: and if nihilism (understood as an ontological doctrine: that all that there *really* is is simple) is true, for example, that won't be the case. If 'exists' means one of the unnatural meanings then some claims of the form 'x exists but it doesn't really exist' will be true, which is what I mean when I say that x exists but that x is not part of our ontology: x is not carved out of the world by its quantificational structure.

There's a sense in which I agree with the neo-Carnapian, then. For both of us, the question as to whether there is some thing that is composed of my right ear, Babe Ruth's bat, and an atom at the core of the Sun, is not so much a metaphysical question as a conceptual/linguistic one: it's a question about how we use the term 'exists,' not about the objective quantificational structure about the world. I think I share with the neo-Carnapian the following advantage, then: we don't need to let the ontologist scare us into doubting the truth of our claim that there are tables, chairs, persons, and so on. These 'Moorean truths' are immune from refutation by the devious ontologist. But I disagree with the neo-Carnapian when they say that there's no ontological question to be asked. There is: it's 'What is there really?' That question is in perfectly good standing. My view is like neo-Carnapianism, but with an anchor of realism to stop us drifting to the perilous shores of pragmatism.

3   Composition and necessity

One advantage of this view is that we can explain what is otherwise a mysterious necessity: the inter-world supervenience of the compositional facts on the non-compositional facts. That is, that any world that is alike to ours in the distribution of mereological simples, and in the non-mereological properties and relations that are had by and hold between those simples, is also alike to ours with respect to the existence, distribution of, and properties of, complex objects.

This inter-world supervenience claim is widely held, but it's not clear why it should hold.[13] Consider some complex object (suppose for the sake of argument that there is at least one) composed of the Xs, call it A. On the face of it, we've got an extra entity here; so why is it impossible for A to fail to exist without there being some other change in the world? Simple combinatorial reasoning about possibilities suggests that there should be a possible world where everything is just like it actually is, except that A doesn't exist.

Anyone who is attracted to the inter-world supervenience of the compositional on the non-compositional needs to account for this necessity. To explain it, our starting thought should be to deny what I just said was on the face of it true: that when you've got a complex object you've got some *extra* entity. It's this thought that is generating the trouble with the combinatorial reasoning, because it's only if you've got an extra entity that combinatorial reasoning says you should be able to take it away whilst leaving everything else the same.

That complex objects aren't really extra entities over and above the simples that compose them is a familiar thought. Armstrong (1997, p. 12) says that complex objects are 'an ontological free lunch ... no addition of being.' But what does it *mean* to say that complex objects are no addition of being? One thing it could be taken to mean is that complex objects are identical to the simples that compose them.[14] On this view, there are true many-one identity statements: A, the sum of the Xs, is numerically identical to the Xs.

Here's why the thesis that composition is identity (CAI) might be thought to entail the inter-world supervenience claim. CAI is necessary if true; CAI entails universalism; the necessity of universalism entails the supervenience claim; so CAI entails the supervenience claim. The problem I have with this is the move from CAI to universalism. It's easy to see why you might think that entailment is okay: CAI says a complex object just is its parts, so of course whenever there are some things (the Xs) there is some thing that is their sum. The sum *just is* the Xs, so that follows simply from the fact that whenever you've got the Xs you've got the Xs.

I don't think this is right. All CAI says is that *when* there is a complex object, it is identical to its parts. This leaves it open that some collections compose and that some don't (both within, and across worlds): that for some collections there's a one that the many are identical to, but that for some collections there's no one that the many are identical to. So on the face of it, CAI allows that there's a world exactly like ours with respect to what simples there are and how they are arranged, and differing solely as to what collections of simples are identical to some one thing.

In making this claim I must respond to an argument that aims to prove that CAI entails universalism.[15] Suppose for reductio that there are some Xs that don't compose. They *could* have composed. So go to the world where they do (w). In w there is a one, A, that the Xs are identical to. Given the (necessity of the) necessity of identity, possible identity entails actual identity. So the Xs are actually identical to A. So there's actually a one the Xs are identical to, so they compose, contrary to our supposition. I don't think this argument works. It shows only that it's actually true that the Xs are A. But it only follows that the Xs are identical to a one if A is actually a one. But all we know is that A is *possibly* a one; we can only conclude that A is *actually* a one if we have the assumption that anything that is possibly a one is necessarily a one. But what right do we have to make that assumption? If we're leaving open the possibility that there's a many that's not a one but could be (and at this stage we must, lest we beg the question), we should also leave open the possibility that there's a many that is a one but might not be. Since the many is the one, this is a one that might not be a one: a one that is a many and that might have been a *mere* many – a many that is identical to no one. This is the status we should think A has in w if we think that the Xs do not actually compose; and so we have no reductio of the hypothesis that CAI is true but that the facts about the simples don't settle the facts about the complexes. We must look elsewhere.

I suggest that if you believe the inter-world supervenience claim you should hold that the fact that the complex object exists is made true not by the complex object itself, but rather by the simples, or perhaps by the simples and certain non-mereological relations (e.g., the spatio-temporal relations) that hold between them. In that case, the inter-world supervenience claim is simply a consequence of truthmaker necessitarianism.

Suppose <A exists> is made true not by A but by the Xs. That's *not* to say that A is identical to the Xs: it is simply to say that the portion of ontology that makes true the proposition <A exists> is no complex object but rather a collection of simples – the Xs. In that case, I say that though A and the Xs all exist, only the Xs *really* exist. It follows immediately, given truthmaker necessitarianism, that you can't take A away and leave everything else as it is, because if you leave everything else as it you leave the Xs, and it's necessary that if the Xs exist then <A exists> is true, since the Xs actually make it the case that <A exists> is true.

The difference between this view and composition as identity can be best illustrated by considering what possibilities my position allows that composition as identity closes off. I have been speaking so far solely as if the fact that some complex objects exist holds in virtue of the fact that its simple parts exist. But you might object that the parts of a thing *don't* necessitate the existence of the thing: scatter the atoms that make up me across the universe and it's not that you've scattered *me* across the universe, rather you've *destroyed* me without destroying my atoms.

So is the existence of a complex object necessitated by the existence of its simple parts or not? Well, perhaps it depends on what kind of complex object it is. It's not uncommon to distinguish between *mere sums* – complex objects which necessarily exist if and only if their parts do, and which are necessarily composed of exactly those parts if they exist – and genuine complex objects like tables and chairs which could fail to exist even if their actual parts all exist and which could exist even if (some, if not all of) their actual parts fail to exist. The mere sum of the atoms that make up the table has the same parts as the table: but *had* the atoms been scattered across the globe, the mere sum would still have existed but the table would not have, and there are possible counter-factual situations where the mere sum and the table both exist but have different parts.

The above is perfectly coherent on my account. Let the simple parts of the table be the Xs. All we need to say is that the Xs make true only that the mere sum of the Xs exists, and that what makes it true that the *table* exists is the Xs together with certain *non-mereological* properties and relations that are had by or hold between the Xs. So <the sum of the Xs exists> is made true by the Xs and <the table exists> is made true, perhaps, by the Xs being distributed as they actually are in space-time. We get the existence of two complex objects, but in neither case do we need complex objects in our fundamental ontology to make it the case that the sentences proclaiming the existence of these two complex objects express truths: the simples, or the simples and their spatio-temporal distribution, are ontology enough. In the world where the Xs are scattered across the globe, then, it is still true that the mere sum of the Xs exist, because *that* it exists is actually made true by the Xs and the existence of the truthmakers necessitates the truth of the proposition which they actually make true; but in this world we *don't* have the actual truthmaker for the fact that the table exists, because it is made true not by the Xs but by the Xs together with the fact that they are arranged the way they are in space and time, and in this new world they are not so arranged, and that's why we are not forced to say that the table exists but we are forced to say that the mere sum exists.

So I have no problem at all in accounting for the truth of the claims that there are two objects here, a mere sum and a table, that share the same parts, but where one could exist without the other. Nor does the theorist who insists that there *really are* two extra elements of our ontology here: that our ontology consists of the Xs and *over and above the Xs* two complex objects which both have exactly the Xs as parts but which differ in their modal relationship to those parts. We can both account for the truth of all those sentences, although I do so with a far less bloated ontology. But the theorist who has trouble saying anything like this is the composition as identity theorist. For if composition is identity then, since both the mere sum of the Xs and the table have the Xs as exactly their parts, both the mere sum and the table are identical to the Xs; and so, since identity is Euclidean, the mere sum simply *is* the table. But then, how can it be that the mere sum can exist without the table; how can it be that the table but not the mere sum could have had different parts?[16] The composition as identity theorist either has to deny that there is a mere sum, or that there is a table, or deny some of the modal claims involved, or reconcile the truth of the various modal claims by adopting something like counterpart theory. Now, maybe that's a cost and maybe it's not; what I'm concerned with here is not so much with scoring points over the composition as identity theorist but rather showing that my position is a genuine alternative. Holding that the existence of complex objects obtains in virtue of the existence of simples and the non-mereological relations that hold between them is not the same as holding that the complex object *is* the simples: options are open to one who accepts the former that are not open to one who accepts the latter.

Let me give another brief example. I think the view I am offering gives us a nice story to tell regarding the problem of the many. There's a cloud in the sky. It's natural to think that the cloud is identical to a sum of water particles. But which sum? There are many sets of water particles that seem to have equal claim to being the cloud: but surely there's only one cloud? The composition as identity theorist is in as much trouble as anyone here, but I offer a simple solution. It's not that the cloud is identical to a sum of water particles (or identical to some water particles); really, there is no cloud – the claim that there is a cloud in the sky is literally true, but it is made true simply by some collection of water particles. Which collection? All of them: each of the collections that the universalist will say has a claim to *being* the cloud. And there's simply no pressure to concede as a result of saying this that there's more than one cloud, for the simple reason that one proposition can have multiple truthmakers.

I'll close by saying something about necessary truths like the truths of mathematics. If the way to find out about the ontological commitments of a sentence is not by looking at what must be counted as a value of a variable in that sentence but rather by looking at the ontological grounds for the truth of that sentence, this means that it's at least a conceptual possibility that a sentence have no ontological grounds and, hence, that its truth brings no ontological commitment, even if it is a truth of the form '... exists.'

What kind of sentences might lack ontological grounds? Some point to negative existentials, like 'there are no unicorns,' but I disagree. The only sentences that lack grounds, say I, are those that are necessary. If a sentence is contingent, if its truth value varies from world to world, then there must be some corresponding portion of ontology that is a contingent existent, whose existence at one world and not at another partially explains the difference in truth value.

I say 'partially,' because it does not follow from the fact that the truthmaker for a sentence S might not have existed that S is contingent, simply because there is not a one-one correspondence between truths and possible truthmakers. It is at least conceptually consistent that S be a necessary truth because it necessarily has a truthmaker, even if there is no truthmaker that it necessarily has. Nevertheless, if S is in fact contingent, this seems to be in part explained by it having a truthmaker that contingently exists. Certainly, S can't be contingent and have a necessarily existing truthmaker, since the existence of the truthmaker necessitates the truth of that which it actually makes true. And if S simply didn't have a truthmaker, there would be nothing to explain why its truth is sensitive to worldly matters, hence why it is contingent.

In Cameron (2008b), I rejected the thought that necessary truths might not need truthmakers. Why, I asked, should some truths need grounding and others not: what is it about the necessary truths that gets them off the hook? But I was, I now think, thinking about things the wrong way round. Take some necessary truth that lacks a truthmaker: it's not that it needs no truthmaker because it's necessary; it's that it's necessary because it has no truthmaker. We've got here a brute truth; ex hypothesi, its truth is not tied to the world; and so you can do what you like to the world and it will still be true.

Note that this allows that there are also necessary truths that *are* grounded, either because they have a necessary existent as a truthmaker or because they necessarily have some contingently existing truthmaker or other. I remain silent on whether there are such cases. Although the potential reduction of modality if there are no such cases – S is necessary iff there is no truthmaker for S – looks attractive enough to make me hope that there are none. Today's ambitions are modest, though: all I want to suggest here is that there are at least some necessary truths that are necessary because they lack grounds; and that means that they have no ontological commitments, even if they are existence claims. I'm thinking in particular of the mathematical truths. Take 'there is a prime number between 8 and 12.' That's true. So there are numbers! Well, yes, there are; but for the ontologist qua ontologist, that's not interesting: the question is whether or not there really are numbers. And to answer that we should look to the ontological grounds of that sentence, and ask whether they include numbers. And they trivially don't, I suggest, because that sentence has *no* ontological grounds (a fortiori none that include numbers). Mathematical truths are 'trivial' in the sense that, in not requiring an ontological ground, their truth simply makes no demands on the world – and that's why they're necessary. And of course, as a result it's necessary that there are numbers. But one shouldn't be in the slightest bit worried, for this is merely the cheap sense of existence. There aren't *really* any numbers: the mathematical truths don't demand there to be *any* real existents – they don't demand *anything!*[17]

4 Conclusion

I'm attracted to an ontology whereby what there really is is just: spacetime, simple substances, and the location relations that fix what substances are at what locations at what times. These simple substances have their intrinsic natures essentially: they do not change in their intrinsic natures over time (thus making it harmless to say that they endure, and hence avoiding the need for temporal parts), nor could they have differed in their intrinsic nature (thus allowing them to be the truthmaker for the fact that they have the intrinsic nature they have, and hence avoiding the need for properties). Everything that is true is true in virtue of the distribution of these simple substances throughout spacetime. Sometimes there exist things arranged so as to make it true that there are people, tables, cities, universities, etc; other times, there are no such things. But more important than any particular ontology is the methodological lesson concerning how to do ontology. Common sense 'Moorean' truths about what there is *can* guide us in ontology; but we must be cautious about how we proceed: the task of the ontologist is to show how a perhaps sparse ontology is nevertheless sufficient for grounding the truth of those existential claims in English.

Notes

Thanks to Elizabeth Barnes, Allan Hazlett, John Heil, Kris McDaniel, Jason 'The Ontological Turner' Turner, and Robbie Williams for many helpful discussions.

1. See especially Heil 2003, 2005, and 2006. I have been much influenced by these works.
2. For discussion of SCQ, see van Inwagen 1990.
3. For a defence of the perdurantist ontology, see Sider 2001; for the constitution view, see Thomson 1998.
4. Obviously, Quine doesn't think that to do ontology we should just look at what appears to be quantified over by everyday sentences of English. We're not committed to dearths by uttering 'there is a dearth of resources'. Rather, we are to look to a regimentation of our language: we should be asking whether there is a sentence that plays the same theoretical role as the one just mentioned that doesn't quantify over dearths (Quine 1960). But this is still to let our focus drift from ontology to conceptual/linguistic matters. The question isn't whether sentences that don't talk about dearths can play the same theoretical role as sentences that do; the question is whether dearths are needed amongst the ontological grounds of the true sentences that make use of dearth talk.
5. See, inter alia, Carnap 1950, Hirsch 2002 and 2005, and Putnam 2004. For discussion, see Eklund 2008 and 2009 and Sider 2009.
6. See Sider 2009.
7. Here I again follow Sider 2009; see especially section 7.
8. See Goodman 1972, pp. 443–4.
9. Lewis 1983.
10. See, e.g., Dorr and Rosen 2003, p. 170.

11. I'm not making a claim here about how 'really' works in English. Think of 'really exists' as a single semantic primitive: the point is just to introduce a quantifier that carves the world at its joints. I am also not claiming that whenever we say 'X really exists' we are using this natural, ontologically loaded, quantifier. When I say that there *really is* global warming, I am merely trying to emphasise the truth of the English sentence 'there is global warming' to sceptics; I am not making the claim that global warming is a constituent of fundamental ontology. I also don't want to claim that the English 'exists' *never* means the natural meaning: it may be that the meaning of the English quantifier is context sensitive so that, for example, when we ask 'what exists?' inside the metaphysics classroom the answer is different from what it would be were we to ask it outside, with the former answer being the answer to the ontological question. I don't want to take a stand on such issues. What I want to insist on are two points: (i) in at least some ordinary uses of 'there exists an F,' the quantifier doesn't mean anything natural; and so we can agree that the ordinary assertion of 'there is a hand' is a Moorean truth without conceding an ontological commitment to hands, (ii) there is a natural meaning for the quantifier, so the 'external' ontological question is in good standing; when using this quantifier, there are no Moorean truths concerning what exists.
12. See Cameron 2008a.
13. For discussion, see Cameron 2007.
14. For a defence of composition as identity in its strongest form, see Baxter 1988a and 1988b; for discussion, and endorsement of a weaker principle, see Lewis 1991, p. 81, and Sider 2007.
15. Merricks 2005, p. 30. See also Sider 2007.
16. How can I account for the fact that the table could have had different parts? Well, remember that a proposition can possibly be made true by some thing(s) which do not actually make it true, so even though it is the Xs being arranged thusly that actually makes it true that the table exists, perhaps in other worlds it is the Ys being arranged thusly that makes that very same proposition true.
17. See Rayo (forthcoming) for a defence of mathematical trivialism, some of which at least is in the spirit of this.

Bibliography

Armstrong, D. M. (1997), *A World of States of Affairs* (Cambridge, UK: Cambridge University Press).

Baxter, Donald (1988a), 'Many-One Identity,' *Philosophical Papers* 17, 193–216.

—— (1988b), 'Identity in the Loose and Popular Sense,' *Mind* 97, 575–82.

Cameron, Ross (2007), 'The Contingency of Composition,' *Philosophical Studies* 136 (1), 99–121.

Cameron, Ross (2008a), 'Truthmakers and Ontological Commitment: Or, How to Deal With Complex Objects and Mathematical Ontology Without Getting Into Trouble,' *Philosophical Studies* 140 (1), 1–18.

—— (2008b), 'Truthmakers and Modality,' *Synthese,* 164 (2), 261–80.

Carnap, Rudolf (1950), 'Empiricism, Semantics and Ontology,' *Revue Internationale de Philosophie* 4, 20–40.

Dorr, Cian and Rosen, Gideon (2003), 'Composition as a Fiction,' in Gale (ed.), *The Blackwell Guide to Metaphysics* (Oxford: Blackwell), pp. 151–74.

Eklund, Matti (2008), 'The Picture of Reality as an Amorphous Lump,' in Sider, Hawthorne and Zimmerman (eds.), *Contemporary Debates in Metaphysics* (Oxford: Blackwell), pp. 382–96.

—— (2009), 'Carnap and Ontological Pluralism,' in Chalmers, Manley, and Wasserman (eds.), *Metametaphysics* (Oxford: Oxford University Press), pp. 130–56.

Goodman, Nelson (1972), *Problems and Projects* (Indianapolis, IN: Bobbs-Merrill).

Heil, John (2003), *From an Ontological Point of View* (Oxford: Clarendon Press).

—— (2005), 'Real Tables,' *The Monist* 88, 493–509.

—— (2006), 'The Legacy of Linguisticism,' *The Australasian Journal of Philosophy* 84, 233–44.

Hirsch, Eli (2002), 'Quantifier Variance and Realism,' *Philosophical Issues* 12, 51–73.

—— (2005), 'Physical-Object Ontology, Verbal Disputes, and Common Sense,' *Philosophy and Phenomenological Research* 70, 67–97.

Lewis, D. K. and Lewis, S. R. (1970), 'Holes,' *The Australasian Journal of Philosophy* 48, 206–12.

Lewis, David (1983), 'New Work for a Theory of Universals,' *The Australasian Journal of Philosophy* 61, 343–77.

—— (1991), *Parts of Classes* (Oxford, UK: Blackwell).

Merricks, Trenton (2005), 'Composition and Vagueness,' *Mind* 114, 615–37.

Moore, G. E. (1959), 'Proof of an External World,' in his *Philosophical Papers* (George Allen and Unwin), pp. 126–48.

Putnam, Hilary (2004), *Ethics without Ontology* (Cambridge, MA: Harvard University Press).

Quine, W. V. (1948), 'On What There Is,' *Review of Metaphysics* 2, 21–38.

—— (1960), *Word and Object* (Cambridge, MA: MIT Press).

Rayo, Agustín (forthcoming), 'Towards a Trivialist Account of Mathematics,' in Bueno and Linnebo (eds.), *New Waves in Philosophy of Mathematics* (Palgrave-Macmillan).

Sider, Ted (2001), *Four-Dimensionalism: An Ontology of Persistence and Time* (Oxford: Oxford University Press).

—— (2007) 'Parthood,' *The Philosophical Review* 116, 51–91.

—— (2009), 'Ontological Realism,' in Chalmers, Manley, Wasserman (eds.), *Metametaphysics* (Oxford: Oxford University Press), pp. 384–423.

Thomson, Judith Jarvis (1998), 'The Statue and the Clay,' *Noûs* 32 (2), 149–73.

van Inwagen, Peter (1990), *Material Beings* (Ithaca, NY: Cornell University Press).

—— (2004), 'A Theory of Properties,' in Zimmerman (ed.), *Oxford Studies in Metaphysics,* vol. 1 (Oxford: Oxford University Press), pp. 107–38.

2
Two Composition Questions in Action

Sara Rachel Chant

1 Introduction

Just as we may ask whether, and under what conditions, a collection of objects composes a single object, we may ask whether, and under what conditions, a collection of actions composes a single action. Peter van Inwagen calls the problem concerning material objects the 'special composition question' (van Inwagen 1985). I have argued elsewhere (Chant 2006) that van Inwagen's question may be applied to actions to pose what I have called 'the special composition question in action.'

In this chapter, I shall introduce a second composition question in action. Here we will also ask whether, and under what conditions, a collection of agents constitutes a single collective agent. In this chapter, I will refer to the first composition question in action as 'CA1' and the second question regarding agents as 'CA2.' One might think, as a number of authors do, that a correct answer to CA1 determines a correct answer to CA2. For it is argued that if there is a single collective action that cannot be reduced to the actions of individuals, then there must be some single collective agent that is the author of that act. If this is right, then a correct answer to CA1 will guide us directly to a correct answer to CA2, or so the argument goes.

In this chapter, I will argue that the two composition questions are not so closely related. In fact, there are excellent reasons to think that CA1 demands a positive solution that does not impose any restrictions on CA2. I will also argue for a solution to CA2; I will conclude that a proper understanding of collective agency helps shed light on issues concerning individual agency.

2   The special composition question in individual action

It will be instructive to compare the special composition question in action with the related problem of action individuation. This problem has seen a number of proposed solutions over the years. Most notably, the accounts due to Donald Davidson (1980), Alvin Goldman (1970), and Carl Ginet (1990) exemplify the three main approaches to the question. To illustrate the problem of action individuation, consider the following well-known example from Davidson. Suppose a submarine commander pushes a button, which causes a torpedo to be launched, which causes the Tirpitz to sink. The problem of action individuation asks how many actions the submarine commander has performed. According to a so-called coarse-grained theory, advocated by Davidson, the submarine commander has performed one action with several different descriptions. That is, the descriptions, 'pushing the button,' 'launching the torpedo,' and 'sinking the Tirpitz' all refer to the very same action. In contrast, a 'fine-grained' theory of action individuation, whose major proponent is Goldman (1970), would say that the commander has performed three distinct actions – in other words, that each description names a distinct action he has performed. Lastly, according to a componentialist theory, advocated by Ginet (1990), the submarine commander has performed a 'large' action that has 'pushing the button,' 'launching the torpedo,' and 'sinking the Tirpitz' as proper parts.

Although there has been a significant literature on the question of action individuation, many philosophers lost interest in it when it was argued – primarily by Alfred Mele (1997) and Carl Ginet (1990) – that nothing substantively depends on its answer. Somewhat ironically, following a detailed account of his componentialist theory of action individuation, Ginet says that

> ...it seems to me that the issue over the individuation of action, though sufficiently interesting in its own right, is not one on which much else depends. ...Moreover, any of the three accounts can be made to work in the sense that, first, each can be spelled out well enough that one can see that it gives a coherent account of the kind of thing it says actions must be, and, second, each can find *some* support in our ordinary talk about actions. (Ginet 1990, pp. 70–1)

If Mele and Ginet are right about the unimportance of action individuation, one might suspect that nothing substantive would depend upon the answer to CA1. After all, CA1, like the problem of action individuation, is a problem of how to count actions; in one case, it is how to count the number of actions performed by an individual. In the second, it is a problem of how to count the number of actions performed by a group of individuals.

However, before concluding that nothing much depends upon the answer to CA1, we should consider exactly why the individual form of the action individuation question is supposed to be unimportant. Fortunately, we do not need to look too far for an answer. Theories of action are supposed to illuminate puzzling features of human agency, intentionality, moral responsibility, and practical rationality, among others. But it is reasonable to expect that no particular theory of action individuation would straightforwardly affect our view of these features of human agency. To return to our example, it is hard to see how a theory of action individuation would affect our view of the submarine commander's action or actions. No matter whether we say he has performed one action or many, we know that he presumably sank the Tirpitz intentionally, he has displayed an appropriate form of practical rationality, he is morally responsible for his action (and the result of his action) in the usual way, and so on. In other words, the features of his agency seem to be independent of how his actions are individuated. So although there may be a metaphysical puzzle about the individuation of individual action, it is a puzzle whose answer will not have any repercussions on the most important issues concerning action.

Now we ask whether the same is true of groups and their collective actions. In other words, are the features of group agency clear to us already, independently of how we individuate the actions performed by the members of the group? Here, I think the answer – even if it is not a resounding 'no' – is at least unclear enough to prevent us from dismissing CA1 out of hand. Unlike in cases of individual action, we know very little about the agency of groups, and this is evidenced by the fact that so many different theories of group agency have recently been defended in the literature. To take a particularly clear example, Kirk Ludwig has argued that, in spite of the fact that our natural language appears to commit us to the proposition that there are groups and distinctively collective actions, this talk can be reconstructed so as to avoid those implications (Ludwig 2007). And because (according to Ludwig), our language constitutes the strongest argument in favour of the existence of collective actions and agents, this semantic reconstruction obviates the need for positing their existence.

On the other hand, some have argued that there is a form of group agency that cannot be eliminated or reduced to the agency of individuals. Advocates of this view – including Philip Pettit and Christian List (List and Pettit 2004) – have argued that certain failures of collective rationality are specific to groups having a particular structure. That is, some groups may consist entirely of rational individuals, each fulfilling any practical or moral obligation in a perfectly consistent manner, in spite of the fact that the group fails to do so.[1] Such phenomena, according to this view, militate in favour of retaining a distinct sense of 'group agency,' 'collective action,' and related concepts.

Thus, whether we say that a group has performed one action or many amounts to the question of whether there is a distinct sense of 'collective action.' And as we have seen, notions of collective agency, collective practical rationality, and collective responsibility are far from clear already, and may reasonably be taken to depend – at least in part – on whether a distinctive form of collective action exists. Thus, we should not be too hasty in dismissing CA1 merely because we may have dismissed a related question concerning individuals.

So regardless of whether action individuation at the level of the individual is important to a complete theory of action, there is an excellent case to be made for the non-triviality of the metaphysics of collective action. In the next section, I will examine CA1 to see whether there is any satisfying solution to it. After offering an answer to CA1, I will go on to discuss its implications for an account of CA2.

3   The special composition question in collective action

In the previous section, I argued that dismissing the question of action individuation for individuals does not justify dismissing CA1. But this raises an important methodological question. That is, when theorizing about collective action and its related concepts, should we model our analysis by analogy to that of individual action? And if so, how closely should such an analogy be followed?

I believe that it would be a mistake to follow an analogy to individual action too closely. The agency of groups – if there is such a thing – would obviously differ in important ways from the agency of individuals. Collective actions would also have an aetiology that is importantly different from that of individual action. So one cannot assume that an analysis of individual action and agency will apply straightaway to group action and agency.

However, that being said, it is also a mistake to dismiss the analogy out of hand. Indeed, the very fact that we pose these questions by borrowing terms and concepts from discussions of individual action suggests that we are looking to exploit some similarities between individuals and groups. So the method I propose here is to find a balance between respecting an analogy between individual and collective action, while simultaneously recognizing that the underlying mechanisms and aetiology of each may yet differ in important ways. Accordingly, I shall assume that when there are well-motivated reasons for recognizing a particular form of action or agency in the individual case, we thereby have good *prima facie* reasons to recognize its counterpart in the collective case. However, we should not assume that the similarities between the two will necessarily be very deep, insofar as we are concerned with the underlying mechanisms and other, more subtle, features of each.

If this methodological assumption is followed, then we are led almost straightaway to the conclusion that there are collective actions, distinct from the individual actions that bring them about. To see this, consider which individual actions would be most relevantly similar to collective actions, if there are such actions. In considering this question, we must ask what features of an alleged collective action are most distinctive of it. Of course, one feature is that it would be authored by more than one individual agent; but obviously, we cannot look for this feature among individual actions. However, another feature of collective actions is that they would be composed of (or generated by, or brought about by) more than one individual action. Let us say, for short, that collective actions are 'composite.'

If there were a corresponding form of individual action – a composite individual action – then it would be what Carl Ginet has called an 'aggregate action,' or what Alvin Goldman has called an action brought about by 'compound generation' (1970). These are actions performed by one individual, typically across time, who performs more than one 'simpler' or more 'basic' action. To take Goldman's example, a person may drive a nail into a wall by hitting it with a hammer five times. Each strike with the hammer is the result of a single action, and the action of 'driving the nail into the wall' is brought about by those five actions. In Ginet's example, a person may type the word 'by' as a result of typing the letter 'b' followed by typing the letter 'y.' There is a difference between how Goldman and Ginet refer to these actions; for Goldman, they are 'generated' by simpler actions, whereas for Ginet, these actions are 'composed of' their constituent actions. But for our purposes here, these differences are not important. What is important is that we are to recognize a form of individual action that is 'composite' in the appropriate sense.

Attention to composite individual actions is certainly warranted. After all, action theory is properly concerned with features of human agency that can be understood only when we consider agents who perform composite actions across time. For example, a rich form of human agency (in contrast to the possible agency of dogs and cats, or of human infants) is shown in our ability to use practical reasoning to make complex plans that will be executed over an extended period of time. To put the point another way, we coordinate our own 'simpler' actions across time in order to bring about a desired result. To the extent that this motivation applies to cases of purported collective action, we have reason to take the existence of collective actions seriously.

Of course, members of groups are often motivated to coordinate their actions with other agents for the same reasons that individuals coordinate their actions across time. Accordingly, accounts of collective action and intentionality typically centre on the role of planning and inter-agent coordination and cooperation to deliberately achieve a collective end. Thus, the coordinating behaviour of individuals within a group is significantly analogous to the practical reasoning employed by an individual across time. Of course, the process of so organizing one's individual actions may be significantly different from the process of organizing a group's actions. But in spite of this difference, the motivation for considering both forms of composite action is similar. That is, we want to better understand a form of practical reasoning that is central to a rich concept of distinctively human agency.

But as I have argued at length elsewhere (Chant 2006), the analogy between individual and collective composite action does not end there. In the case of individual composite action, we want to understand the difference between intentional and unintentional action. That is, we recognize cases in which a composite action is brought about by an individual in accordance with a plan, as well as cases in which the composite action was unintentional. These are cases in which, although each 'simpler' action may have been intentional, it was not the agent's intention to thereby perform any composite action at all; but in spite of this fact, some composite action was performed.

Thus, we may distinguish between two forms of unintentional composite action – a 'weak' form and a 'strong' form. In the weak form, a composite action may be unintentional in much the same way that a non-composite action may be unintentional. These are cases in which the agent intentionally performs some composite action, but it has an unintended consequence. We would say that the agent's bringing about that unintended consequence is an unintentional (composite) action. For example, a person may paint her house by performing many 'simpler' actions, and thereby perform the intentional composite action of 'painting her house.' But suppose that, because the colour is so garish, she also lowers the value of her house. If she did not have the intention to do so, then 'lowering the value of her house' is (or denotes) a composite action as well, albeit a weakly unintentional one. In this way, an intentional composite action can give rise to an unintentional one.

In the 'strong' form of an unintentional composite action, a person may perform several 'simpler' actions that are each intentional (under some description, perhaps), without having an intention to perform any composite action at all. To take an example I have discussed elsewhere (Chant 2006), a person may intentionally flip each of two light switches, without having any intention regarding the combined effects of doing so. But if it turns out that the two switches have been wired together in a particular way – for example, so that they set off an alarm if they are both flipped – then she may thereby perform a composite action denoted by 'setting off the alarm.' I shall refer to such cases as 'strongly' unintentional because no intention existed to perform any composite action whatsoever.

In cases of individual composite actions that are strongly unintentional, we are naturally led to assume that a composite action has been performed because we want to discuss issues of responsibility – both causal and moral – for the result of the action.[2] Returning to the example, we may want to know whether the person is causally responsible for setting off the alarm (in contrast, say, to the person who wired the switches together), morally responsible for doing so, or in any other way culpable. Attributing a strongly unintentional composite action to the individual in such cases makes it sensible to ask such questions.

Similarly, one should presume that there are strongly unintentional composite *collective* actions for much the same reason. If the switches are flipped by two agents, then the same motivations exist for saying that a composite action has been performed – but this time, the motivations speak in favour of attributing a (strongly unintentional) *collective* action to the group. Given the clear similarity between these two forms of strongly unintentional composite action, it would be arbitrary to allow the existence of one without also allowing for the other.

3.1   Desiderata of the account

At this point, we should pause to take up a few related issues. First, we should note that the best argument for the existence of strongly unintentional collective actions proceeds from the analogy to individual action. The conclusion that such actions exist in the collective case is something with which the vast majority of writers on this subject would disagree. For those authors, the very possibility of such strongly unintentional collective actions is actually defined away; for the standard approach to the subject of collective action is to stipulate as a necessary condition that the set of actions be performed with the (collective) intention to thereby perform a collective action. Although the specifics vary significantly from one account to another, it is remarkable how much agreement there is on this point.[3] However, the position for which I shall argue here is that such a stipulation is a mistake. Given the existence of strongly unintentional individual (composite) action, we cannot simply build into the definition of collective action that no corresponding class of actions exists. If it turned out to be the case that strongly unintentional collective actions did not exist, this conclusion should be the result of an argument, not the immediate consequence of a stipulation.

The second point is that it is a mistake to argue from the existence of collective moral or causal responsibility to the existence of collective action or collective agency. This strategy proceeds from the temptation to argue that in certain situations – say, 'tragedy of the commons' cases – that a group bears moral responsibility for producing some undesirable outcome. Then, from the principle that one is only responsible for one's *actions* (as opposed to non-actional events), one might conclude that the group must have performed a collective action if it is to bear moral responsibility for the outcome. Similar arguments might be made for collective agency, collective causal responsibility, and so on.

Even if such arguments turned out to be sound, this general strategy is not a good one.[4] Specifically, suppose one were to argue, as above, that groups bear moral responsibility, and must thereby be able to perform collective actions or have collective agency. If one were uncomfortable with this conclusion, it would be possible to consistently maintain that there is no distinctively 'collective' moral responsibility at all; instead, one would argue, it is the individual group members – not the group as a whole – that bear moral responsibility. Thus, the debate comes down to the issue of whether there is collective, 'non-distributive' moral responsibility – that is, moral responsibility borne by the group as a whole, but not by the individual members *qua* individuals. And of course, the issue of whether there is such non-distributive moral responsibility is at least as murky as whether there are collective actions, collective agents, and so on. So this argumentative strategy is not a good one. I shall have more to say about this line of argument later in this chapter.

If these considerations are correct, we cannot analyze the concept of collective action by looking to the intentions of individuals within the group, nor can we look to derive an analysis from such related concepts as collective moral responsibility or collective agency. Instead, the proposal for which I shall argue is that a set of actions performed by individuals may be a collective action because of the causal structure of that set of actions, not because of its origins or moral properties.

However, we need to digress briefly before getting to the analysis. The reason for this digression is that we have to address the question of how we are to evaluate a proposed analysis of the concept of collective action. This is a difficult issue, because it would seem that our ordinary usage of the term 'collective action' and the circumstances in which it appears reasonable to attribute collective actions are quite diverse – so diverse, in fact, that it is implausible to suppose that ordinary usage will entail any specific account.

Consider the following cases in which ordinary usage would suggest that a collective action has been performed. Two people walk together, hold a conversation, compete with each other in a boxing match, or carry a heavy table across the room. A larger group of individuals might parade down the street in a highly organized way, and an unruly mob might riot in a chaotic scene. People who are not even aware of each other's existence might collectively bring down a computer network by accidentally overburdening it. Finally, a collective action can, in some sense, be performed by a single person; such would be the case when a lawyer representing a large corporation negotiates a contract and commits the corporation to the agreement. Thus, if ordinary usage is to be our guide, we would have to assume that collective actions can be organized or disorganized, laden with normative considerations or free of them, cooperative or competitive; ordinary usage also suggests that collective actions can be performed in a highly cooperative manner, or by individuals who are not even aware that the others exist, much less that a collective action is being performed. And, lastly, a collective action could be performed by individuals according to an express agreement of which all parties are aware, or by a single person representing a group whose members are implicitly committed to follow the representative's lead.

Rather than stipulate a particular subset of (what ordinary language suggests are) collective actions as the target of the analysis, or be constrained by ordinary usage, a different strategy is appropriate. We should take note of the fact that collective action is of particular interest because of its central place in a cluster of related concepts, some of which I have mentioned above. When we study collective action, we do so because we hope that the analysis will not merely be consistent with our analyses of related concepts, but will additionally help us to better understand those concepts. In fact, this is why it is unacceptable to stipulate that collective actions *must* be the result of a group's members so intending to act collectively. The stipulation, by simply assuming a particular (and highly restrictive) relationship between intentions and collective action, forfeits any chance of clarifying any wider set of concepts.

Furthermore, there is a deeper assumption underlying accounts of collective action and its cohort of related concepts. This assumption is that issues concerning the behaviour of groups of agents can be understood in analogy to the behaviour of individual agents. In part, what we are doing when we discuss collective action is trying to give a reconstruction of our pre-analytic, 'folk psychological' theory of group behaviour. For just as we try to understand and predict an individual's behaviour by attributing beliefs, desires, intentions, and other mental states to that person, so, too, we attribute a corresponding set of attributes to groups of agents.

It is important to keep in mind that this is, in fact, an assumption – or perhaps more accurately, a working hypothesis. For it could turn out that there simply is no way to understand group behaviour through such an analogy to individual behaviour. Or to say the same thing a different way, it could turn out that, in order to make the analogy work at all, we would need to characterize these group analogues of individual mental states so differently that the analogy would be rendered meaningless.

This working hypothesis, like others, will be vindicated only if an adequate analysis of these concepts is informed by the relationships among them in the same way that our theories of the 'individualistic' concepts are so informed. For example, an analysis of individual intention, in order to be judged successful, would have to help us understand the aetiology of individual action, without trivially entailing a particular view of it. If we are to test the assumption that there are group analogues of 'individualistic' concepts such as action and intention, then we must aim at an analysis of those group-level concepts that plays a

similar role in shedding light on related issues. Thus, the most important test of an account of collective action will be whether it does end up
informing us – or at least laying a productive framework for studying –
about these related concepts.

3.2   The causal proposal

The proposal I am endorsing here is a simple one. To a first approximation, we may say that a set of individual actions is a collective action if
its component actions are related to each other so as to bring about a
particular kind of consequence, which I will call a 'non-additive' consequence.

Consider the following example. Suppose that two technicians working in a lab each pour a chemical into a test tube, and the two chemicals combine in such a way as to produce a cloud of smoke. I think
it is relatively clear that the descriptive phrase, 'producing a cloud of
smoke' denotes a collective action on the part of the two lab technicians. The reason why this is a case of collective action is that the
event of the smoke cloud appearing is non-additive in the following
sense. Consider a pair of counterfactual situations in which each lab
technician pours their chemical into the test tube without the other.
Now consider all of the causal consequences of each of these isolated
actions. The union of those two sets of actions will be the set of additive consequences, and anything that denotes a member of that set will
not be taken to denote a collective action. For instance, 'two chemicals
being poured into the test tube' denotes an additive consequence; and
we would accordingly say that this does not denote a collective action –
it is simply the description of a pair of individual actions. But 'producing a cloud of smoke' denotes a non-additive consequences – for in
each of the two counterfactual situations, the smoke would only have
been produced by the combination of both chemicals, whereas only
one is present in each instance. Thus, we say that 'producing a cloud
of smoke' denotes a non-additive consequence, and hence, it denotes a
collective action.

By characterizing collective actions according to the production of
non-additive consequences, we correctly identify a core set of cases.
Consider the following example, which is clearly not a collective
action. Suppose there are two people, and each person lifts a weight
individually and puts it down again. If we ask whether 'lifting two
weights' denotes a collective action, the proposal correctly gives a negative answer. For the union of the consequences of each action taken
separately will contain the lifting of two weights. Hence, we would say

that the lifting of two weights is merely an additive consequence of the actions of each person; so 'lifting two weights' does not denote a collective action.

The class of collective actions will shrink or expand, depending upon how broadly we interpret 'non-additive consequences.' In the two examples given here, I have considered only what we might call *'causal* non-additive consequences,'* in which the component actions cause an event that is not merely the 'sum' of the two component actions. There are other kinds of non-additive consequences, however. To take an example I have discussed elsewhere (Chant 2006), suppose that two people each sign a contract and thereby enter into a binding agreement with each other. The phrase, 'entering into an agreement' should clearly count as a non-additive consequence, even though it is not caused by the component actions, but is instead 'generated' by the two signings, plus the legal conventions concerning contracts. That is, legal conventions bring the agreement into existence only as the result of both parties signing the contract.

3.3   An objection

It might be argued that the proposal is too broad in that it always will say that in every case in which more than one agent acts, a collective action has thereby been performed. Consider the two weight lifters once more. There may be some trivial non-additive causal consequence of their actions; perhaps some dust particle is moved in such a way that 'moving the dust particle' will count as picking out a non-additive causal consequence. If so, the objection goes, the two weight lifters have performed a collective action after all – namely, the action denoted by the phrase 'moving the dust particle.' But this is wrong, since it is intuitively clear that no collective action has been performed at all.

The answer to this objection relies upon a point about the ontology of action. Suppose that collective actions were to be identified with particular sets of bodily movements. Then, returning to our example, the two phrases, 'lifting two weights' and 'moving the dust particle' could be taken as denoting the same set of actions. Thus, if 'moving the dust particle' really does pick out a collective action, then the two agents' actions of lifting their respective weights would be a collective action. And since 'lifting two weights' picks out that collective action, it would turn out that the movement of that dust particle really does render this a case of collective action – a very undesirable result, especially when one considers how easily the example generalizes to virtually every other case.[5]

To see what is wrong with such an objection, we consider Davidson's account of intentional action. As I have said earlier in this chapter, Davidson's account is that a phrase such as 'sinking the Tirpitz' is the description of an intentional action if the effect named in the description rationalized the agent's acting in the way she did. In his example, the submarine commander pushes a button, which launches a torpedo, which sinks the Tirpitz. The commander did this in order to sink the Tirpitz, so 'sinking the Tirpitz' picks out an intentional action on Davidson's account. But of course, the button-pushing has other causal consequences as well, which may also be used pick out the submarine commander's action. For example, a cloud of smoke may have been created by the explosion, so 'causing a cloud of smoke to appear' is also a phrase that can be used to pick out the submarine commander's action. But 'causing a cloud of smoke to appear' will not normally pick out an *intentional* action.

At this point, a similar objection might be offered against Davidson's theory. Let us say that the submarine commander's action is to be identified with a particular bodily movement of his. So if 'sinking the Tirpitz' picks out an intentional action, then that bodily movement is an intentional action. And since 'causing a cloud of smoke to appear' also picks out that bodily movement, then it picks out an intentional action. Of course, this is an incorrect result for the theory, since we recognize that 'causing a cloud of smoke to appear' is unintentional (although certainly foreseeable).[6]

However, the objection only gains whatever plausibility it has by making an error about the ontology of action, and the manner in which actions are denoted. Specifically, the objection assumes that the various descriptive phrases such as 'sinking the Tirpitz' or 'launching the torpedo' refer to a specific thing – the action itself. The objection would have it be the case that the action itself unambiguously bears either the property of being intentional, or the property of being unintentional. And since actions are either intentional or not, depending upon the descriptive phrase referring to them, it would be possible on this assumption that the very same entity could be both intentional and unintentional when two or more descriptive phrases are used to pick it out.

Of course, it is now a familiar point that actions are not entities bearing the property of being intentional or unintentional. Rather, calling an action 'intentional' – being dependent on the manner in which the action is described – is really an assertion about the action 'under a description' and not an assertion about a property borne by some metaphysical entity, the action.[7]

A similar point applies to descriptions of collective actions. Merely describing some non-additive consequence or other that was brought about by two or more agents' individual actions does not have the undesirable result that whenever two or more agents act, they perform a collective action. Like attributions of intentionality for individual action, whether or not a set of actions performed by various individuals is a collective action will depend upon the manner in which that set of actions is described. Putting the point another way, it is not that there is an entity – the collective action – that is brought into being and made to bear the property of being a unified action by virtue of its being referred to in a particular way. Instead, sets of actions performed by individuals are either collective actions or not only 'under a description.' We may think of 'collective actionhood' as a relation determined not only by the individual actions, but also depending upon the description used to pick out that collection.

Of course, even if one accepts this view of the ontology of collective action, it is still possible to reasonably worry that in some cases, we shouldn't say that there is any collective action at all in any sense. Returning to the example given earlier, if our two weight-lifters each lift their individual weights without any regard of the other person, one may want to say that there isn't any collective action at all. Accordingly (the objection would go), the mere discovery of some insignificant non-additive consequence should not give us any means whatsoever of referring to this pair of actions as a collective action.

However, I think that this worry is not important. Although we may find it counterintuitive to say that the two weight-lifters performed the collective action of 'moving the dust particle,' this uneasiness is not the result of referring to the actions as a collective action. Rather, this feeling arises because of the triviality of the consequence we use to refer to the set of actions. We would never, under any reasonable circumstances, be concerned with this tiny consequence; so it should not be surprising that we find the example odd or counterintuitive. But suppose that, due to a structural failure of the building, the sudden shifting of the weights causes the floor to buckle. According to the proposal I am defending here, we are to conclude that the phrase, 'buckling the floor' picks out their actions as a collective action (albeit a strongly unintentional one).

I think it is safe to say that the feeling of uneasiness surrounding this attribution is less than in the previous example, although we have to acknowledge that some uneasiness may yet remain. But there is a good explanation for this. In everyday cases of collective action, we often tie attributions of collective action to the moral responsibility borne by the group or its members. In the case of the two weight-lifters, as the story is told we would conclude that there is no reason to hold them morally responsible. And of course, one way in which we signal that we should let them 'off the hook' is by not thinking of their individual actions as composing a collective action at all. For example, if a bystander were to say, 'those weight-lifters buckled the floor,' it would be reasonable to expect someone to respond by saying, 'it was just an accident; they didn't *really* buckle the floor.' But the reason why this is a reasonable response is because the responder is conversationally implying that it would be wrong to attribute moral responsibility to them. And as I have argued already, the existence of strongly unintentional collective actions emphasizes the fact that moral responsibility does not determine whether a collective action has been performed. Rather, we frequently perform collective actions for which there is no moral responsibility at all.

3.4 Benefits of the causal proposal

Clearly, this proposal allows for the existence of strongly unintentional collective actions, since it does not require any intention on the part of the agents, other than whatever intention would have to be present in order for each to perform her individual action. And as I have argued above, this is a desirable feature for any account of collective action. We must now consider how the proposal fares on some other important criteria.

Understanding the concept of collective action in terms of non-additive consequences has an important benefit – specifically, it coheres well with economic and game-theoretic models of cooperation and coordination. For example, consider the Prisoner's Dilemma, which is often used as a simple model of a situation in which cooperation is a desirable outcome. Recall that in a Prisoner's Dilemma, each individual faces a choice between cooperating with the other player and defecting. In order to be a Prisoner's Dilemma, a few simple conditions must be satisfied. First, the act of defection must strictly dominate cooperation, meaning that an individual receives a higher payoff for defecting, regardless of what the other player does. And just as importantly, the very best outcome for either player occurs when she defects while the other cooperates (this is the so-called Temptation to defect); conversely, cooperating while the other player defects must yield the worst possible outcome for that player (this is referred to as the 'Suckers Payoff'). Third, mutual cooperation (yielding the

'Reward' payoff) must yield a higher payoff than mutual defection (the 'Punishment'). These conditions guarantee that it will be individually rational for both players to defect, but collectively rational for both to cooperate.

But another condition is frequently overlooked in discussions of the Prisoner's Dilemma. This is the condition that the 'reward' payoff for mutual cooperation must be higher than the average of the 'temptation' and 'sucker' payoffs.[8] This condition entails that, if we think of payoffs as quantifying the effect of the players' actions[9] then the outcome most often associated with a collective action – namely, mutual cooperation – will also count as a collective action under the current proposal. This is because the total effect of the players' combined actions must be greater than the combined effect of their actions if they act individually – that is, if at least one player defects.

Indeed, this is a common feature of other games that are used as models of cooperative behaviour and collective action. For example, in the Stag Hunt game – which may also plausibly be used as a model of collective action (Skyrms 2001) – it is also a necessary condition that the sum of the two players' payoffs when both cooperate is higher than the sum of their payoffs in any other condition. The fact that the current proposal coheres so closely with this formal work on cooperation is an important virtue; after all, if we have the correct analysis of the concept under study, the features figuring into that analysis should be present in an abstract model of it.[10]

Additionally, if we understand collective action in terms of non-additive consequences, we also get the explanatory relationship between collective intentions and collective actions right. Typically, the reason why a group of individuals will form the intention to act together is because they collectively aim at bringing about a desirable non-additive consequence. To take a very simple example, suppose that two people want a certain heavy table to be moved across the room, and neither person can move it alone. When they move it together, they have brought about a non-additive consequence, according to the criteria I have given above. In fact, one way of understanding a non-additive consequence is by recognizing it as a consequence to which no individual can contribute 'her fair share' alone. For example, it would be less intuitively clear that 'moving the table' refers to a collective action if each person were somehow able to move it half the required distance individually; that would be a case in which each of the two individuals in the group is capable of bringing about one-half of the desired consequence by herself.

4   The special composition question for collective agents

We now consider the question, 'when, if ever, is a group of individuals a collective agent?' Before providing an answer to this question, we must first address a simple form of argument that has been deployed to answer it. I shall argue that in spite of the popularity and simplicity of this approach, it does not establish any conclusion about the existence or non-existence of collective agents.

4.1   The linking argument

The form of this argument – which I shall call the 'linking argument' – is simple. First, it begins with the premise that only agents have a particular capacity, such as the ability to perform actions or to bear moral responsibility. Second, an argument is provided that groups of agents possess the relevant property. Then, we are to conclude that there are collective agents.

Instances of this strategy are easy to come by. Among the properties that are supposedly tied to agency are 'rational unity,' the ability to perform actions, and the ability to bear moral responsibility. For example, David Copp (2006) has argued that there is a form of collective moral responsibility that is possessed by groups, and which cannot generally be distributed among the members of the group. For Copp, the property that establishes that there are collective agents is (what he calls) 'moral autonomy,' which in other discussions is sometimes called 'collective, non-distributive' moral responsibility.[11]

The cases described by Copp originate in theoretical results regarding judgment aggregation, which were first rigorously described in the seminal work of Kenneth Arrow (1950). These formal results describe a surprisingly wide range of cases in which a group of rational individuals comes to a collective judgment on some matter, but the collective judgment is something which no individual in the group would have endorsed. In the example used by Copp (and which was first discussed in this literature by Pettit and List (2004, 2007) a university committee must decide whether to recommend Mr. Borderline for tenure. University policy stipulates that tenure will be granted only if the candidate is judged to have achieved excellence in each of the three categories of teaching, research, and service.

Suppose that the three members of the committee are Alice, Bob, and Carol. We are to suppose that the committee will make its decision by majority vote. In considering their individual decisions on how to vote on this issue, each member of the committee comes to the decision that Borderline has failed in exactly one of the three areas, but has achieved excellence in the other two. However, each believes that he has failed to achieve excellence in a different area. Specifically, Alice believes that he has been deficient in teaching; Bob believes that he has been deficient in research; and Carol believes he has been deficient in service. Thus, when they vote, they unanimously come to the conclusion that Borderline should be denied tenure.

However, Copp argues that Mr. Borderline has a legitimate complaint against the committee.[12] For consider what would have happened if the committee had voted on each of the three areas separately. If they had, then the vote would have been 2–1 that he had achieved excellence in each of the three areas of research, teaching, and service. Thus, the committee would have judged that he had met the necessary criteria, and Mr. Borderline would have been granted tenure.

Now, let us assume that the morally and rationally correct procedure was the latter one, which would have granted tenure to Mr. Borderline. If so, Copp argues that the moral or rational blame cannot fall on the members of the committee as individuals, since (we assume) each was fully rational in his or her vote, and each followed the university procedure for deliberating and voting. Rather, the fault must lie with the committee as a whole. In Copp's terms, the committee has 'moral autonomy.'

Although it is possible to take issue with Copp's interpretation of this particular case, here, we are interested only in how the example is used to support the conclusion that there are collective agents. Copp summarizes the form of his argument in the following way:

1. There are possible cases in which (i) individuals act in official organizational roles on behalf of collectives, (ii) the choices and actions of these individuals are entirely rational and morally innocent.... (iii) there is moral or rational fault that must be assigned somewhere, and (iv) the only plausible candidate for the assignment of such fault is the collective.
2. If the collective is at fault, it must have acted.
3. Agency individualism is false (i.e., the group is capable of intentional action). (Copp 2006, p. 216, parenthetical comment mine).

Although it is certainly possible to object to premise (1), I will grant that there are cases of collective 'non-distributive' moral responsibility. And although one might be concerned about other premises, the one I will focus on here is (2), which is tantamount to the claim that only entities that act can bear moral or rational fault.[13]

This is an intuitively plausible assumption; but it is worthwhile to locate the origins of its plausibility. I think it is safe to say that whatever plausibility (2) enjoys is the result of our experience with the agency of individuals. For example, one might be interested in a sense of individual agency according to which adult humans are agents, but not small infants or non-human animals. It might be observed that (e.g.) the property of bearing moral responsibility coheres well with this conception, insofar as adult humans (typically) possess both agency and moral responsibility, but neither infants nor non-human animals possess either agency or moral responsibility. Cases that are less clear may then be examined. For instance, we would say that a person who (say) lashes out violently because of a high fever is not morally responsible for her action; correspondingly, it is at least reasonable to assert that her agency – at least for that time – is absent or at least significantly impaired. Furthermore, it might be thought that, having established the link between moral responsibility and agency for individuals, an analysis of collective agency should follow an analogous principle. This thought is even more reasonable if one accepts – as I have argued earlier in this chapter – that analyses of collective action and agency should be at least somewhat analogous to corresponding analyses of individual action and agency.

However, an important problem with the linking argument is that much weaker premises are equally compatible with our experiences and intuitions with individual agency; but those weaker premises would not support the linking argument. For example, let us assume that at least in the individual case, it is true that only agents can be the bearers of moral responsibility for their actions (or the outcomes of those actions, etc.). But this assumption does not provide compelling evidence of any general principle that can be deployed in the linking argument. For consider the proposition that 'only agents or groups of agents can bear moral responsibility for actions.' If we consider only individual actions, this weaker principle would (trivially) yield the same conclusions in all cases; thus, it is compatible with all our experience and intuitions of individual action and agency.

However, the weaker principle is unable to support any conclusion about collective action and agency. For let us grant that in some case, there is moral responsibility for a collective action. According to the weak principle, the existence of such moral responsibility only supports the conclusion that some agent (or agents) were involved in the production of the action. And even someone who was unfriendly to the existence of collective agents would readily agree that there are agents who contributed to the action – after all, the individuals in the group did contribute to the performance of the action, and they are presumably agents. In this way, any principle – including Copp's – that is used as part of a linking argument can be weakened in such a way as to yield another principle that is equally well-justified, but cannot support the desired conclusion.

4.2   Towards the positive account

In the remainder of this chapter, I will offer a programmatic suggestion for understanding the concept of collective agency. Although this suggestion will fall short of a full-blown analysis, we can at least get the broad strokes of an analysis in place.

First, let us begin with what I take to be a reasonable default position regarding the existence of collective agents – that they do not literally exist. An advocate of this negative view would hold that whenever we talk about groups in such a way as to suggest that they are agents, this is only a metaphor.[14] More specifically, a proponent of this view could hold that we tend to understand the behaviour of groups by way of analogy with the behaviour of individuals. But the reliance on an analogy to individuals is merely a heuristic, not evidence that groups are agents.

This view – which I shall call 'collective nihilism' – is far from untenable. Given considerations of parsimony, I think that the burden of proof is on the proponent of collective agents; and as I have argued above, it is not enough to cite our ordinary language when arguing for this thesis. However, I shall argue that much of the plausibility of collective nihilism comes from introspecting about our own individual agency in ways that are dubious.

The plausibility of collective nihilism rests, at least to an important extent, on a line of reasoning that I shall illustrate by an analogy to another dispute in metaphysics. This is the problem of whether we should consider two or more material objects as constituting a single object. Although I cannot do justice to this large literature here, let us consider a very simplified line of reasoning, just by way of providing a useful illustration. Suppose that I take a paradigmatic case of a 'unified' material object to be that of an ordinary table under ordinary conditions. I now consider the question of whether a set of chairs – perhaps the chairs that are arranged around the table – should count as constituting a 'unified' material object. Suppose that as a first attempt at an analysis, I propose that a set of objects composes an object just in case there are no spatial 'gaps' among the constituent objects. This might be seen as cohering well with my intuitions: a set of chairs has spatial 'gaps,' but the table does not. Accordingly, we intuitively judge – in agreement with my proposed analysis – that the table is a 'unified' material object, but the set of chairs is not.

However, a moment's reflection reveals that the proposal is untenable. For it may be pointed out to me that, despite appearances, the table is filled with spatial 'gaps' as well. In fact, someone may correctly inform me that, if we consider the entire volume of the table, it is mostly empty space. So ironically, it has turned out that the very feature (having spatial gaps) which I intuitively thought distinguished the set of chairs from the table – and which I made the centre of my analysis – is actually shared by the table. In this case, because the proposed condition – having no spatial gaps – is not met by any paradigmatic cases of a unified object, we would probably be right to conclude that the proposal has little to show for itself.

I think that a similar line of reasoning is present (although it is kept in the background) in discussions of collective agents. We begin by considering a paradigmatic example of an agent, namely, a fully competent adult human being who carefully considers her actions in detail. If we begin from what I have called the 'default position' of collective nihilism, then we might begin by supposing that a disorganized mob is a fairly clear case of a group of agents that does not constitute a collective agent.

We now should consider what property distinguishes between the two cases. As many authors have pointed out (using different terminology and with different emphases), there is a clear candidate for separating the competent adult from the disorganized mob. That is, that there is a certain 'unity' to the deliberative process undertaken by the individual, which may not be present in the group. Specifically, when we are considering a single adult, we suppose that the set of considerations, desires, beliefs, attitudes, and other mental states are 'wholly present' to the individual; it is one subject who has access to all of the data underlying her intentions and actions, and it is the combination of many mental states that is responsible for bringing about her subsequent action. Let us say that the various mental states that figure into the deliberations of a fully competent adult are 'transparent' to her insofar as she is aware of all of them, and deliberately employs these beliefs, desires, and other mental states in determining what actions to undertake.

In this sense, the various mental states that figure into the mob's behaviour are not 'transparent' to the group as a whole. So in order to distinguish this feature of the mob from the transparency of the group, let us say that the mental states of the individuals in the mob are 'opaque' to the group. Thus, it is reasonable to suppose that this 'opacity' is responsible for our judgment that the group should not count as a unified agent.

However, as with our proposed analysis regarding material objects, it might not actually be so clear whether the paradigmatic case really possesses the feature we have supposed it to have. Thus, we do well to reconsider more carefully whether the deliberative, individual agent really possesses the 'transparency' that we have supposed her to have.

Unlike when I described the table and chairs, here it is quite unclear whether, or to what extent, a normal, competent adult human being really possesses this transparency. After all, it is a commonplace observation that a normal human being – even a well-functioning adult – may frequently lack the power to introspect into her own beliefs, desires, dispositional attitudes, and the like. As we informally say, a person may be 'in denial' about her own beliefs, and her actions may only be rationalizable on the assumption that she is acting out of motives that she herself would be quick to sincerely deny. Indeed, although cases of delusion, psychosis, panic, and the like are easy examples of this phenomenon, we do not need to consider such extreme cases; our ordinary lives are full enough of these cases. Thus, it is as least questionable whether our paradigmatic individual agent really possesses the property that we have taken to distinguish her from (supposedly) clear cases of entities that are not agents.

If we were to follow the material composition example, then we might conclude that this proposal is a non-starter; for if it cannot distinguish between fully competent adults and unruly mobs, then we might suspect that it is not useful at all. However, I think we would be acting too quickly to simply dismiss this proposal out of hand. After all, the property of possessing 'transparency' is not an all-or-nothing affair; this is a vague property that an individual might have to various degrees. A similar observation holds with respect to groups of individuals. A highly organized and deliberative group may have very high levels of transparency, whereas an unruly mob may be highly opaque. Indeed, I think it is not unreasonable to suspect that there may be cases in which the transparency of a group is greater than that of an individual.

Being a matter of degree, it may be possible to salvage the suggestion that transparency is the crucial feature in determining whether there is a unified agent behind an action. We might say that an individual or a group is an agent to the extent that transparency accounts for its actions (perhaps 'in the right way'). This would allow the possibility that a thoroughly deluded individual might not be rightly considered an agent at all, whereas a highly deliberative and well-informed group may yet count as an agent.

This suggestion will require some adjustments, if it is to succeed as part of an analysis of the collective agent. Besides the obvious need to clarify the very loose concept of 'transparency,' we must address a difficulty that arises from using a vague concept to determine whether a particular entity – the agent – exists or not. Specifically, we need to make a choice among three options, each of which may have its own advantages and disadvantages. First, we might say that the vague concept of 'transparency' determines a similarly vague answer to the ontological question of whether a particular entity is an agent, or whether a particular kind of agent exists. Second, we could avoid the necessity of giving a vague answer to the ontological question by fixing a threshold level of transparency above which the entity is to count as an agent. Or, third, we might try to change the subject, so to speak, by stripping the issue of collective agents of its ontological presuppositions.

The first option – to say that an entity's being an agent comes in degrees – will offend many people's metaphysical views, and for a good reason. As has been pointed out in other literature, whether a thing exists or not cannot be a matter of degree – it is absolutely and unambiguously true or false that a particular entity exists. And if we are considering the question of whether there exists a collective agent in such-and-such circumstances, then this principle makes non-sense of any degreed conception of an agent. For obvious reasons, I think that the second option, to establish a threshold level of transparency, is not workable. Such a line separating agents from non-agents would have to be defended against the charge of arbitrariness, and it is not clear how such a defence could be mounted.

Thus, I think we are better off endorsing the third option. That is, we must replace the question, 'when does a group of individuals compose an agent?' with the less ontological question, 'how do we determine what degree of agency is possessed by a group of individuals?' This change of subject replaces the ontological question of whether or not a particular kind of agent exists with the subtly different question of determining to what extent an entity possesses the property of agency. On this view, we consider agency as a kind of power that may be possessed by an entity – whether an individual or a group – to varying degrees. Of course, this change will have at least one entailment that many would find highly counterintuitive. Specifically, if we adopt the view that there is no satisfactory way to make sense of the concept of a collective agent, then the same view will almost certainly apply to the concept of an individual agent. Thus, if we are right to say that, strictly speaking, there is no such thing as a collective agent (only groups possessing agency to varying degrees), then we would also have to say that strictly speaking, there is no such thing as an individual agent – only individuals who possess agency to some degree.

Although some would be loath to abandon the existence of agents, I do not think that we are losing anything of value in doing so. Of course, we can still make perfect sense of our ordinary way of speaking about agents as a kind of shorthand referring to entities that possess a particular level of agency, where that requisite level of agency will be vague and change from one situation to the next. Similarly, every philosophically interesting question about the ability of agents to act, bear moral responsibility, and so on can be rewritten as a question about the relationship between agency, action, moral responsibility, or any other power or property that was supposed to apply to agents.

5   Conclusion

In this chapter, I have argued for several theses: that the right analysis of collective action will make use of the causal consequences of the alleged collective action; that an analysis of collective action does not settle any important issues regarding collective agency; that an analysis of collective agency needs to be argued independently of questions regarding collective moral responsibility; and finally, that we may get closer to an account of collective agency by stripping the question of some of its ontological presuppositions.

We may say a bit more about the last argument in an attempt to tie together some of the separate threads of this chapter. Earlier, I said that the existence of collective action and agency is really best thought of as a working hypothesis – that is, it is a working hypothesis that there is an informative analysis of the behaviour of groups that makes recourse to a vocabulary like that of the folk psychological theory of individual behaviour. If this working hypothesis is to be vindicated, then we have an additional reason to shift our attention from the question of collective agents to one of collective agency. For if we keep the question focused on the existence of a thing – the agent – then we will undoubtedly lose much of the relevant similarity between individuals and groups. After all, although I do not know what, from the perspective of metaphysics, a collective agent would turn out to be, I am reasonably confident that it would turn out to be extremely different from an individual agent. In other words, the similarity (if there is such) between individual and collective agents is not that the same thing exists in both cases. Rather, the similarity is that there is an important property or characteristic shared (at least sometimes) by both individuals and groups. The working hypothesis amounts to the assumption that this shared property can play the same explanatory role in accounting for the behaviour of individuals and for groups. Whether this hypothesis is borne out over the long run will depend on whether the details of the analysis yield a useful general theory of individual and group behaviour. If the arguments in this chapter are correct, then we have at least a roadmap for deriving such a theory.

Notes

1. This recent work owes much to the earlier work of Kenneth Arrow, whose impossibility theorem ushered in these considerations (1950). The work of Pettit and List is notable for generalizing the impossibility theorem, and relating it in a sophisticated way to philosophical, as opposed to economic, problems.
2. Although the desire to ask questions of (e.g.) causal and moral responsibility is a motivation for considering the actions as a single composite action, I will argue below (p. 41) that this does not provide a sound argument for the existence of composite actions.
3. For instance, see Tuomela 1984, 1989, 1991, 1995, 2002, 2004, 2005, Tuomela and Miller 1988, and Miller 2001b. For these authors, the central concept in collective action is that of a collective intention ("or joint intention" or "we-intention"). With the proper account of that concept – according to these authors – an analysis of collective action follows almost immediately.
4. I do not believe that such arguments are sound. Below later in this chapter, I shall argue that even the premise that there are collective actions does not suffice to show that there are collective agents.
5. Perhaps there would be rare examples in which the individual actions are causally isolated from each other.
6. If one wants to assert that the submarine commander did intentionally cause a cloud of smoke to appear (perhaps because it was forseeable), choose some other, trivial consequence that was unforseeable.
7. The rather obscure notion of ' "under a description" description' was introduced by Elizabeth Anscombe (1958), and later clarified (or adapted) by Davidson.
8. This condition is important because if it is not met, it would be possible for the two players (in an iterated game) to mutually benefit by taking turns as Defector and Cooperator.
9. Of course, we are never forced to think of payoffs in this way. However, there are many cases in which the story is told in such a way that this interpretation is very natural.

10. We should note here that the usual strategy of analyzing the concept of collective action in terms of the collective intentions of the group has no hope of systematically cohering with these game-theoretic models. For these analyses are purely etiological – they do not depend upon the consequences of the alleged collective action, only on how it was generated. Thus, an analysis in terms of group intentions is at best orthogonal to formal work on collective action and cooperation.

11. See (e.g.) Feinberg 1991, Lewis 1991, May and Hoffman 1991, Mellema 1988, Miller 2001a, Narveson 2002, and Sverdlik 1987 for discussions of collective, non-distributive moral responsibility.

12. Or against the university as a whole. Here, I shall sidestep the issue of whether the committee serves as a kind of ' "proxy agent" ' for the entire university.

13. Throughout his discussion, Copp does not distinguish between the ability to act intentionally, and status as an agent. For example, Copp defines ' "agency individualism" individualism' as ' "the doctrine that ... collectives are not agents and are not capable of intentional action" action'(2006, p. 195). Because this is the doctrine against which is arguments are directed, and because there is no suggestion that he is arguing that collectives are either agents or capable of intentional action (which is the negation of the doctrine as stated), I shall interpret Copp as treating both as equivalent.

14. A recent example of this is Kirk Ludwig's view that all talk of collectives can be rewritten into a language that does not include reference to groups as such (Ludwig 2007).

Bibliography

Anscombe, G. E. M. (1958), *Intention* (Cornell University Press).

Arrow, K. (1950), 'A Difficulty in the Concept of Social Welfare,' *The Journal of Political Economy* 50 (4), 328.

Chant, S. R. (2006), 'The Special Composition Question in Action,' *Pacific Philosophical Quarterly* 87, 422–41.

David Copp, D. (2006), 'On the Agency of Certain Collective Entities: An Argument From "Normative Autonomy," ' *Midwest Studies in Philosophy* 30, 194–221.

Davidson, D. (1980), *Essays on Actions and Events* (Oxford, UK: Clarendon Press).

Feinberg, J. (1991), 'Collective Responsibility,' in May and Hoffman (eds.), *Collective Responsibility: Five Decades of Debate in Theoretical and Applied Ethics* (Rowman and Littlefield Publishers), pp. 53–76.

Ginet, C. (1990), *On Action* (Cambridge: Cambridge University Press).

Goldman, A. I. (1970), *A Theory of Human Action* (Englewood Cliffs, NJ: Prentice Hall).

Lewis, H. D. (1991), 'Collective Responsibility,' in May and Hoffman (eds.), *Collective Responsibility: Five Decades of Debate in Theoretical and Applied Ethics* (Rowman and Littlefield Publishers), pp. 17–33.

List, C. and Pettit, P. (2004), 'Aggregating Sets of Judgments: Two Impossibility Results Compared,' *Synthese* 140, 207–35.

Ludwig, K. (2007), 'Collective Intentional Behaviour from the Standpoint of Semantics,' *Noûs* 41 (3), 355–93.

May, L. and Hoffman, S. (eds.) (1991), *Collective Responsibility: Five Decades of Debate in Theoretical and Applied Ethics* (Savage, MD: Rowman & Littlefield Publishers).

May, L. (1990), 'Collective Inaction and Shared Responsibility,' *Noûs* 24, 269–78.

Mele, A. R. (ed.) (1997), *The Philosophy of Action* (New York: Oxford University Press).

Mellema, G. (1988), 'Causation, Foresight, and Collective Responsibility,' *Analysis* 48 (1), 44–50.

Miller, S. (2001a), Collective Responsibility, *Public Affairs Quarterly* 15 (1), 65–82.

—— (2001b) *Social Action: A Teleological Account* (Cambridge: Cambridge University Press).

Narveson, J. (2002), 'Collective Responsibility,' *The Journal of Ethics* 6 (2), 179–98.

Skyrms, B. (2001), 'The Stag Hunt,' *Proceedings and Addresses of the American Philosophical Association* 75 (2), 31–41.

Sverdlik, S. (1987), 'Collective Responsibility,' *Philosophical Studies* 51 (1), 61–76.

Tuomela, R. (1984), *A Theory of Social Action* (Dordrecht, The Netherlands: D. Reidel Publishing Company).

—— (1989), 'Actions by Collectives,' *Philosophical Perspectives* 3, 471–96.

—— (1991), 'We Will Do It: An Analysis of Group-intentions,' *Philosophy and Phenomenological Research* 51 (2), 249–77.

—— (1995), *The Importance of Us: A Philosophical Study of Basic Social Notions* (Stanford , CA: Stanford University Press).

—— (2002), *The Philosophy of Social Practices: A Collective Acceptance View* (Cambridge: Cambridge University Press).

—— (2004) 'Joint Action,' in *Proceedings of the Workshop on Holistic Epistemology and Theory of Action* (University of Leipzig).

—— (2005), 'We-Intentions Revisited,' *Philosophical Studies* 125, 327–69.

Tuomela, R. and Miller, K. (1988), 'We-intentions,' *Philosophical Studies* 53, 367–90.

van Inwagen, P. (1990), *Material Beings* (Ithaca, NY: Cornell University Press).

3
Another Look at the Reality of Race, By Which I Mean *Race$_f$*

Joshua Glasgow

Bucking previous trends, more and more researchers have been coming to endorse the proposition that race is real. Realist *constructivists* maintain that our practices' astoundingly significant consequences compel us to recognize that race has a social reality. As the saying goes, try telling a black person trying to hail a cab that race isn't real.[1] It's real enough for discrimination, for reduced or privileged access to health care and education and car loans, and for being the glue that bonds identities. And that, say constructivists, is real enough to be real. At the same time, *biological racial realism* has also mounted a comeback lately. Fascinating new scientific data and complementary theoretical architecture, along with a commitment to relegating racist science to the past, have jointly provided powerful support for the doctrine that races are, very roughly, biologically real breeding populations.

Despite the advances partisans of these views have been making, here I want to bolster the case for *racial anti-realism*. I'll go about this indirectly, by getting into some conceptual troubles that seem to have afflicted all three of these camps in the debate over race's ontological status. In discussing these troubles, my primary stalking horse will be biological realism, so I'll have less to say about constructivism. However, a quick look at a basic argument against constructivism provides a glimpse of the thorny conceptual background against which our discussion takes place.

The constructivist's basic thesis is that races are *social kinds*. Now constructivists disagree amongst themselves on exactly *how* races are social kinds, but the common thread is that if we think that some other social kinds are real, we should grant that races are real, too: if we allow that professional kinds, such as *journalist* or *justice of the peace,* though not biologically real, are nevertheless real in some other (social) sense, then we should also allow that races are real in the same (social) way. In very rough outline, Al Gore and Tony Blair are both white because certain social facts about them are true, while the Dalai Lama and Kofi Annan are not white, because other social facts are true of them. In this way, the relevant social facts, which might revolve around our practices of classification, access, discrimination, privilege, and so on, make race real as a social category.

One objection to this view is that the groups structured by social forces – to which constructivists rightly direct our attention – are not races, because racial terms, by definition, are meant to refer to something biological, rather than social. We might follow Lawrence Blum (2002) and others who call those groups structured by *social* forces 'racialized groups,' but whatever we want to call them, they aren't appropriately called 'races,' at least if one constraint on appropriate labelling is conformity to ordinary discourse.[2]

As this objection illustrates, the truly metaphysical debate over race often boils down to semantic issues. Ron Mallon (2006) points out that otherwise opposed race theorists have actually formed an 'ontological consensus' concerning many facts about race, such as that there are no racial essences and that race-related social forces affect us. Thus the real question about specifically racial constructivism is not whether groups structured by social forces are real, but whether it is appropriate to call them 'races.' More broadly, pursuing what Mallon calls the 'semantic strategy,' many of the participants in the race debate aim to constrain the meanings of racial terms such that, when joined with some ontological premises, those meanings either allow race to be real or guarantee its illusory status. So generally speaking, anti-realists maintain that 'race' is defined biologically, which is to charge that when constructivists talk about something social that they call 'race,' they aren't really talking about race, at least not in the relevant, ordinary, folk sense of the term.

Again, I will not be defending this criticism of constructivism here,[3] but it illustrates how the semantic strategy might be used. What I want to do next is to pursue that strategy in another direction, by defending some of the conceptual premises in a parallel argument against the new biological realism, premises that have been called into question lately by Robin Andreasen, arguably biological realism's most dedicated partisan in philosophy. Since these issues are the bedrock source of a significant chunk of the contestation, the hope is that if we make progress at the conceptual level, we might make some metaphysical headway.

1   Biological racial realism and the mismatch argument

Biological racial realism has recently received the prominent endorsement of philosophers, scientists, and even a science writer for the paper of record, the *New York Times'* Nicholas Wade (2006).[4] Many such views are variants of what is sometimes called *populationism,* the thesis that races are real as breeding populations or as clusters of breeding populations. Scientists can use our genetic data to reconstruct elements of our species' history, and part of that history includes identifiable patterns of breeding isolation, where people reproduced within their population at substantially greater rates than they reproduced with those outside of their population. The cumulative effect of this isolation – *relative,* rather than *absolute,* reproductive isolation, which can result from everything from geographic separation (oceans, deserts, mountains) to social pressures – has been to pool us into populations, and clusters of populations, which frequently are marked by distinctive genetic and phenotypic traits.[5] Roughly speaking, then, populationists conclude that the data on human populations suffice to show that race is biologically real (though like constructivists, they disagree amongst themselves on some crucial details).

One criticism that some of us levelled against populationism is the 'Mismatch Argument.' David Hull (1998, pp. 364–5) makes the central point vividly: 'Several groups of people who are considered Caucasoids by anthropologists would rouse all the anxiety and hostility in ordinary white racists that blacks do. Their skin is black. They look black. But technically, they are Caucasoids. But such observations are not likely to persuade the members of the admissions committee of an all-white country club.' Below we will expand on Hull's observation and note several ways in which populationism's concept of race seems not to be our ordinary concept of race – among other things, it might require saying that there is no Asian race, and it seems to abandon the core idea that races are organized according to their visible traits. But before we get to that, here's the more basic argument:

The Mismatch Argument

(1) For the race debate, the relevant metaphysical question is whether the commonsense concept of race picks out something real.

(2) The breeding populations identified by science are not picked out by the commonsense concept of race.

Thus,

(3) Those breeding populations are not races in the sense relevant for the race debate.[6]

Andreasen's sustained defence of populationism recently has devoted several pages to challenging the Mismatch Argument (Andreasen 2005). To see its relative modesty, though, begin with the first, meta-analytical premise.[7] We focus our attention on the commonsense concept of race because of the aims of our inquiry. The debate over the reality of race has largely been about the kind of thing that we normally talk about when we use racial terms. We want to know whether *that* sort of thing is real. There might be some *other* kind of thing that is real. In fact, there probably are other real kinds of thing – there is titanium and water and everything else. But we in the race debate have been particularly interested in whether race in the ordinary sense is real. One of the reasons that this has been the traditional scope of relevancy is that the back-and-forth over race's reality is often animated by a prior ethico-political debate about whether we should eliminate racial discourse. The underlying connection between these debates is evident: if race in the ordinary sense is, like Medusa, not real, then plausibly this is one reason that we – we in the public sphere, not a few academics holed up in dusty offices – should stop using *our* racial discourse. Thus the metaphysical debate about race traditionally has had a particular concern with whether the *ordinary* concept of race picks out anything in this world.

Many presentations of the Mismatch Argument (including my original discussion of it (Glasgow 2003)) take this dialectical context for granted, which might make the argument appear weaker than it is. For instance, Andreasen (2005, p. 97; 2007, p. 477) writes that my earlier presentation of the Mismatch Argument rejects the claim that we defer to scientists to tell us the referent of 'race,' that is, she interprets my argument as denying that semantic deference is appropriate for racial terms. But this is not accurate: while the Mismatch Argument is committed to saying that our folk racial discourse is the *relevant* one for the race debate, it is not committed to the anti-deferential claim that the 'underlying nature' of what we purport to talk about with our folk racial discourse should not be identified by scientists. To say that we should focus on the ordinary concept of race is not yet to say anything about the content of that concept or about whether and to what extent the linguistic community has conferred upon some experts the authority to identify its content. Semantic deference enthusiasts (e.g., Putnam 1975) hold that we turn to scientists to tell us the referents of our (lay scientific) terms. That is to say, scientists tell us some of the *content* of our concepts. But they are still *our* concepts. So semantic deference to science may be entirely appropriate; changing the terms of the debate by talking about non-folk, scientific concepts and terms of art is another matter entirely. Thus the mismatch worry is *not* that scientists cannot identify the underlying natures of the groups that we purport to refer to with racial terms, should any such underlying natures exist; it is that, in their research on human breeding populations, they have stopped talking about those groups and started talking about something else.[8]

If two laypeople are arguing about whether some person, George, is what they call 'schizophrenic' by trying to sort out whether he has multiple personalities, a psychologist might step in and say, 'Ah, but that's irrelevant, because "schizophrenia" refers, not to having multiple personalities, but (according to our diagnostic authority, the *DSM-IV*) to a condition that includes at least one month of at least two of the following symptoms: delusions, hallucinations, disorganized speech, grossly disorganized or catatonic behaviour, as well as a marked deterioration in functioning – which you agree George does not display. What you're calling "schizophrenia" is actually what psychologists call "multiple personality disorder." ' While that specialist information is all fine and good, the laypeople would not be conceptually confused to ignore this bit of 'mere semantics' and continue discussing whether George is schizophrenic in *their* sense. It is convenient fortune that the folk name, 'schizophrenia,' and the expert name, 'multiple personality disorder,' refer to what turns out to be the same thing. I don't know if scientists have another term for what the folk are purporting to talk about when they talk about race, but the point of the Mismatch Argument is that 'breeding population' is not it.

Here is another illustration of the point that setting which concepts are relevant is different than setting the content of the relevant concepts: if we – the folk – were to debate the reality of water, it would be irrelevant for scientists to tell us that water is real because they identified it as the chemical compound NaCl (Glasgow 2003, pp. 466–7). We would be within our linguistic rights to say, 'That doesn't show that water is real. We call the stuff, S, whose underlying nature you've identified as NaCl, "salt," and we use "water" to talk about that *other* kind of stuff, W. Please tell us if that other stuff, W, is an identifiable chemical compound.' If the scientists responded by saying, 'Forget W – in the lab we refer to that stuff, S, which is composed of NaCl and which you call "salt," as "water," ' we would be right to insist that their specialist labelling of S as 'water' is irrelevant to the debate we were having, which was about W. We and the scientists would simply be referring to two different things with the same word, 'water.' We would not have a disagreement with the scientists; we would have a misunderstanding.

As a convention that will be useful in avoiding such misunderstandings, let's say that the definition of 'water' as these imagined scientists use the term – referring to NaCl – is given by the concept water$_s$, while the definition of 'water' as we (the folk) in the original water debate were using it – referring to H_2O – is given by the concept water$_f$. The debate we ordinary folk were having was not over whether water$_s$ picks out anything real, but whether water$_f$ picks out something real. In this way, again, the nature of our inquiry constrains which concepts are relevant. And, again, in the case of the race debate, the relevant concepts are the folk concepts. I will have more to say about this below, but for now I only want to emphasize that this does not reject semantic deference: saying that we're focused on race$_f$ – race in the folk sense – allows that the folk might defer to scientists to identify the referent of 'race$_f$.' As long as scientists are informing us about the reference of 'race$_f$,' their investigations may be entirely relevant, but as soon as they start talking about race$_s$ – race in the specialist sense – the information they give us is irrelevant to the debate we are having. It would only be relevant to some other debate – quite possibly an interesting, useful, and even closely related one, but a different one nevertheless. So the Mismatch Argument is most plausibly construed not as rejecting semantic deference, but as constraining the scope of relevant discourse so that semantically deferring to experts might tell us something that bears on our discussion.[9]

That said, some might be tempted to argue that since we might defer to science, we should listen to whatever scientists say about race$_f$. Now to whatever extent this is true, it must conform to what I believe is another constraint on semantic deference: we can usefully defer to experts only when there is an agreed upon set of relevant experts and when there is a consensus amongst them to which we can defer. But this too is a claim with which Andreasen (2005, p. 103) takes issue, on the grounds that '[d]isagreement among scientists should not be a problem for semantic deference, provided that there is a fact of the matter about the nature of the kind.' Of course, I should, and do, agree that we defer to scientists only because we think they are the best source for learning about the natural world. Nonetheless, the mundane practical truth is that there is no way to get a useful expert judgment on the nature of race if either there is no determinate and identifiable set of experts or the experts can't agree on the referent and know its underlying nature. To return to the water example, if there was ever a time when scientists generally disagreed on whether 'water' refers to H_2O, or simply going back to the time when they had no idea that this was the case (assuming for the sake of illustration that 'water' does refer to H_2O), it would have been useless to appeal to science to tell us the facts of the matter. In the very superficial sense, there simply is no useful authority to defer to in situations of authoritative ignorance or indeterminacy.

Arguably there is no clear authority to defer to in the race debate – should it just be scientists, or social theorists too? (Haslanger 2003) – and even more decisively, whatever reasonable set of experts you might choose, they have not come to any sort of consensus on the nature of race$_f$. Neither biologists nor anthropologists nor social theorists have any sort of agreement on whether or not race$_f$ is real, and, among the realists, there is no agreement on what *kind* of thing race$_f$ is (allegedly). So it's not much use to defer to the experts, *even when semantically deferring to them is otherwise appropriate,* to tell us about the referent of 'race$_f$.' Obviously, race$_f$ *might be* biologically real while the experts to whom we defer are ignorant or divided about that fact, but if someone wants to compellingly argue that race$_f$ *is* some biological kind *b*, it can't be on the grounds that the experts *have actually* agreed, with anything approaching the zip code of univocality and determinacy, that race$_f$ is *b*.

A similar response is fitting for Andreasen's (2005, p. 103) claim that the Mismatch Argument maintains that expert disagreement justifies privileging commonsense over science (when, she notes, commonsense is just as confused as science). The Mismatch Argument is not committed to such a hierarchy. Instead, it only needs to claim that if we want to know the referent of the folk term 'race,' it's no use appealing to scientists when they give no answer or an indeterminate answer. In the case of race$_f$, the problem is that we're stuck in this rut: whatever group of experts you want to (plausibly) choose, they do not provide useful, univocal judgments about whether it is real and, if so, what its nature is. We simply have nothing determinate to which we can defer. Or, we might be deferring to the *ideal* expert judgment, the one that by hypothesis taps into the way the world is, but when in the non-ideal real world of sadly imperfect knowledge, *this* world where we're trying to sort out the metaphysical status of race$_f$, we have no idea what that ideal judgment would be.

So we cannot say that race$_f$ is biological entity *b* just because science says it is. What we need to do, instead, is look at our racial language and see if science can point us to something that we might independently judge to be an adequate referent for our racial terms. That is, we need to see if premise 2, the claim that biologically-identified breeding populations do not sufficiently match those groups ordinarily identified as racial, is true. Some of Andreasen's (2005, pp. 103–4) concerns about this premise also raise fundamental questions in the theory of reference, including some issues related to the causal-historical theory of reference. Now whether or not you find the causal-historical theory of reference plausible, whether or not it is *true,* racial anti-realism, and the Mismatch Argument in particular, are orthogonal to it. According to the causal-historical theory of reference, many names get their referents through a 'baptism,' a naming ceremony where we rigidly designate an object (or its kind or nature) as the referent of the name. If we associate with that object a description of it that turns out to be false, so much the worse for our association; the referent is anyway set independently by the baptism. The Mismatch Argument has fewer commitments than this: it only relies on the intuitive point that the reference and meaning of our racial$_f$ terms are constrained by our use of terms like 'race,' 'white,' or 'Asian.' So if scientists identify the existence of something that doesn't fit those linguistic practices, then that something won't be race$_f$.

Andreasen objects to my view here on the grounds that, first, historians don't agree on the linguistic and temporal origin of the term 'race,' and that, second, it has had a 'diversity' of meanings, and our ignorance about this history means that we don't know 'what was in the minds of speakers during the baptismal procedure.' However, if I have understood her correctly, this appears to be a red herring: the Mismatch Argument, and, for that matter, the causal-historical theory of reference, are each independently compatible with this kind of historical ignorance and variation. First, both allow that a term's reference can shift (see Kripke (1980, p. 163) on 'Madagascar,' for example) – 'baptism' just being a caricature of patterns of language use. Second, we don't need to know the etymology of a term (even assuming our usage of it hasn't changed) in order to know that to which it refers. Even those of us who have no idea where the term 'water' came from can know that 'water' refers to H_2O. We know this because our use of 'water' reliably indicates what stuff 'water' is intended to refer to, and science has (we suppose) univocally told us that the underlying nature of that stuff is H_2O. What matters for the Mismatch Argument is that our racial terms are attached to certain groups of people. How we got these attachments handed down to us is relevant insofar as it is the process by which the attachment, and therefore the term's extension, became fixed, but we don't always need to know the history of the process in order to know that it is fixed. And all of this is consistent with the causal-historical theory.

Again, then, the Mismatch Argument shouldn't be read as importing any controversial assumptions from the philosophy of language. Instead, to see if it succeeds, the real questions are what the scientifically identified breeding populations are and what the folk concept of race is. The answers to those questions will show us whether the breeding populations in question dovetail sufficiently with our referential practices regarding race$_f$ (contrary to the substantive claim of premise 2). On these questions, as well, premise 2 has proven controversial. One plausible reason for asserting it is that morphology is central to and ineliminable from the ordinary concept of race (Glasgow 2003, pp. 459–61; Glasgow 2009). In principle, this could provide considerable ammunition against those (many) forms of populationism that do not require that breeding populations bear distinctive visible traits, for if 'race$_f$' is defined such that the different races$_f$ must have distinctive morphologies, and if scientifically identified breeding populations don't necessarily have those distinctive morphologies, then those breeding populations won't be races$_f$. But is the conceptual claim accurate? Andreasen (2005, 98) claims that in my focus on morphology, I 'overlooked other [commonsense] definitions that focus solely or primarily on genealogy.' Now I don't agree with that claim. To my great detriment, I have often been guilty of overlooking commonsense definitions. But I don't think that this is one of those cases. (I feel reassured on that front by the fact that, in the exact same paragraph, Andreasen explicitly writes that 'Glasgow himself provides examples of folk conceptions that rely on genealogy alone.') But the interesting question here isn't whether I overlooked genealogy; it's what the Mismatch Argument requires in order to succeed. On this count we should be clear: the important claim is *not* that ancestry is not a crucial part of the ordinary conception of race (and I reject such an exclusionary claim (Glasgow 2003, p. 461)); rather, the claim is that our visible traits, such as skin colour, are, *inter alia,* crucial parts of the ordinary concept of race.

Now as a separate matter Andreasen rightly notes that this latter claim, that visible traits are central to the ordinary concept of race, itself must be vindicated. Towards that end, one might be content to simply make the armchair observation that it is 'intuitive' and 'obvious' that 'race$_f$' is defined at least partly in terms of visible traits (Glasgow 2003, pp. 459–60, n. 11). But such a presumption might be perceived as rash. (Although, for whatever dialectical context is worth, Andreasen (1998, p. 212; 2000, p. S663) agrees with this characterization, anecdotal evidence confirms what we both agree on, and very many people in the literature on race agree as well.) It is additionally noteworthy, then, that the claim that morphology is central to ordinary race-thinking has also been confirmed by a good deal of empirical psychological literature on this question (Hirschfeld 1996; Condit, Parrott, Harris, Lynch, and Dubriwny 2004; Shulman and Glasgow forthcoming).

But in case that's not enough, further argument is available (Glasgow 2009). It proceeds with a basic thought experiment. Imagine that radical egalitarians infuse the global water supply with a chemical agent that causes our bodies to take on a relatively uniform appearance, so that we all are instantaneously and permanently made to look roughly like (say) the Dalai Lama. And allow that until this point, we are members of a few paradigmatic breeding populations. Now given that, post-infusion, we all look more or less alike, should we say that there is still a racial$_f$ difference between us? Suppose that we even continue to roughly maintain our previous breeding patterns for awhile, but our offspring, like us, all look similar to the Dalai Lama. Populationism implies that we should say that we are still racially$_f$ different, but this appears to be counterintuitive: if we all look the same, there is no racial$_f$ difference between us – there are no racial$_f$ groups, no black race$_f$ or white race$_f$, for instance. Note, importantly, that this is one way in which the concept of race$_f$ as a group comes apart from the concept of race$_f$ as the property of an individual. It might be that an individual can bear the visible traits of a race$_f$ other than her own; but if the entire race$_f$ bore the visible traits of 'another' race$_f$, they wouldn't constitute *another* race$_f$ – though they might well be a different ancestral or ethnic or religious group.

Now, so far as I know, no surveys have been done to see if this judgment is widely shared, and if it turns out to be idiosyncratic, this argument will take a (non-decisive) hit, for that will undermine evidence that the ordinary concept of race requires morphological differentiation. But until such data are in, consult your own intuitions. If you agree that such a scenario would mean the end of racial$_f$ groups, then you should agree that, as a conceptual matter, visible traits are part of the concept race$_f$. As part of entertaining this thought experiment, predict how people would behave in such a world. They might continue to separate themselves, discriminate, and privilege based on cultural practices or religion or any number of other categories. But, after some time has elapsed, would they *racially$_f$* discriminate? Would there still be oppressors that target *black* people, or would they instead target orthogonal (if sometimes coincidental) groups, perhaps focused on certain cultural objects or ancestral homes? Would there still be groups devoted to ending anti-*black* racism? Importantly, our concepts' contents are in part revealed by our practices (Haslanger 1995, 2005, 2006), and my strong suspicion is that, in our imagined world of radical racial upheaval, we would abandon classificatory practices surrounding terms like 'black' and 'white,' perhaps focusing instead on other, ancestrally or ethnically related practices, which would indicate that race$_f$ is inescapably tied to visible traits.

If this suggestion is correct, a key – perhaps *the* key – subsidiary premise in the Mismatch Argument is vindicated: what counts as a race$_f$ is, *inter alia,* supposed to be distinguished by certain visible traits, in which case breeding populations, which don't necessarily have those distinguishing visible traits, won't count as races$_f$.

Moreover, there appears to be a second (not unrelated) point of mismatch: extensionally, the groups we ordinarily identify as races$_f$ are different from the breeding populations identified by scientists (Glasgow 2003, p. 459; Glasgow 2009, Ch. 5). One point of contention here is the suggestion that most common racial$_f$ classificatory schemes in America pick out no more than four or five races$_f$; often, anyway, those in the debate agree that Africans, Asians, and Caucasians are supposed to be races$_f$, and many consider Latino/as and Native Americans distinctive races$_f$. This claim provides important ammunition for the Mismatch Argument. Scientists have so far found little evidence for, and significant evidence against, the proposition that Latino/as constitute a distinctive breeding population. In addition, the scientific data rarely show Asians to constitute a unified and distinctive breeding population (some data generate the result that Southeast and Northeast Asians are distinct races, while others separate Northeast Asians from those west and south of the Himalayas, who are lumped in with Caucasians). So if the biological data entail that there is no Asian or Latino/a race and that those in southern and western Asia are of the same population as those from Norway, and if the ostension of 'race$_f$' requires either that there is an Asian or Latino/a race$_f$, or that southern or western Asians are not racially$_f$ the same as Norwegians, then once again we have a mismatch – the data on breeding populations will bypass the concept race$_f$.[10]

In reply, Andreasen (2005, pp. 100–1) claims first that the history of the U.S. census and intellectual theory do not always align with what I claim to be the extension of 'race$_f$.' But that is, I believe, irrelevant; what dialectically matters is whether *our* (current, folk) concept of race$_f$ aligns with it. On that score, Andreasen further claims that the 2000 census does sufficiently align with one plausible carving of breeding populations, according to which there are Africans, Caucasians, Northeast Asians, Southeast Asians and Pacific Islanders, and Native Americans.

However, this degree of alignment may not be sufficient: if the folk consistently and *non-negotiably* identify Northeast and Southeast Asians as a race$_f$ or Latinos as a race$_f$, and if science indicates not only that Latinos or Asians are not a race, but also that Northeast Asians are racially closer to Caucasians than to Southeast Asians, then we're no longer talking about race$_f$.[11] Unfortunately, robust conceptual evidence on this question is hard to come by, so it is left to you: if you think that on the concept of race$_f$, a concept that you can probably deploy competently, Asians (say) constitute a race$_f$ and the Amish do not, and that if someone denied those claims they'd have stopped talking about race in the ordinary sense, then you'll possess a piece of evidence that populationism can't help vindicate race in the relevant sense (race$_f$); if you don't have those judgments, then this plank in the mismatch case against populationism is weakened.

I think that there is depth to the mismatch beyond what I've discussed here (for more, see Glasgow 2009, ch. 5), but hopefully at least the *prima facie* case is made: there is intensional mismatch regarding the importance of visible traits to race$_f$, and there is extensional mismatch regarding categories like *Asian*. In saying this, it should be emphasized that, first, none of this means that, in our ordinary discourse, we cannot make mistakes that need to be corrected, or that, second, what prompts those corrections might be dictated by the world, since the world can sometimes determine the referents of our terms. What it does entail is that *some* propositions will be conceptually non-negotiable. This is why some concepts simply pick out *nothing* in the world – manatees will never be picked out by the concept mermaid.[12] And hopefully a starter case has been made that, in the case of race$_f$, there appear to be widespread and relatively non-negotiable conceptual commitments, which gain expression in our language use and practices, that prevent us from understanding race$_f$ in the way required by populationism (Glasgow 2009). Instead of being a plausible re-characterization of race in the ordinary sense, populationism changes the subject to another category altogether, just as we change the subject from mermaids when we start talking about manatees.

Andreasen has recently made some comments that suggest something quite similar to this basic claim. Strikingly, she takes this to provide a rejoinder for populationism. According to this rejoinder, if there is a scientifically vindicated concept of race, then even if it deviates from the folk concept, that is enough to establish the reality of race, given that the two concepts are, as she puts it, 'autonomous' and that the term 'race' is ambiguous between these two 'meanings' (Andreasen

2005, pp. 102–6; 2007, p. 477). Let's call this the *ambiguity thesis*. When we see the kind of divergence in usage that motivates the ambiguity thesis, which is often due to the different functions and classificatory principles of science and commonsense and which happens with respect to many other, non-racial categories, 'there is often no revision (nor any expectation of revision) to science or [commonsense].'

Andreasen takes the ambiguity thesis to be not only a defence of her view, but also a theoretical option that I have 'overlook[ed],' and to that extent I have allegedly 'misrepresent[ed]' her view and in the Mismatch Argument presented a critique that 'does not apply' to her view. I am confused by this accusation, for *the ambiguity thesis is, in effect, the central claim of the Mismatch Argument.* The Mismatch Argument states that to the extent that populationism gives us any concept of race at all, it gives us a concept of race that is different than the folk concept of race – that, effectively, there are two 'meanings' for 'race,' and, in addition, only the folk concept is relevant for the purposes of the race debate. Since we've arrived at a puzzling crossroads in this discussion, let's take a moment to assess the overall dialectic.

In her earlier articles pioneering populationism, Andreasen explicitly aimed to articulate a new way of thinking about race that would render biological realism a plausible alternative to anti-realism and constructivism. Now, as she acknowledges, the contention of most anti-realists and constructivists is that (what we here are calling) race$_f$ – not some other concept of race, but race$_f$ – is not biologically real (Andreasen 2004, p. 428), and it is this claim that she wants to, as she says, 'disagree' with (Andreasen 1998, p. 200; cf. 2000, p. S655). But to the extent that she is arguing against anti-realists and constructivists – to the extent that she is providing a new perspective on an existing debate and truly disagreeing with anti-realists and constructivists – she must argue that race$_f$ is biologically real. (Otherwise she would just be talking past them! And it is also worth noting that Andreasen (2005, p. 102) herself considers the ambiguity thesis to be a stronger claim than what she claimed in her earlier articles.) To that same extent, though, it would be dialectically significant if, while populationism might show that race$_s$ – race in some non-folk, specialist sense – is real, it does not show that race$_f$ – race in the folk sense – is real. That is, although populationists and the folk might use the orthographically and phonologically identical word, 'race,' and even though their uses of the word might even overlap to a significant extent, the two concepts are, as Andreasen would say, autonomous. The word has two different meanings. In that case a realist vindication of one concept does not entail the vindication of the other.

Now, Andreasen also sometimes says – sometimes in the very same article – that populationism is 'not in competition' with either constructivism or anti-realism (1998, p. 218; cf. 2000, pp. S664-S665). So there is an interpretive question here: at the end of the day, is Andreasen disagreeing with constructivists and anti-realists, or not? Here I believe that either way, there is a problem. If populationism is an attempt to disagree with the other parties to the race debate, it fails to do so because it only provides evidence for the existence of something that is picked out by a concept other than ('autonomous' from) the one they are debating about. If, instead, populationism is not supposed to be a competitor to the other parties, then it fails to engage the race debate, which Andreasen claims to be engaging. Here I've only addressed in any detail one version of populationism, but if this dilemma can be extended to other forms, then populationism more generally won't be a viable alternative to anti-realism and constructivism.

The streets of metaphysics are littered with positions that have been discarded because various parties slid nearby but distinct concepts into the discussion and ended up talking right past each other. So perhaps we advocates of the Mismatch Argument should make our case as clear as possible by saying that populationism does not show the reality of $race_f$, as opposed to saying more vaguely that it does not show the reality of *race,* in order to explicitly signal that we are using 'race' in the way relevant to the pre-existing debate about what to do with (seemingly erroneous) folk racial discourse. And none of this is to say that there's no point in discussing a non-folk, scientific specialist concept of race. It's just to say that the specialist concept of 'race' isn't the same as the folk concept of race. If this is right, then populationists can either engage the $race_f$ debate and defend *only* the view that scientific discoveries about human breeding populations show that $race_f$ (rather than $race_s$) is real – that is, they can focus their arguments solely on rejecting the claim that there is too little of a match – or they can stop trying to enter the debate that anti-realists have been having with realists about $race_f$. I don't think that the first strategy is going to prove very fruitful, and I think that $racial_f$ anti-realists and constructivists as such do best to remain silent on debates that aren't about the metaphysics of $race_f$.

2   Around the horn

I suggested earlier that other parties to the race debate have flirted with structurally similar proposals. Consider first that while most constructivists acknowledge the depth of biological race-thinking, some go all the way down to the conceptual sea floor. For example, according to Linda Martín Alcoff, '[i]nherent to the concept of race is the idea that it exists there on the body itself, not simply on its ornaments or in its behaviors' (Alcoff 2006, p. 196). While I agree with this claim, it is couched in a book where one of the main theses is that race is real, but not because it exists – or at least not because it *merely* exists – on our bodies themselves. On Alcoff's particular brand of constructivism, our bodies' visible traits are essential parts of race, as ordinarily conceived, but the ways in which they determine our races are a function of our socially constructed perceptual habits. For Alcoff, race is real, but not because race is biologically real; instead, race is real because of the impact that constructed patterns of visually-based racial classification have on our lives.

So, while of course Alcoff may have been writing for effect, if we should read her literally, as saying that it is conceptually true that race exists 'on the body itself,' then taking that conceptual truth for granted, what exists by virtue of *us imposing* racial categories on the body isn't race at all. For that is something that *doesn't* exist on the body itself; it is a construction we perceive to be on the body. That construction is something close to race, perhaps what Blum and others would call our *racializations*. But whatever it is, it's not race in the ordinary sense.

At the other end of the theoretical spectrum, Naomi Zack has long advocated for anti-realism, in part by consistently arguing that the concept of race$_f$ purports, but fails, to pick out a certain kind of biological entity (Zack 1993, 1995, 1997, 2002, 2007). Generally this is an argument for which I have a lot of sympathy (although sometimes for very different reasons than those provided by Zack). So I am pretty much on board with the broad strokes of her view, up until the point at which she claims that 'race is real in society, but no more than a social construction' (Zack 2002, p. 106). That sounds like a constructivist claim to me, and it violates the premise that the concept of race$_f$ purports to pick out some biological reality. If that's truly the purport of the folk concept of race, and I agree that it is, then whatever might be 'real in society' as a social construction isn't race$_f$.

I think that the best way to avoid this problem is to abandon the claim that race$_f$, strictly so-called, is 'real in society.' Correlatively, I do not believe that populationism or constructivism can solve their versions of this problem without fatally undermining themselves as views that purport to engage the race$_f$ debate. Instead, I think that at the end of the day, we'll have to say that races$_f$ are, as a conceptual matter, supposed to be biological, thus undermining constructivism, and biological in a morphologically-centred way that, even populationists acknowledge, is not vindicated by our most advanced science, thus undermining populationism.

Notes

Thanks to participants in a seminar at Victoria University of Wellington and in the 2009 APA New Waves in Metaphysics session, and especially Allan Hazlett, for helpful feedback on prior versions of this chapter.

1. Recently, this bromide got some empirical validation (Dao 2003).
2. I use single quotation marks when mentioning words and phrases and small caps when naming concepts.
3. For the expanded argument, see (Glasgow 2009, esp. ch. 6).
4. I will be focusing on Andreasen's work; for other populationist literature, see Arthur 2007, ch. 2; Burchard et al. 2003; Kitcher 1999; Mayr 2002; and Sarich and Miele 2004.
5. Henceforth I will, only for simplicity, talk of breeding populations, omitting talk of *clusters* of breeding populations.
6. Different commentators focus on different aspects of the mismatch, but other versions of this argument can be found in Appiah 1996, pp. 71–4; Blum 2002, pp. 133–44; Condit 2005; Feldman et al. 2003; Glasgow 2003; Glasgow 2009, ch. 5; Hirschfeld 1996, p. 4; Jorde and Wooding 2004; Keita et al. 2004; Keita and Kittles 1997, p. 538; Montagu 1964, p. 7; Zack 2002, esp. chs. 2, 4, and 5.
7. For further motivation of premise 1, see Glasgow 2009, esp. ch. 3.
8. Note, then, how the Mismatch Argument should be less controversial than, say, John Dupré's (1981, 1999) 'promiscuous realism.' This view holds that there are multiple, equally legitimate carvings of the world, so that if folk classifications say that whales are fish (an antecedent he has come to deny of late), then, relative to that classificatory system, whales are fish, even if on another, scientific system, whales are mammals. Thus for him fishy whales can be real, in a promiscuous sense of 'real.' The Mismatch Argument, by contrast, only requires that the terms of the debate in which we are engaging set which concepts are *relevant*. It only holds that to the extent that folk concepts differ from scientific concepts, the folk, rather than scientific, concepts of race will be the relevant ones.
9. Of course, specialist and folk concepts will often be identical. Whether they are will be significantly constrained by the ways that the relevant communities use the associated terms.
10. In considering the extensional mismatch, I originally compared what I take to be the commonsense notion of race with nine populations identified in Andreasen (1998, 2000). Andreasen more recently indicates that she is not committed to those nine races (Andreasen 2005, p. 100), so in my discussion here, I just focus on the populations that are most recently vindicated by science and most *helpful* to populationism.
11. Whether a particular racial category is conceptually non-negotiable may depend on who is the semantic authority for that category within our linguistic community. If, for example, some Latinos non-negotiably claim that they belong, not to the black or white or any other race but to the *Latino* race

(López 2005), and if Latinos hold the authority to determine at least some of the content of the concept Latino, then that may be sufficient to render their claim non-negotiable.
12. I owe this example to Allan Hazlett.

Bibliography

Alcoff, L. M. (2006), *Visible Identities: Race, Gender, and the Self* (Oxford: Oxford University Press).

Andreasen, R. O. (1998), 'A New Perspective on the Race Debate,' *British Journal of the Philosophy of Science* 49, 199–225.

—— (2000), 'Race: Biological Reality or Social Construct?' *Philosophy of Science* 67, Supplementary Volume, S653–66.

—— (2004), 'The Cladistic Race Concept: A Defence,' *Biology and Philosophy* 19, 425–42.

—— (2005), 'The Meaning of "Race": Folk Conceptions and the New Biology of Race,' *The Journal of Philosophy* 102, 94–106.

—— (2007), 'Biological Conceptions of Race,' in Matthen and Stephens (eds.), *Handbook of the Philosophy of Science: Philosophy of Biology* (Amsterdam: Elsevier), pp. 455–81.

Appiah, K. A. (1996), 'Race, Culture, Identity: Misunderstood Connections,' in Appiah and Gutmann (eds.), *Colour Conscious: The Political Morality of Race* (Princeton: Princeton University Press), pp. 30–105.

Arthur, J. (2007), *Race, Equality, and the Burdens of History* (Cambridge: Cambridge University Press).

Blum, L. (2002), *'I'm Not a Racist, but ...'* (Ithaca, NY: Cornell University Press).

Burchard, et al. (2003), 'The Importance of Race and Ethnic Background in Biomedical Research and Clinical Practice,' *The New England Journal of Medicine* 348, 1170–75.

Condit, C. M. (2005), '"Race" Is Not a Scientific Concept: Alternative Directions,' *L'Observatoire de la génétique* 24.

Condit, C. M., et al. (2004), 'The Role of "Genetics" in Popular Understandings of Race in the United States,' *Public Understanding of Science* 13, 249–72.

Dao, J. (2003), 'Report Cites Persistent Bias Among Cabbies in Washington,' *New York Times*, Oct. 8, A19.

Dupré, J. (1981), 'Natural Kinds and Biological Taxa,' *The Philosophical Review* 90, 66–90.

—— (1999), 'Are Whales Fish?,' in Medin and Atran (eds.), *Folkbiology* (Cambridge, MA: MIT Press), pp. 461–76.

Feldman, M. W., et al. (2003), 'Race: A Genetic Melting Pot,' *Nature* 424, 374.

Glasgow, J. (2003), 'On the New Biology of Race,' *The Journal of Philosophy* 100, 456–74.

—— (2006), 'A Third Way in the Race Debate,' *The Journal of Political Philosophy* 14, 163–85.

—— (2009), *A Theory of Race* (New York: Routledge).

Haslanger, S. (1995), 'Ontology and Social Construction,' *Philosophical Topics* 23, 95–125.

—— (2003), 'Social Construction: The "Debunking" Project,' in Schmitt (ed.), *Socializing Metaphysics: The Nature of Social Reality* (Lanham, MD: Rowman & Littlefield), pp. 301–25.

—— (2005), 'What Are We Talking About? The Semantics and Politics of Social Kinds,' *Hypatia* 20, 10–26.

—— (2006), 'Philosophical Analysis and Social Kinds: What Good Are Our Intuitions?,' *Proceedings of the Aristotelian Society Supplementary Volume* 80, 89–118.

Hirschfeld, L. A. (1996), *Race in the Making* (Cambridge, MA: MIT Press).

Hull, D. L. (1998), 'Species, Subspecies, and Races,' *Social Research* 65, 351–67.

Jorde, L. B. and Wooding, S. P. (2004), 'Genetic Variation, Classification and "Race,"' *Nature Genetics* 36, Supplement, S28–33.

Keita, S. O. Y., and Kittles, R. A. (1997), 'The Persistence of Racial Thinking and the Myth of Racial Divergence,' *American Anthropologist* 99, 534–44.

Keita, S. O. Y., et al. (2004), 'Conceptualizing Human Variation,' *Nature Genetics* 36, Supplement, S17–S20.

Kitcher, P. (1999), 'Race, Ethnicity, Biology, Culture,' in Harris (ed.), *Racism* (Amherst, NY: Humanity Books), pp. 87–117.

Kripke, S. (1980), *Naming and Necessity* (Cambridge, MA: Harvard University Press).

López, I. H. (2005), 'Race on the 2010 Census: Hispanics and the Shrinking White Majority,' *Dædalus* 134, 42–52.

Mallon, R. (2006), '"Race": Normative, Not Metaphysical or Semantic,' *Ethics* 116, 525–51.

Mayr, E. (2002), 'The Biology of Race and the Concept of Equality,' *Dædalus* 131, 89–94.

Montagu, A. (1964), 'The Concept of Race in the Human Species in the Light of Genetics,' in Montagu (ed.), *The Concept of Race* (New York: The Free Press), pp. 1–11.

Putnam, H. (1975), 'The Meaning of "Meaning,"' in his *Mind, Language and Reality: Philosophical Papers,* vol. 2 (Cambridge: Cambridge University Press), pp. 215–71.

Sarich, V. and Miele, F. (2004), *Race: The Reality of Human Differences* (Boulder, CO.: Westview Press).

Shulman, J. and Glasgow, J. (forthcoming), 'Is Race-Thinking Biological or Social, and Does It Matter for Racism? An Exploratory Study,' *Journal of Social Philosophy*.

Wade, N. (2006), *Before the Dawn: Recovering the Lost History of Our Ancestors* (New York: The Penguin Press).

Zack, N. (1993), *Race and Mixed Race* (Philadelphia, PA: Temple University Press).

—— (1995), 'Life After Race,' in Zack (ed.), *American Mixed Race: The Culture of Microdiversity* (Lanham, MD: Rowman and Littlefield), pp. 297–307.

—— (1997), 'Race and Philosophic Meaning,' in Zack (ed.), *Race/Sex: Their Sameness, Difference, and Interplay* (New York: Routledge), pp. 29–43.

—— (2002), *Philosophy of Science and Race* (New York: Routledge).

—— (2007), 'Ethnicity, Race, and the Importance of Gender,' in Gracia (ed.), *Race or Ethnicity? On Black and Latino Identity* (Ithaca, NY: Cornell University Press), pp. 101–22.

4
Brutal Individuation

Allan Hazlett

There are several debates in metaphysics that centre on issues of arbitrary boundaries. Consider the question of composition: when do several things $x_1 ... x_n$ compose another thing? We want to draw a line between those sets of things that compose another and those sets of things that don't compose another. But where to draw the line, without being arbitrary? We want to rule in the set that contains (only) the jacket and the trousers of my suit, but rule out the set that contains (only) the trousers of your suit and the trousers of my suit. But this seems, in some inchoate way, metaphysically arbitrary: there seems to be no real, objective difference between the two sets. (The issue isn't quite the same as the problem of vagueness, since even a vague boundary would seem arbitrary.)

Three possible views, then. Mereological nihilism draws the boundary *way* to one side: it says that no set of putative parts is a set whose members compose something else. And mereological universalism draws the boundary *way* to the other side: it says that every set of putative parts is a set whose members compose something else. Finally, restricted composition says that there is a real, objective boundary between those sets whose members compose something else and those sets who members don't compose something else, *and* that that boundary lies somewhere between the two extremes.

There are two ways of developing the thesis of restricted composition. The first is to propose some unifying principle (or principles) of composition: putative parts compose only when they are touching each other, or stuck together somehow, or 'caught up in a life' (cf. van Inwagen 1990). The second is to reject any such unifying explanation of composition, and say that the many specific facts of composition are brute (Markosian 1998).

A structurally similar issue arises when we consider the individuation of individual things in modal space. Given a plurality of possible worlds, we can ask after the modal boundaries of any individual thing: what merely possible things count as 'the same thing' as *this* particular individual? To stay neutral on issues of trans-world identity (vs. counterpart theory), we can ask which things are *versions* of a given individual. To ask whether a possible thing y is a version of some actual individual x is just to ask whether x could have had all the properties of y.

The problem of arbitrariness arises here as well. We want to draw my modal boundaries so that I, with a haircut, lie inside the boundary, but so that the atoms that presently compose me, scattered across the universe a few hundred years from now, do not. But this seems metaphysically arbitrary. Three possibilities, then: to draw the boundaries of individuals in the extremely minimal way (so that no merely possible things count as versions of me); to draw the boundaries of individuals in the extremely maximal way (so that everything counts as a version of everything else); or, finally, to say that there are real, objective modal boundaries of individuals, and that these boundaries lie somewhere between the two extremes.

One way of developing this thought is by talking about *essential properties*. We find this idea in Aristotle, where he writes that 'the essence of each thing is what it is said to be in virtue of itself,' and that '[w]hat … you are by your very nature is your essence' (*Metaphysics* Z, 1029b14). The modal boundaries of a thing extend just as far as those things that share that thing's essence, and it is the possession of this essence that explains why a thing's boundaries lie where they do. (More on this idea later.)

The aim of this essay is to motivate the rejection of individual essences, in their traditional form. My argument against them has two steps. First, I argue that we have prima facie reason to reject individual essences of two types: sortal properties and historical properties (Section 1). Then I criticize three arguments that suggest we need to posit essential properties, in spite of this (Section 2). I then consider alternative solutions to the problem of modal boundaries (Section 3). The view that I favour is *brutal individuation,* which is the modal analogue of Markosian's brutal composition: individuals have objective modal boundaries, but these facts don't admit of any further explanation.

1   Sortal and historical properties not essential properties

I am going to talk about essential properties; something's essence is just the set of all and only its essential properties (or perhaps the conjunctive property of having all its non-conjunctive essential properties). And I am going to talk exclusively about the essential properties of individuals, leaving aside the matter of whether kinds have essences.

Now this is yet to say what an essential property is, and I should apologize up front for the fact that I am nowhere going to say what *exactly* an essential property is. This is in large part because there are competing accounts of essential properties, and I aim for my criticism of them to apply to all the competing accounts. But all parties agree that any essential property of something is a property necessarily had by that thing. In other words:

Necessity of essence (NE): For all x and F, if being F is an essential property of x, then, necessarily, x is F.

Even a critic of modal conceptions of essences (e.g., Fine 1994) would agree to NE. It is a minimal commitment of anyone who believes that there are essential properties of individuals.

Some say that, essential properties must be sufficient to distinguish one individual from any other. For example, I am necessarily self-identical, but we should not count this as part of my essence, since *everything* is necessarily self-identical. I'm going to confine my attention to material things and to macroscopic, composite things. And I am going to concede that such things are necessarily material, and necessarily macroscopic, and necessarily composite. Perhaps there is some sense in which such things are essentially material, macroscopic, and composite. But I think not: if essences are to distinguish individual things from each other, than properties like *being a material thing* are not fit to be essential properties. But in any event, I make no claims about such properties here.

The essential properties that I *am* against are, first, the usual suspects: sortal properties of individuals, such as the property of being human, or the property of being a shed, or the property of being a creature capable of conscious thought. (These are the properties that people first bring up, if you say that there aren't any essential properties.) Second, I'll consider historical properties, and in particular origin properties, such as the property of having been constructed out of a particular piece of wood.

There is no room for essential properties of individuals within the austere empiricist metaphysic championed by David Lewis, known as Humean Supervenience. On this picture, 'all there is in the world is a vast mosaic of local matters of particular fact,' and '[t]here is no difference without difference in arrangement of qualities. All else supervenes on that' (Lewis 1986, pp. ix–x). But facts about essences would necessarily need to supervene on something more. No arrangement of local qualities could ground facts of the sort the essentialist posits. This is obvious if we are actualists (nothing in the actual particular arrangement of qualities makes it the case that such-and-such properties of me are essential to me), but this is also true even if we allow a plurality of possible worlds, so long as we keep insisting (as Humean Supervenience says we must) that there is nothing anywhere save particular arrangements of qualities. So if one is antecedently committed to Humean Supervenience, then one will have reason to deny the existence of individual essences. And one might think that we have independent reason to embrace Humean Supervenience, at least tentatively, on the grounds that it is best supported by our best scientific theories. This is what Lewis suggests (1986, pp. x–xi), and philosophers attracted to the thesis are generally of the scientific, naturalistic variety, those attracted to the most simple and austere metaphysical pictures available, at least when they are consistent with our best science.

Alternatively, one might be opposed to individual essences on epistemic grounds. Those with epistemological qualms about the possibility of modal knowledge, in general, will find knowledge of essences equally problematic.

My strategy here is different from either of these ways of resisting individual essences. Indeed, in some sense it is incompatible with the epistemological objection. For I am going to assume, at least for the sake of argument, that modal knowledge is possible.

I aim to undermine the idea that sortal and historical properties are essential properties by appeal to thought experiments in which we imagine individuals lacking these properties. What is want to show is that we have prima facie reason to think that certain properties are not essential properties of any individual. I'll appeal to:

Principle of imagination (PI): If you can imagine *p*, then you have prima facie reason to believe that *p* is possible.

We should accept this – or something like it – because if something like this isn't true, then modal knowledge seems impossible. All modal knowledge is grounded, in one way or another, in our imaginative capacities. Since it seems crazy to deny that there can be modal knowledge, we should accept PI (or something like it).

1.1 Sortal properties and transformation

Consider the property of being human. This is as plausible a candidate as any for being an essential property of human beings. But recall

Kafka's story, in which '[w]hen Gregor Samsa awoke one morning from troubled dreams he found himself transformed in his bed into a monstrous insect' (2000, p. 64). Now there is nothing special about Samsa that makes him particularly susceptible to this transformation; you can imagine *any* human being undergoing such a transformation. For any human being, we can imagine her being transformed into a non-human being. So, given NE, we have prima facie reason to think that its possible for any human being to be non-human. Therefore, we have prima facie reason to think that being human is not an essential property of human beings.[1] (The same point obviously applies to any 'bodily' properties more specific than the property of being human.)

What Kafka's story shows, you might argue, is just that my essence is psychological, not bodily. Consider Descartes' claim, in the Second Meditation, that 'were I totally to cease from thinking, I should totally cease to exist.' Is the property of being a thinking thing essential to thinking things?

Here I think we need not even appeal to NE. I was *actually* not a thinking thing, when I was very young, and I won't be a thinking thing, when I am a corpse. There might be, of course, interesting reasons stemming from some philosophical theory to deny that I was a fetus or that I will be a corpse. But that's not the way we ordinarily think and talk. We may speak of when we were in the womb (Liz Lemmon: 'They think I might have eaten my twin'), and we may worry about what will happen to us when we are dead ('I want to be cremated'). It seems that I not only could fail to be a thinking thing, but that I was once a non-thinking thing, and I will most likely be a non-thinking thing again.[2,3]

What about more specific psychological traits: memories, personalities, character traits, values? Again, consider the possibility, indeed the actuality, of transformation. For any specific psychological feature of mine, I can imagine changing so that I no longer have that feature. Despite frequent philosophical denials of this, it seems *obvious* that I could have my memory erased, either in whole or in part. When Grandfather loses his memory, I lament what is happening *to Grandfather*. I don't think that Grandfather is slowly fading out of existence, being replaced by some other qualitatively similar entity. You can imagine *yourself* losing your memory, and it is not something that you want to happen *to you*. And this point holds even more obviously when it comes to personality and values. It is sometimes surprising or even upsetting, but our personalities and values often change over time. At the very least, we can imagine this happening. Given NE, then, we have *prima facie* reason to think that no specific psychological features are essential to me.

So far I've considered some candidate essential properties of human beings. But it is important to see that similar arguments can be given for other material things. Consider Simon Starling's 'Shedboadshed,' in which the artist disassembled a shed, built a boat from the shed's parts, sailed the boat down the Rhine, and reassembled the shed at a museum in Basel. Is the property of being a shed essential to sheds? It's not essential to Starling's shed, because Starling's shed was a boat and not a shed during its trip down the river. But if it's not essential to that particular shed, because it actually was a non-shed for a time, then it's not essential to any shed, because any shed could be transformed into a non-shed, in exactly the same way Starling transformed his.[4] More carefully, because we can imagine any shed being transformed into a non-shed, we have prima facie reason to think that no shed is essentially a shed.

We can see that the same point applies to any composite material thing with respect of any property the having of which depends on the arrangement of a thing's parts. Call these *arrangement* properties. Here is the strategy:

R1. Take any composite material thing x that has the arrangement property of being F. Imagine that x is disassembled, and from x's parts something is built that is not F. Then this composite is disassembled, and from its parts something F, indeed something qualitatively indistinguishable from x, is built.

R2. During the process of transformation, we imagined a situation in which x wasn't F.

R3. Therefore, we have prima facie reason to think that it's possible for x to not be F, and thus that being F is not essential to x.

R4. Therefore, we have prima facie reason to think that no arrangement property is ever an essential property of any composite material thing.

Consider, again, Starling's shed. It seems that the shed in the museum is the same individual, indeed the same shed, as the shed that stood on the bank of the Rhine. (I mean that it seems so to our naïve imagination.) R2 claims that the riverside shed is the same individual as the boat that Starling built. If we say otherwise, then we face an embarrassing question: where was the shed during the time between its stay on the bank of the Rhine and its stay in the museum? The natural answer to this question, I submit, is that the shed was being steered down the river by Starling, in the form of a boat. But this is just to say that R2 is correct: that the shed was, for a time, not a shed. (See Hazlett 2006 for a more detailed version of this thought.)

My aim in this section has been to present a prima facie case against the essentiality of sortal properties: properties like being human, being a thinking thing, and arrangement properties, like being a shed or a table.

1.2   Historical properties and alternative origins

Consider Saul Kripke's example of an ordinary wooden table, which he claims could not have been made from any other piece of wood. Consider some nearby table, or some table that is dear to you. Kripke's claim is not prima facie plausible, since we can imagine said table being made from a different piece of wood. Consider factory mishaps ('it could have been made from the flawed piece'), design decisions ('we could have made it from oak, but we settled on cherry'), and table envy ('I wish my table had been made of mahogany'). Given that these situations are imaginable, we have prima facie reason to think that they are possible. Therefore, we have prima facie reason to think that the table's origins are not essential to it.

If we have reason to reject the essentiality of the origins of individuals, then we have reason to reject the essentiality of any historical properties, since origin properties are the most plausible candidates for being essential historical properties of individuals.

The main objection to taking appearances at face value here comes from Kripke:

> Let 'B' be a name (rigid designator) of a table, let 'A' name the piece of wood from which it actually came. Let 'C' name another piece of wood. Then suppose B were made from A, as in the actual world, but also another table D were simultaneously made from C. [...] Now in this situation B ≠ D; hence, even if D were made by itself, and no table were made from A, D would not be B. (Kripke 1980, p. 114)[5]

The argument has three steps. In the first step, we're asked to consider the actual world, in which table B is made from piece of wood A. In the second step, we're asked to imagine a possible world in which B is made from A, and in addition a second table D is made from a second piece of wood C, and in which obviously B ≠ D.

Now in the third step Kripke says: 'even if D were made by itself, and no table were made from A, D would not be B.' I think that on the most straightforward reading, this is just a non-sequitor. What we wanted to say, above, on the basis of our naïve imagination, was that B could be made from C. Kripke here directs our attention to a world – or to all the worlds – in which some other table D exists, and rightly points out that D is not B. But this leaves open the possibility of worlds in which B is made from C.

What Kripke must have in mind is that any table made from C would have to be D. If we grant that, then we can attribute to Kripke a valid argument:

K1. In a world where B is made from A and D is made from C, B ≠ D.
K2. Identity claims are necessarily true.
K3. So, necessarily, B ≠ D. (From 1 and 2)
K4. Any table made from C would have to be D.
K5. Therefore, any table made from C would not be B. In other words, B could not have been made from C. (From 3 and 4)

But the crucial premise – K4 – is unmotivated, and question-begging against anyone suspicious of origin essentialism.[6] And we should be suspicious of origin essentialism, given our prima facie reason to think that tables can be made of different materials. K4 says that any table made from a particular piece of wood is the same table. This is stronger than origin essentialism itself.

Essentialists will not be swayed by these considerations. But my aim here is just to see if there is a good argument for origin essentialism, an argument that would overturn the appearance of possibility described earlier.

It can seem like resisting Kripke's argument involves a linguistic blunder. One might argue that although in some sense there appears to be an object, 'the table,' which could have been made of different kinds of wood, the sense in which this is true is like the sense in which the 2008 Democratic Presidential Nominee could have been a woman – which (on the most natural reading) is not to say that Barack Obama could have been a woman, but to say that Hilary Clinton could have been the nominee. There is not some entity, 'the nominee,' which could have been a man or a woman, and there is not some entity, 'the table,' which could have been made of cherry of made of oak. There are two entities, Obama and Clinton, who could have been the nominee, and there are two entities, the cherry wood table and an oak table, which could have played similar roles, looked similar, been placed in the same room, or whatever.

But I do not think this gives us a reason to think that a table, actually made of one kind of wood, could not have been made from a different kind of wood. What this gives us is a way to explain the sense in which a table, actually made of one kind of wood, could have been made from a different kind of wood, *if we are already convinced that this is strictly speaking impossible.* The objection appeals to our prior commitment to the distinctness of Obama and Clinton to make its point; but we have no prior commitment to the distinctness of the actual cherry wood table and the possible oaken table. Indeed, I have argued that we have prima facie reason, based on naïve imagination, to think that the two are not distinct. What this objection shows is that the thesis of the essentiality of origins is not *crazy*, since it has an account of what we mean when we say that a particular material thing could have had different origins than it actually had. But this doesn't give us positive reason to accept the thesis of origin essentialism.

Let us take a step back from these considerations. We know there is a set of possible tables, call it *S1*, that includes this particular actual cherry wood table, as well as a possible table similar in every way to this one save being made from oak. And we know there is another set of possible tables, call it *S2*, that includes this one, but does not include the aforementioned oak table, and indeed only includes tables made from the particular piece of cherry from which this table was actually made. When we ask whether this table could have had such-and-such properties, we are asking: which set of possible tables is the set of possible tables that are possible versions of this one? Now I have argued, above, that modal appearances – based on what we can imagine – suggest taking *S1* to be this set. Is there any non-question-begging argument against this?

2   Brutal individuation

The foregoing should make us suspicious of the idea of individual essences. We have prima facie reason to reject the traditional, familiar sorts of essential properties that philosophers talk about: sortal properties like being human or being a table, and historical properties like being made from a particular piece of wood. But other considerations might give us reason to reconsider, and posit essential properties after all. I turn now to three arguments for precisely that conclusion; in criticizing these arguments I will develop the proposal I am calling 'brutal individuation.'

2.1   The argument from individuation

Individual essences have been posited to explain the distinctness of individuals. Consider two individuals x and y, where $x \neq y$. There must be something that explains why x is distinct from y, something that individuates x as distinct from y. Something must explain why x is the thing that it is (and likewise for y), why x is *this* thing (and y is *that* thing). What is needed here, so the argument goes, are essential properties of x and y, which distinguish the one from the other. (See Locke, *Essay Concerning Human Understanding*, III.iii.15, Yablo 1987, p. 297, and Fine 1994, pp. 2–5.)

There is a cogent objection to this line of reasoning, which I'm made to understand was first offered by the fourteenth-century philosopher Peter Auriol (Nielsen 2003, p. 498). Suppose that H is the essential property (or conjunction of properties) the possession of which explains why I am distinct from you. We can now ask, given NE: what explains my necessarily having H? It can't be some general truth, like NE itself, or the claim that everything is self-identical, or whatever, because what we are trying to explain is why *I* am *distinct* from everything else. The question we are asking is not why I have an essence at all, but why I have the essence that I have. No general truth about essences can explain that.

So suppose that some more specific (necessary) truth explains why I have H. But whatever this is, we will be able to ask what explains this. And whatever that truth is, we will be able to ask what explains it. And so on. If we needed an explanation for the (necessary) fact that I am distinct from you, and we offered my necessarily having H, then presumably we need an explanation for why I necessary have H. But once we allow that, then we run into an infinite regress of explanations. The solution is to stop things at the beginning, and reject the idea that we need an explanation for the (necessary) fact that I am distinct from you. We don't need to appeal to some further fact, beyond the necessarily truth that you and I are distinct, to explain our individuality. The argument from individuation rests on a mistaken demand for explanation, where none is needed. The necessary distinctness of individuals is where explanations come to an end; in other words, individuation is brute. This is the crux of what I am calling 'brutal individuation.' The essentialism to which I am opposed maintains that the necessary fact that $x \neq y$ is explained by the fact that x and y differ in their essences. Brutal individuation says that the explanatory buck stops with the necessary fact that $x \neq y$. (This implies a proliferation of specific necessary facts of individuation. But this is no worse than the proliferation of specific necessary facts of essence that would be required otherwise.)

But does conceding that, necessarily, $x \neq y$ entail that x and y have essential properties? If we are liberal in the positing of properties, then it entails this much: that necessarily, x has the property of being diverse from *y*, and of being identical to *x*, and the same, mutatis mutandis, for *y*. What is important, for my purposes here, is that even if we are liberal in that way, that *x* has the 'essential property' of being identical to *x* does not *explain* why *x* ≠ *y*.

2.2   The argument from persistence

Individual essences are well-motivated posits given a certain picture of persistence through change. Persistence through change requires something to remain the same while not remaining the same (i.e., while changing). An obvious way to disambiguate here is to conceive of cases of persistence through change as cases in which some individual retains some unchanging core of properties (i.e., stays the same), while gaining and losing other properties (i.e., changing). In other words, on this picture, necessarily, an individual *x* changes from being *F* to not being *F* only if there is some *G* such that *x* remains *G* through the change. Now what explains any given persisting individual's capacity for persistence? Individual essences would explain this: the essential properties of *x* provide the unchanging core of properties required for *x*'s persistence through change.[7]

Consider a case of personal identity over time. I woke up earlier today, feeling groggy and disoriented, was naked in the shower, then clothed and walking to the station, no longer groggy and disoriented, then on the 4 train, then hungry, then eating lamb and rice, then not hungry, and so on. What accounts for my being the same, despite all these changes? It is natural, if sameness of properties is required for persistence, to posit an essential core of properties: perhaps some unchanging elements of my character and personality, or my deepest commitments and fundamental values, or some physical properties of my body, like the kind of DNA inside it, or whatever.

The argument from persistence appealed to this premise: that, necessarily, *x* changes from being *F* to not being *F* only if there is some *G* such that *x* remains *G* through the change. But I propose that this premise is subject to the following counterexample:

In Buenos Aires the Zahir is a common twenty-centavo coin into which a razor letter opener has scratched the letters *N T* and the number *2*; the date stamped on the face is 1929. (In Gujarat, at the end of the eighteenth century, the Zahir was a tiger; in Java it was a blind man in the Surakara mosque, stoned by the faithful; in Persia, an astrolabe that Nadir Shah ordered thrown into the sea; in the Prisons of Mahdi, in 1892, a small sailor's compass, wrapped in a shred of cloth from a turban, that Rudolf Karl von Slatin touched; in the synagogue in Córdoba, according to Zotenberg, a vein in the marble of one of the twelve hundred pillars; in the ghetto in Tetuán, the bottom of a well.) (Borges 1999, p. 237)

The Zahir persists through changes – it is at one time a tiger, than at another time a coin – without retaining any essential core of properties.[8] What we need to reject the argument from persistence is for the story of the Zahir to be possible. But again, it's obviously imaginable, and so we should conclude that it's possible, unless we have some special reason to think that it isn't.

It might be objected that the Zahir possesses a hacceity, an intrinsic, non-qualitative 'Zahir-ness,' that makes it the same thing, through its various changes. But this would be an *ad hoc* defence of the premise about persistence, and more importantly, Auriol's argument applies here as well. I want to say that the Javan Zahir is the Persian Zahir. If this requires some explanation, some further account – beyond just the necessary truth that the Javan Zahir and the Persian Zahir are one and the same – then won't the fact that they each have Zahir-ness also require some explanation, some further account? Why not stop at the fact that the two are necessarily one and the same?

It might be objected that, in supposed cases of transformation akin to that of the Zahir, there is no way to tell that supposedly identical things (the Javan man and the Persian astrolabe, for example) are identical. There is no way to tell whether the one individual was, say, destroyed, and replaced by a distinct individual, not only qualitatively different, but also numerically different. However, in general, it is possible to be aware of a genuine possibility, without there being a possible means of distinguishing it from alternative possibilities. There is no way to distinguish a situation in which the world uniformly doubles in size from a situation in which it doesn't, but such a situation is possible. So from the fact that it is hard, maybe impossible, to tell whether a given thing is the Zahir or not, we shouldn't conclude that there couldn't be such a thing as the Zahir.

But what explains persistence, then, if not an unchanging core of essential properties? As suggested above, I think we should say that *nothing* explains persistence, because persistence doesn't need to be explained. Facts about persistence are necessary truths (they're identity claims, after all), and there is no good reason to ask for further explanation of them. That the Javan Zahir and the Persian Zahir are one is a brute fact, admitting of no further explanation. (The point about explanation applies here as well: even if we posit 'Zahir-ness,' it can't do any explanatory work that wasn't done already by the necessary identity of the various versions of the Zahir.)

2.3   The argument from destruction

Essential properties are sometimes appealed to in explanations of destruction – to explain why certain changes result in the destruction of a thing, while other changes do not. Why is it that I survive a change of shirts, but not being blown to bits by an explosion? Why do some changes result in the end of a thing's existence, while others don't? If being blown to bits would eliminate one of my essential properties, and changing shirts would not, then we have an explanation of why the one change results in destruction, while the other doesn't.

Plato posits essential properties in connection with precisely this issue. Heat and cold are 'opposite forms'; they are 'not willing to endure' one another and if one 'approaches,' then the other is forced either to 'retreat' or is destroyed by the approach of its opposite. Plato continues:

> not only do opposite [forms] not admit each other, but this is also true of those things which, while not being opposite to each other[,] *always contain the opposites,* and it seems that these do not admit that Form which is opposite to that which is in them; when it approaches them, they either perish or give way. (*Phaedo* 104b, my emphasis)

An essential property of *x* is a property that, in Plato's language, *x* 'always contains.' A piece of snow, for example, 'always contains' coldness, and a flame 'always contains' heat. Thus when a flame is brought near to a piece of snow, the snow must either retreat (i.e., be moved away from the flame) or be destroyed. In the case in which the snow is destroyed, we may appeal to the fact that it was essentially cold to explain why it was destroyed. This is a bit hard to say, but we want to say something like this: that had the snow been warmed, then it would have lacked its essential coldness, but of course that is impossible, therefore the snow was destroyed by the heat. We can't exactly say that the snow was destroyed by being warmed, because it (the snow) was not warmed (that would have been impossible), nor even that the snow was destroyed because it would have been warmed (for, again, that is impossible), but the basic idea is clear enough. (If it's not clear enough, so much the worse for positing essential properties to explain destruction.) So, the argument goes, we need something to explain why some changes result in an individual's destruction, and others don't. And essential properties can do this explanatory work.

As above, I say we should not accept this demand for explanation. Everyone agrees that the destruction of piece of snow can (at least sometimes) be explained by saying that it was warmed. The argument from destruction goes further, asking for an explanation of *why* being warmed was sufficient for the snow's being destroyed. But why should we think that the previous explanation – that the snow was warmed – was insufficient?

This question is complicated by the fact that, as I argued above, it's nearly impossible to come up with non-historical properties that, intuitively, can't be lost. We can cook up a story in which a snowball intuitively survives being warmed: you land a vicious blow with a powerful snowball, I vow revenge, I melt your snowball and refreeze it to make it harder or more aerodynamic or something, and then I cathartically attack – using the very same snowball with which you attacked me. In general, context will determine our intuitions about such cases: the scattered pieces of a Cartier Tank, destroyed in a fit of jealous rage, are intrinsically the same as the scattered pieces of a Cartier Tank, still in existence while spread out on the repairperson's table.

Brutal individuation says that there are objective conditions under which particular individuals are destroyed, and these conditions, given a complete enough description of things, are sufficient for destruction. If we are looking for an explanation of why an individual was destroyed, the fact that those conditions, however elaborate, were met is explanation enough. There is no further need to explain why those conditions were sufficient for the destruction of that individual.

In most circumstances, it's unnecessary to explain everything. It's sufficient to explain the destruction of some piece of snow, in an ordinary case, to say that it was warmed. We don't need to add anything more, in spite of the fact that being warmed alone isn't sufficient for snow's destruction (consider the revenge attack, above). In general, *explanans* doesn't need to be sufficient for *explanandum*; background assumptions are allowed.

Brutal individuation says that destruction sometimes (objectively) occurs. From this it follows that, for a given individual x, there is a condition C such that the obtaining of C would suffice for x's destruction. It follows from this that, necessarily, x has the property of its not being the case that C obtains. Isn't this then an essential property of x?

As earlier, this depends on how liberal we are in the positing of properties. If I am right that melting can destroy a snowball in some cases, but not in the case of the revenge attack, then the proposed essential property of any given snowball will not be an intrinsic property (like being cold, as Plato argued), but a rather awkward and hard-to-specify property (like the property of being cold, unless its one of those situations in which coldness doesn't suffice for destruction, etc.). But the defender of brutal individuation can concede that, in this sense, there are individual essences. Two points distinguish this view from traditional essentialism. First, we have given up on the usual suspects for essential properties of individuals: sortal properties and historical properties. Second, we have abandoned the idea that essential properties explain destruction. For the defender of brutal individuation, the necessary truth that *x* would be destroyed, given *C*, explains why the property of its being the case that *C* doesn't obtain is necessarily had by *x*, not the other way around.

3   Alternatives

One possible response to all this would be to offer an alternative conception of individual essences, on which NE is false. Consider this passage from Robert Paul Wolff:

> I am not a person who just happens accidentally and irrelevantly, to be a man, forty years old, the husband of a professor of English literature, the son of two aging and sick parents, the father of two small boys six and four, a comfortably well-off member of the upper middle class, American-Jewish, born and raised in New York. I am *essentially* such a man. (Wolff 1976, pp. 136–7)

The conception of individual essence presumed here is clearly incompatible with NE. Wolff highlights the properties he claims are essential to him (being a man, being a parent, being American and Jewish) not because of his necessarily possessing them, but because of their *relevance*, because of their importance to his understanding of himself, to his identity – not in the metaphysical or logical sense, but in (what I would call) the phenomenological sense. It is quite implausible that Wolff would be destroyed were he to lose these features, and equally implausible that he couldn't have lacked them. He would be qualitatively different – and in deep, subjectively significant, and powerful ways – if he lacked these properties, but he could easily lack them while being numerically the same individual. Still, if my essence is just those properties which define my identity, in this phenomenological sense, then I have no reason to doubt that there are such things as individual essences.[9] (What is clear, however, is that on this conception of individual essences, they are not motivated by the arguments from persistence and destruction.)

Brutal individuation is a way of drawing the modal boundaries of individuals somewhere between the two extremes described at the outset. But given that accepting brutal individuation carries a heavy burden – a proliferation of specific necessary facts of individuation – we should consider the two extremes.

To draw individual modal boundaries in the most minimal way (the modal analogue of mereological nihilism) would entail that I could not have been, in any way, other than the way that I am. This avoids the profligacy of brutal individuation, but only at the cost of badly violating our modal intuitions; if there are any modal truths at all, surely one of them is that I could have had one lump instead of two in my coffee this morning. But the other extreme – drawing individual modal boundaries is the most maximal way (the modal analogue of mereological universalism) – is equally repugnant to common sense. If this view were right, nothing would or could be destroyed.

Now an alternative to all of these positions is to reject the objectivity of modal boundaries. The lesson of Sections 2 and 3, on such a view, is that there are no *de re* essences, but that there are non-objective essences. Consider Lewis's contextualism about the counterpart relation (1983, pp. 42–3). On this view, which properties of a thing are to be counted as essential fundamentally depends on how that thing is described. The counterpart relation varies from context to context, and so the truth of claims about essences will vary from context to context as well, as will claims about persistence and destruction. So if you are wondering whether your favourite shed still exists, because you want to take a Rhineland vacation, then the true answer is that the shed no longer exists, but if you are wondering whether your favourite shed still exists, because you always wondered what it would look like in a museum, then you'd better believe it still exists! Different contexts determine different modal boundaries of individuals, and thus different truth conditions for claims about essences and persistence conditions.[10]

This is an attractive picture, particularly from the linguistic point of view, where it seems to capture some of our ordinary use quite nicely. I think there are two considerations that speak against Lewis's view, and indeed against any theory that posits essential properties but is non-objectivist about moral boundaries.

First, the very idea of an essential property comes from an objectivist metaphysics: one that takes such things as individuation, persistence, and destruction to be objective features of the world. On Lewis's view, these end up being projections of our language. It does violence to the notion of an essential property to give a contextualist treatment of 'essential property.' Since the idea of an essential property is at home in metaphysics (and not in ordinary language), there's no reason to give a charitable reinterpretation of our talk about essential properties. If we reject *de re* essences, we should reject essences altogether, and stop talking about them.

This is possible for Lewis, for all he needs to do is to retain his contextualist understanding of the counterpart relation, and account for individuation, persistence, and destruction directly in terms of counterparts, without appeal to the (now contextualized) notion of an essential property. This leaves the heart of Lewis's position untouched: the contextualist treatments of individuation, persistence, and destruction.

Second, and more important, is a worry about the plausibility of non-objectivism about individuation, persistence, and destruction. It is a well-known consequence of the Lewisian picture that answers to questions of personal survival are, in some cases, true or false only relative to the contextual specification of a counterpart relation. If I am due for one of the ghastly operations dreamed up by metaphysicians (having my brain transplanted into another body, say), the question of whether *I* will survive will have different true answers depending on the contextual specification of the counterpart relation: on a conservative drawing of my boundaries, no stages of me exist past that time when my brain and my body are parted, but on a liberal drawing of my boundaries, I have stages past that point, stages consisting of (what is uncontroversially) my brain and the new body into which it has been implanted. But I want to know: *will I survive the operation?* The problem is not that contextualism fails to deliver an answer here; we shouldn't ask for a clear answer to such a question. The problem is that contextualism says that the answer to this question depends on context. And there is something deeply counterintuitive, worse *unthinkable*, about that claim. It is not hard to imagine that there is no objective fact about whether the Javan Zahir and the Persian Zahir are one and the same – perhaps in some sense they are, but in another sense they are not. But it just cannot be that, in some sense, I will survive, and that, in some sense, I will not, and that is the end of the story. It seems there *must* be more to the story, in this case. The point here is the same as that made by Chisholm, when he considered the view that personal identity might be a matter of convention:

> Suppose that others came to you – friends, relatives, judges, clergyman – and they offer the following advice and assurance [prior to one of these ghastly and identity-wise ambiguous operations]. 'Have no fear,' they will say. ['W]e will lay down the convention that the man on the table is not you, Jones, but is Smith.' What *ought* to be obvious to you, it seems to me, is that the laying down of this convention should have no effect at all upon your decision [whether to undergo the operation]. For you may still ask, 'But won't that person be I?' and, it seems to me, the question has an answer. (Chisholm 1967, p. 111)

There is something unthinkable about the idea that personal identity is a matter of convention, and there is something equally unthinkable about the idea that personal identity is a matter of context. If this is right, then I think the most attractive view of modal boundaries is brutal individuation.

Notes

Thanks to Bryan Frances, Uriah Kriegel, and Alyssa Ney for valuable help on this chapter, as well as to the folks at Leeds and in Vancouver for their input, when I spoke there in 2008 and 2009, respectively.

1. This clearly applies to any more specific 'bodily' properties.
2. I say 'most likely' just in case the end of my existence and the end of my thinking happen to coincide, for example, if I am blown up by a bomb.
3. Corpses are dead, so to say that I will be a corpse implies that I will be dead. Some philosophers balk at this: to be dead is to not exist, so no one can be dead. But this isn't the ordinary sense of 'dead' that I am using here. Nothing I'm saying implies that I will survive the end of my existence. (Nor am I saying that my existence will never end.)
4. Sartre claimed that human beings are unique in lacking essences, owing to our unique subjectivity and capacity for free choice. Although human beings are perhaps the only things in the world that can choose to transform (i.e., the only things that transform themselves), I am arguing that they are not the only things capable of being transformed – and so not unique in lacking individual essences.
5. See Salmon 2005, pp. 229–52, for a reconstruction of the argument, and Robertson 1998 for a critique.
6. Robertson calls this the 'sufficiency premise.'
7. This picture is Aristotelian. See *Physics* I.7 and II.1.
8. The Zahir I'm imagining here differs from Borges's version in two ways. First, in his story, the Zahir has some unchanging features: its ability to drive men

mad, for example. Second, Borges never insists that 'the' Zahir is actually one thing, as opposed to many.

9. My discussion of Wolff here draws heavily from Velleman 2002.

10. Uriah Kriegel (p.c.) suggests another non-objectivist theory of essences, on which essentiality (a property of properties) is response-dependent. Roughly, a property F is essential to x iff: if x lost F, we would (under normal conditions) intuit that x has gone out of existence. The objection below (to Lewis) is also an objection to Kriegel's idea.

Bibliography

Borges, J. (1999), 'The Zahir,' in his *Collected Fictions* (Penguin), pp. 237–49.

Chisholm, R. (1967), 'Identity through Possible Worlds: Some Questions,' *Noûs* 1:1, 1–8.

—— (1976), *Person and Object* (London : Allen and Unwin).

Cooper, J. M. (ed.) (1997), *Plato: Complete Works* (Indianapolis: Hackett Publishing).

Fine, K. (1994), 'Essence and Modality,' *Philosophical Perspectives* 8, 1–16.

Hazlett, A. (2006), 'Disassembly and Destruction,' *The Monist* 89:3, 418–33.

Kafka, F. (2000), *The Metamorphosis and Other Stories* (New York: Penguin).

Lewis, D. (1983), *Philosophical Papers*, vol. 1 (Oxford: Oxford University Press).

—— (1986), *Philosophical Papers*, vol. 2 (Oxford: Oxford University Press).

Locke, J. (1975), *An Essay Concerning Human Understanding* (Oxford: Oxford University Press).

Markosian, N. (1998), 'Brutal Composition,' *Philosophical Studies* 92 (3), 211–49.

McKeon, R. (ed.) (1941), *The Basic Works of Aristotle* (New York: Random House).

Nielsen, L. O. (2003), 'Peter Auriol,' in *Blackwell Companion to Philosophy in the Middle Ages* (Blackwell), pp. 494–503.

Robertson, T. (1998), 'Possibilities and the Arguments for Origin Essentialism,' *Mind* 107, 729–50.

Salmon, N. (1989), 'The Logic of What Might Have Been,' *Philosophical Review* 98, 3–34.

—— (2005), *Reference and Essence,* 2nd edn. (New York: Prometheus).

Yablo, S. (1987), 'Identity, Essence, and Indiscernibility,' *Journal of Philosophy* 84 (6), 293–314.

van Inwagen, P. (1990), *Material Beings* (Ithaca: Cornell University Press).

Velleman, J. D. (2002), 'Identification and Identity,' in Buss and Overton (eds.), *Contours of Agency* (Boston: MIT Press), pp. 91–123.

Wolff, R. P. (1976), 'There's Nobody Here but Us Persons,' in Gould and Wartofky (eds.), *Women and Philosophy: Toward a Theory of Liberation* (G.P. Putnam's Sons), pp. 128–44.

5
Bringing Things About
Neal Judisch

> The origin of action – its efficient, not its final cause – is choice, and that of choice is desire and reasoning with a view to an end.
>
> —Aristotle, *Nicomachean Ethics*

> The stick moves the stone and is moved by the hand, which is again moved by the man; in the man, however, we have reached a mover that is not so in virtue of being moved by something else.
>
> —Aristotle, *Physics*

1 Natural agency

In this essay, I hope to dissolve a problem for naturalistic theories of human action. The problem I aim to dissolve is generated when two independently plausible theses concerning human action are combined: on the one hand, it is plausible that action consists in sequences of suitably related events – desires and beliefs give rise to mental events such as choices, or states such as intentions, which choices or intentions subsequently cause the agent's body to move in ways aimed at satisfying her goals. On the other hand, actions are distinct from 'mere happenings' in that they are brought about by the agents whose actions they are: actions are things agents *do*, not things that merely occur to or within their bodies.

To put the latter point another way, when a person acts she is not simply the locus of a series of reflexes, whether mental or physical or both, but is (as Taylor indicates) an initiator of action herself: 'In describing anything as an act there must be an essential reference to an agent as the performer or author of that act, not merely in order to know whose act it is, but in order even to know that it is an act at all. ... Another perfectly

91

natural way of expressing this notion…is to say that, in acting, I make something happen, I cause it, or bring it about' (1966, pp. 109, 111). This manner of description is naturally conjoined with the metaphysical intuition that actions are distinct from mere happenings-involving-agents, at least in part, because actions are brought about by agents in a way that differs in kind from the mechanical outworking of causally related event patterns within them. For the mere unfolding of events within a person, however complex, does not obviously add up to an agent's making anything happen, and from this it follows (according to Chisholm) that 'at least one of the events that is involved in any act is caused, not by any other event, but by the agent, the man' (1966, p. 29). Taken literally, these sentiments express the contention that any person who acts must enjoy the possession of a unique capacity the exercise of which cannot be reduced to any sequence of event-causes: necessary to the performance of any action is a direct causal contribution emanating from the agent herself, and nothing *about* the agent – whether mental or physical – is causally sufficient for it.

Such 'agent-causation' theories are not without their difficulties, and the majority of action theorists are not prepared to accept them. A widely popular alternative thus seeks to specify the necessary and sufficient conditions for action without recourse to an 'agent-causal' power of the sort envisaged here. On this approach, human action is constituted by the right kinds of events being related in the right kinds of ways, which does not require the aetiology of any act to include a special variety of causation occurring nowhere else in nature.[1] Theories operating within these parameters are often called 'causal theories' of action, since they attempt to analyse action in causal terms whilst making use of event-causal relations only within their analyses. They are also called 'naturalistic theories' of action. But it is important to recognize that these approaches are 'naturalistic' only in the sense that their theorising is confined by the strictures imposed by an exhaustively event-causal ontology. 'Naturalism' so understood is therefore not equivalent to ontological materialism: there is nothing inconsistent about rejecting materialism in favour of strongly dualistic theories of mind, for example, and nevertheless accepting that action is analysable in terms of appropriately related mental and physical events. The difficulties for naturalistic theories of action should therefore be distinguished from whatever problems besetting materialist theories of mind (or persons) specifically there may be. Thus when N. M. L. Nathan says, strikingly, that 'materialism is false if anyone ever performs an action' (1975, p. 501), he should be understood as registering the conviction that materialism cannot allow 'agent-causal' powers, and that, since powers of this sort are required for action, materialism is not consistent with action. If, however, a given anti-materialist metaphysics is no more hospitable to 'agent-causal' powers, then such an anti-materialism would likewise be false if anyone ever performs an action, and for the same reason. 'Materialism,' in this instance, isn't the primary culprit.

Similar remarks apply to the issue of mental causation. One of the ironies of the last few decades has been the emergence of the problem of mental causation as a difficulty for materialist theories of mind, not just for overtly dualistic ones. Yet although it is clear that any naturalistic theory of action is committed to the reality of mental causation (inasmuch as it relies upon mental causes in its analysis), an acceptable solution to the latter problem will not solve the problem of interest here. For our problem concerns, not how mental events could be causes, but how, even when they are, such events occurring within an agent could amount to the agent's making anything happen.[2]

Closer to home, but still distinct from our difficulty, is a challenge to naturalistic theories that is often supposed to be the chief hurdle they must overcome. This is the problem of causal deviance, and it challenges us to explain exactly *how*, or in what *way*, mental states must cause bodily movements in cases of intentional action. The concern is that an agent may form an intention to perform some action A in order to bring about a state of affairs S, and that very intention may in fact cause the agent to A and S to obtain as a result, but the causal trajectory between the intention and A may be such as to preclude the agent from exercising control over what she does, rendering her behaviour unintentional. The intention in question might produce in the agent a state of nervousness, for example, which causes her temporarily to lose control over her behaviour but which, fortuitously, also causes her body to move in just the way she had intended it to. And in cases like this the agent either does not act intentionally, or, if all actions are intentional, fails altogether to act.

Examples of deviance tend to vitiate the hope that sufficient conditions for intentional action might be framed without appeal to a form of agency that cannot be analysed by way of the interplay between an agent's desires, intentions and motions; and to that extent they too pose a problem for naturalistic action theories.[3] Yet even granting that this difficulty may by itself be thought to undermine naturalism about action, this isn't the only thing that might jeopardize a naturalistic orientation. For a successful solution to the problem of deviance may specify the 'right way' for mental events to cause bodily movements without thereby illuminating how these rightly-related happenings amount to a doing. Simply put, the deviance problem is essentially concerned with explaining how mental and physical events are related when a person (intentionally) acts, and our problem is concerned with how action can consist of 'happenings' and nothing more, quite apart from the precise manner of the relation between the happenings.

A final clarification. The question before us is naturally of concern to philosophers interested in the metaphysics of free will, insofar as there can be no free agency unless there is such a thing as agency 'period.' But it is not a problem afflicting one theory of human freedom only. Specifically, although philosophers inclined towards 'agent-causation' in action theory may also be inclined towards libertarianism about free will, the challenge of explaining how actions are distinct from mere happenings is neither generated by libertarian theories of freedom nor uniquely applicable to them. It is a problem, in other words, that the libertarian faces qua action theorist, not qua libertarian, for it applies in the first instance to agency simpliciter and to free agency only secondarily. (I shall return to this point and address its significance in the final section.)

Our puzzle, then, although easily conflated with the foregoing topics, is distinct from and rather more general than them. Irrespective of a person's stance on the mind/body relation or the freedom of the will, it confronts anyone who wishes to locate instances of agency within nature, or to explain what goes on in a world of events when someone acts: 'Of course action differs from other behaviour in that the agent brings it about, but the problem is how to accommodate such bringing about within a naturalist ontology' (Bishop 1989, p. 69).

2   Can agency be reduced

Broadly speaking there are three available naturalistic strategies for accommodating the intuition that actions are assignable to agents, as being in a special sense their causes. The first involves identifying agents with the complexes of states and events, or some subset of them, which are productive of action. The second is similar, but takes on a distinctively functionalist cast. It attempts to specify the characteristic causal role played by agents in cases of action, and then to identify a state or disposition causally relevant to behaviour that satisfies the agent's functional description. And the final strategy tries first to solve the problem of causal deviance and then to argue that because no further (reductive) analysis of action is possible, no further analysis is necessary. I take them each in turn.

One interesting version of the first strategy has been formulated by Ekstrom (1993), whose 'coherentist' theory of the self is targeted at explaining how an action may be said to derive from an agent as its 'source.' To forestall confusion it must be acknowledged that Ekstrom's proposal is geared specifically towards explicating the conditions for 'self-determination' in a sense that confers *autonomy,* and a mildly refined version of it is put into service of the (naturalistic) libertarian account of free will developed in her (2000). I have argued that the problem of 'bringing things about' is not equivalent to worries about autonomy or free will, and that it ought not be tied to any particular conception of them. But although Ekstrom's overarching goal is to specify the conditions for autonomous action, it should be noted that the uniquely libertarian aspects of her theory can with propriety be dissociated from those aspects of it that are directly related to the more fundamental problem we have isolated, and it seems to me that her analysis of self-determination may offer the resources for a promising first run at its solution. So I shall examine only the elements of her theory relevant to our question in what follows.

Note first that Ekstrom's account is 'reductive' in a twofold sense, since 'agent-causation' is in her view 'an ontologically and conceptually reducible notion' (2000, p.114). It is *ontologically* reducible because an agent's causing an action, or causing an intention to act, consists in events (involving agents) causing her behaviour, or prior deliberative events causing her intentions to act. And it is *conceptually* reducible because all we have in mind when we say that an agent causes something, according to Ekstrom, is that some event involving the agent causes the something in question to occur:

> Surely we do have experience of people doing things, *bringing about* events and states of affairs.…. But in speaking of ourselves as being the cause of these events…what we really mean is that certain events caused other events…. Speaking of an object or an agent as the cause of some event is just shorthand for the more specific event-causal explanation upon which the agent causal explanation supervenes. (p. 94)

Readers familiar with the mental causation literature will be alive to the concern that a 'supervening' state (or explanation) may sometimes be eclipsed by the underlying causal process upon which the state (or explanation) supervenes. For given the causal sufficiency of the underlying process, and the corresponding sufficiency of the causal explanations couched in their terms, it is tempting to dismiss the 'supervening' states and explanations as superfluous – unless, of course, the 'supervening explanation' is demonstrably just a restatement of the lower-lying one.[4] The conceptual reducibility of agent-causation is therefore not peripheral to her project: to see that the 'agent causal explanation supervenes' in a way that secures the agent's contribution to action, a conceptual reduction of the 'agent' or the 'agent-cause' is required.

And this is precisely what she seeks to provide. Under her analysis, an agent is identifiable with a 'character-system,' which is comprised of preferences, beliefs, and desires, along with a capacity to fashion and refashion the character via critical evaluation. Of particular significance are the agent's *preferences,* understood as 'specially processed desire[s]' that have been 'formed by a process of critical evaluation with respect to one's conception of the good' (p. 106). A preference is thus a second-order desire that some first-order desire of the agent be effective in action, namely, whichever first-order desire coheres with her evaluation of what is good to want, and what sorts of desire she reflectively believes ought to move her to act.[5] It is the preferences in particular which underwrite the thought that the agent herself is the source of her behaviour when she acts upon them, because the preferences she endorses are most expressive of her character, or the sort of person she is: 'Since a "preference" represents what an agent wants as the outcome of her reflection on what is good...when an agent acts on a decisively formed preference...she is involved in the action – she is its source' (p. 107). Given the reducibility of agents to these character-systems, then, we can specify that 'an intention is agent caused just in case it results by a normal causal process from a preference for acting as specified in the content of the intention, where the preference itself is the output of an uncoerced exercise of the agent's evaluative faculty, the inputs into which (various considerations) cause...the decisive formation of the preference' (p. 114).[6]

Part of what lends appeal to Ekstrom's proposal is the attractive idea that when an action is attributable to the agent who performs it, her conduct should be reflective of who she is. And insofar as her preferences and acceptances form a comparatively resilient and coherent system, which is supported by her values or entrenched convictions, there is reason to think that her character is identifiable with this causally relevant set of psychological states.[7] Yet if the agent can likewise be reduced to her character, then we can affirm that the agent herself brings her behaviour about whenever her character-system plays a causal role in generating it. The question is whether this series of reductions goes through.

There is cause for concern that at least one of these reductions fails. It is not, I think, excessively naïve to protest that the beliefs, wants, and even the enduring values of a person, however closely connected with his 'character' they may be, remain for all that characteristics *of* the person – things had or possessed by him – and therefore at any rate not *conceptually* equivalent to the person who possesses them. To be sure, Ekstrom does not intend to deliver a theory of 'persons,' so much as a theory of 'agents' or the 'self.' And it may be that, on her theory, the person should be seen as causing his actions 'qua' agent, as opposed to 'qua' person or enduring object. Nevertheless, the intuition underlying this protest, I take it, is that it must *be* the person – 'the man,' to borrow from Chisholm – who is causally responsible for what he does, and not simply the complex of traits or beliefs and desires 'characteristic' of him. To the extent that 'the man' isn't conceptually reducible to some subset of properties or states he exemplifies, to that extent the man resists reductive analysis – and so therefore does the man-as-cause.

Perhaps this anti-reductive intuition may be shaped into a specific objection. It seems that a conceptual reduction of the agent will fail, if what an agent does when he weighs his reasons and preferences, forms intentions to act in their light, and then acts accordingly, is distinct from what his reasons and intentions themselves accomplish when he acts. Notice how natural it is to say (as indeed Ekstrom says above) that an agent 'acts on' his preferences, after having 'formed' them by way of his evaluation of the good. These locutions reflect the fact that, at least in idea, 'Intentional causation is in certain important respects unlike billiard-ball causation. Both are cases of causation, but in the case of desires and intentions, in the case of normal voluntary actions, once the causes are present they still do not compel the agent to act; the agent has to *act on* his reasons or on his intention' (Searle 2001, p. 231). Thus despite the ineliminable causal contribution his mental states undoubtedly provide, the agent's characteristic role is intuitively to mediate between his reason states and his intentions, by forming his intentions in light of his wants and beliefs, and again, to mediate between his intentions and his behaviour by executing his intentions in act. Yet his reasons cannot 'mediate' between themselves and his intentions, nor can his intentions sensibly be said to 'act upon' themselves.

This is not yet to decide that the ontological reduction of agency cannot be matched with a corresponding conceptual reduction of the agent's causal contribution to action. What it does suggest, according to Velleman, is that involvement of the kinds of mental states that have so far been articulated fails to capture the agent's distinctive involvement in generating his conduct, because what the agent does 'is to intervene between reasons and intention, and between intention and bodily movements, in each case guided by the one to produce the other.... When reasons are described as directly causing an intention, and the intention as directly causing movements, not only has the agent been cut out of the story but so has any psychological item that might play his role' (1992, p. 463). Since the agent's characteristic role is to mediate between the occurrences to which standard naturalistic theories appeal, the agent will fail to participate in his actions unless he – or his agential role – can be reduced to some state or event within him, which performs the work we suppose him to do. A second attempt at the conceptual reduction of agent-causation may thus remain in the offing, if we can add to the mix of action-generating states a state or disposition that is functionally identical to the agent, in the sense that it plays the 'intermediary' role ordinarily ascribed to him.

According to Velleman we should view the agent's definitive role as being 'that of a single party prepared to reflect on, and take sides with, potential determinants of behaviour at any level in the hierarchy of attitudes' (p. 477), so as to ensure that the motives which provide the best reasons for acting 'prevail over those whose rational force is weaker' (p. 478). The psychological state that fills this bill, he argues, cannot be identical to any of the reasons or motives that may potentially come up for evaluation, but must be a distinct state *by* which the agent evaluates his motives: a state with sufficient motivational force to 'throw its weight' behind what the agent considers are his best reasons for acting, by selecting and actuating the superior motivations 'in the agent's name.' What might this state be? It 'can only be a motive that drives practical thought itself' (p. 477), a desire to act in accordance with reasons, 'to do what makes sense, or what's intelligible to [the agent], in the sense that [he] could explain it' (p. 478). 'Only such a motive would occupy the agent's functional role, and only its contribution to his behaviour would constitute his own contribution' (p. 477).

The form of reductive strategy driving Velleman's procedure is I think unquestionably the most promising one. The specifics of his reductive analysis, however, suggest that the problem he solves is not the problem with which he began; it is not the problem of 'bringing things about.' As a general matter, one might worry that it makes little sense to identify a desire as performing the work ordinary parlance attributes to agents since, as Mele points out, even granting that a person's deliberations and decisions are motivated by something akin to the desire figuring centrally in this account, the desire itself 'cannot play [the agent's] role because no desire can deliberate and decide' (2003, p. 225). Whatever it is that is caused *to* evaluate motives by the desire to behave rationally, in other words, may not itself be reductively identifiable with the desire that moves the agent to engage in his evaluative efforts, and it is 'engagements' of precisely this sort that the critics of naturalism contend are irreducibly actional. But there is a more telling indication that Velleman's solution misses its mark. Notice that akratic or weak-willed actions are not such that the agent's disposition to ensure the victory of his rationally superior motivations contributes decisively to their occurrence, nor indeed is any action that the agent does not 'throw his weight behind' in Velleman's sense. Yet akratic acts are most certainly actions agents perform, even if they are not paradigms of rational, self-controlled agency.[8]

The central difficulty with Velleman's solution can best be appreciated if we borrow a bit of his terminology. What began as an attempt at 'finding an agent at work amid the workings of mind' turned quickly into a theory of 'full-blooded' human action, or human agency *'par excellence,'* within which the basic activity of the agent remains unanalysed and in effect presupposed. This tendency to slide from the relatively more fundamental phenomenon of 'doing' to a special form of agency, wherein the agent may be considered more 'fully involved,' is similarly in evidence when he remarks that 'full-blooded human action occurs only when the subject's capacity to make things happen is exercised to its fullest extent' (2000, p. 4), where the extent of his involvement is to be appraised along normative lines. But our problem is not primarily normative. It emerges most clearly when we consider the analogies Velleman formulates in an effort to convey that human agency is of a piece with other varieties of 'behaviour' that fit less problematically within event-causal schemes. Thus a person counts as the 'initiator' of his actions in the same sense that a person counts as a digester of food or a fighter of infections: namely, by virtue of the fact that some proper part of the person contains a food-digesting system, an infection-fighting system, and an 'action-initiating system' – a system which itself 'performs the functions in virtue of which he qualifies as an agent' (1992, p. 475–6). But these analogies invite the very misgivings that induce scepticism concerning naturalism in the first place; for the goal of a naturalistic theory should be to 'earn the right to make jokes about primitive agent-causation' (p. 469), precisely by explaining how naturalism can accommodate the distinction between actions on the one hand and mere sub-actional physiological processes (such as digestion) on the other. To presuppose the distinction can be accommodated, and then proceed to differentiate agency simpliciter from action 'par excellence' is one thing; to accommodate the distinction is something else.

When reductive analyses persistently fail, it is natural to revisit the item targeted for reduction with an eye towards greater clarification of just what this phenomenon is supposed to be, and why it creates such persistent trouble. It's reasonable, too, to ask whether the item in question either needs no more reduction than whatever degree it has already received, or whether for that matter it ever really needed any reduction to speak of at all. Suppose for example we succeed in answering the argument from deviance, by establishing criteria the satisfaction of which entails that, in any naturally possible world, a person whose behaviour is caused in *that* way is a person who intentionally acts. What more about agency requires reduction, if intentional action has already been reduced?

John Bishop (1989) asks and answers this question by arguing that once the challenge of causal deviance has been addressed it is no longer reasonable to entertain doubts about the compatibility of naturalism and agency. His own analysis of (basic) intentional action, he allows, may not apply to any possible worlds containing subjects with irreducible agent-causal powers, but he claims that the conditions he sets forth do apply 'to all possible worlds *that have the same kind of ontology and causal order that science understands the actual world to have.*' In judging the merits of his theory, then, what the reader has to do is 'to ask whether, within a natural scientific ontology, you could *conceive* of just those conditions it specifies applying without being prepared to attribute a basic intentional action to the agent, or conversely.' And if we're ready to concede that the absence of intentional action is inconceivable under such circumstances, we must a fortiori be prepared to admit that agency as such is compatible with naturalism: 'Postulating that agency involves a nonnatural factor (agent-causation) may be quite sensible while we lack uniform correlates for actions; but it becomes plain silly once we can understand how such correlates may be obtained' (p. 179). Whatever additional factors may be fuelling 'agent-causation syndrome' – or the urge to view agency as nonnatural, irreducible – 'dwindle by comparison' with the challenge of causal deviance, says Bishop (p. 180), and may at this point permissibly be ignored.

I have voiced my agreement that specifying normality conditions on the event-causal relations involved in cases of action is insufficient to allay fears that something essential to agency – viz., its 'initiation' by the agent – has been overlooked. At the same time, Bishop's position is perhaps closer to my own than are the reductionist approaches we have already examined. Bishop does not think any 'more' conceptual reduction of agency is required than what he (let us grant) has already achieved, and here I am prepared to agree. Where we part ways, however, is on the reasonableness of persistent scepticism concerning natural agency. For if there remains something about agency that cannot be reduced, then we want an explanation for this failure of reducibility. In particular, we want an explanation for this failure that is consistent with the naturalism which was thought initially to require it, for supposing a person is 'on the fence' about ontological naturalism, she may well view the irreducibility of (some features of) agency as providing reason to reject the naturalism assumed in Bishop's account and his theory of action along with it.

The point is not merely a dialectical one. Here I tip my hat to Sydney Shoemaker, whose remarks in another connection I find equally applicable to our situation: 'To a large extent, the mind-body problem, including the problem of personal identity, arises because of considerations that create the appearance that no naturalistic account could be true; and I think that solving the problem has got to consist in large part in dispelling that appearance (while acknowledging the facts that give rise to it)' (1984, p. 71). What's missing from Bishop's presentation is not necessarily some aspect of the metaphysics of action that has escaped his analytic attention, but an explanation for the appearance that 'natural agency' somehow leaves out its agent, and why agent-causation syndrome remains hard to shake.

3   The phenomenology and conceptual Irreducibility of agency

I propose we attempt to dispel the appearance that naturalism could not be true by acknowledging that when we conceive of action as a 'natural' phenomenon we no longer conceive it as centred upon the agent as its source. Hornsby is no doubt correct when she says that 'Our conception of a person as an agent is a conception of something with a causal power... to initiate series of events containing some we want. An action is the exercise of such a power, and a person's actions are the events at the start of those series she initiates' (1993, p. 164). But the question is how such a conception can be maintained alongside a very distinct conception, according to which the agent's 'initiation' of any act is a matter of particular states within her being caused by prior events. Viewed far enough 'from the outside,' as Nagel rightly notes, nothing of agency looks to remain within this causal network, for both the agent and her putative initiating powers are inevitably engulfed in the relentless tide of occurrences: 'Something peculiar happens when we view action from an objective or external standpoint. Some of its most important features seem to vanish under the objective gaze. Actions seem no longer assignable to individual agents as sources, but become instead components of the flux of events in the world of which the agent is a part' (1986, p. 110).

Once more, the problem cannot with justice be laid on the doorstep of 'materialism' per se. Stipulating the presence of a robustly efficacious non-physical mentality does not alter the fact that '*my doing* of an act – or the doing of an act by someone else – seems to disappear when we think of the world objectively…. Even if we add sensations, perceptions, and feelings we don't get action, or doing – there is only what happens' (p. 111).[9] The anxiety about agency to which this alienating vision leads thus stems fundamentally from our being situated within a purely event-causal nexus; a 'nexus' from which we seem unable to coherently imagine escaping, but within which we likewise cannot conceive of ourselves as genuine springs of activity.

The conceptual disorientation that attends viewing our world 'objectively' is not unfamiliar. Many of philosophy's 'hard problems' involve something recognizably similar – normativity, meaning, and conscious experience are prime examples of phenomena that, each in their own way, prove uneasy to cognize in terms of the 'natural' facts thought to 'give rise' to them. Between these things and the natural world is a notorious 'explanatory gap.' And what lies behind the gap isn't necessarily a dearth of pertinent empirical knowledge – of a sort that might be rectified by conservative extension of the stock of empirical concepts we currently possess – but rather an intuitive failure of conceptual *fit*.

The conditions that invite this conceptual displacement may vary from case to case. What is naturalistically recalcitrant about normative or teleological phenomena (e.g.) probably isn't what makes phenomenal consciousness difficult to naturalistically explain. But although agency certainly involves normative and telic dimensions, I do not see that these features are responsible for the problem of 'bringing things about.' Rather, I claim, the conceptual residue of agency, which remains even after the deviance problem is pushed past, derives from something like what plausibly generates the 'explanatory gap' between phenomenal consciousness and our physical makeup.

On the approach I have in mind, the celebrated gap between conscious states and physical ones is conceptual, not ontological. 'Dualism-syndrome' (as we may call it) urges us to infer the metaphysical irreducibility of phenomenal qualia from their conceptual irreducibility. But this urge can itself be diagnosed, according to this approach, without undermining the naturalism it presses against. It derives in effect from a sense/reference confusion: from reflecting on our conscious experience – itself a natural phenomenon – from the internal point of view, under a mode of presentation that is very unlike modes presenting it *as* a natural phenomenon. More specifically, the 'phenomenal concepts' we deploy when we attend introspectively to the 'feel' of our conscious states are not reducible to the third-person concepts of, say, brains and central nervous systems; nor do the functional roles these sets of concepts play in our thinking coincide. The gap between these items might thus be categorized as unreal, a 'cognitive illusion' to which we succumb when we fail to appreciate the special character of phenomenal concepts and the way these concepts function within our cognitive hierarchy.[10]

How precisely phenomenal concepts should be understood is a matter of dispute.[11] But this question need not delay us. What appears undeniable is that phenomenal concepts, however exactly they should be construed, are not reducible to third-person, purely 'natural' ones, that there is no a priori connection between 'what it's like' for a subject of conscious experience and the physical (functional, representational) states with which his conscious experience is related. Yet whether or not this recognition safeguards materialism in the mind/body case, it may be extended to explain why agency seems to disappear under 'the objective gaze.'[12]

I suggest, accordingly, that it is because the phenomenology of agency is absent from third-person conceptualizations that action theories developed from this perspective will inevitably appear to ignore something significant.[13] And in a sense they do. What they leave unaddressed is how things *seem* to us when we act; they ignore what Carl Ginet (1990) has called the 'actish phenomenal quality.' Of course, a theory of action *need* not include a description of what it's like to act, because it needn't be judged incomplete as a metaphysical theory if it fails to include such a description. Our problem may therefore be contrasted with the problem of consciousness, because in this case the phenomenal feel of conscious experience is itself the thing that needs explanation; and the action theorist, for her part, is simply concerned with action. But it does not follow that the phenomenology of agency is irrelevant to an assessment of naturalism about action. For it may be that what is apparently missing from the naturalistic account is a particular *phenomenal* conception of ourselves as sources of our conduct – one that we come by from the internal point of view – and which cannot in the nature of the case be conceptually reduced to any item given in a third-personal analysis.

Here I'm indebted to Horgan et al., who identify 'three especially central elements of the phenomenology of doing: (i) the aspect of self-as-source, (ii) the aspect of purposiveness, and (iii) the aspect of voluntariness' (2003, p. 323). Not surprisingly, the phenomenology they describe is so pervasive as to recede into the background. It may however be surfaced by way of contrast with defective cases. You can imagine being the subject of a deviantly caused action: you can appreciate the experiential difference between involuntarily shaking and rapidly moving your hand, or losing your grip and releasing some item on purpose. And what it's like to trip is very different from what it's like to pretend to be tripping. In typical cases of doing, the phenomenology represents a subject (to herself) as an embodied agent whose behaviour is generated, guided, voluntarily controlled from within – it 'tells us,' so to say, that things are working properly, or that we're at the helm of the ship.

If the phenomenology of doing is in this way intentional, then it has veridicality conditions; it can accurately reflect and it can misrepresent how things are. And it is initially reasonable to believe that the aspect of self-as-source, which Horgan et al. dub the phenomenology of 'immanent generation,' satisfies its veridicality conditions only if some component of any act is in Chisholm's sense 'immanently caused' – produced immediately by the agent, and not by any mere event at all. Indeed, this intuition is I think what's principally responsible for the feeling that naturalism fails to account for 'bringing things about' and gives us mere happenings instead.

Compare Timothy O'Connor, who remarks that a preference for agent-causation over causal theories of (free) action:

> may be bolstered by a simple appeal to how things seem to us when we act. It is not, after all, simply to provide a theoretical underpinning for our belief in moral responsibility that the agency theory is invoked. First and foremost ... the agency theory is appealing because it captures the way we experience our own activity. It does not seem

to me … that I am caused to act by the reasons which favor doing so; it seems to be the case, rather, that *I* produce my decision *in view of* those reasons…. Such experiences could, of course, be wholly illusory, but do we not properly assume, in the absence of strong countervailing reasons, that things are pretty much the way they appear to us? (1995, pp. 196–7)

But this intuition may not be as trustworthy as it looks. Certainly it must be admitted that action is not phenomenologically represented *as* a sequence of events wherein, say, the subject experiences an occurrent desire to A, and then idly watches as her body moves about in an A-ish way. Nor does the experience of action present it *as* consisting of bodily motions *being caused by* pertinent mental states – granting that causal processes are sometimes perceived *as* causal processes, and not simply as strings of contiguous occurrences. Experiences of either sort, Horgan et al. (p. 328) rightly point out, would be unfamiliar and indeed alienating. Still, this does not imply that the phenomenology of doing is non-veridical if, in fact, an agent's 'bringing things about' consists in suitably related psychological and physical events.

Consider here that most 'agent-causation' theories locate the agent-caused event at the start of an extended action, but not as being operative throughout it. Thus according to Chisholm (1964) what the agent causes is a cerebral event of some kind, subsequent to which standard event-causal processes (constituting the action proper) unfold as a consequence of the cerebral event produced by him. Or again, on O'Connor's (1995) approach what the agent causes is an 'action-triggering intention,' which itself causes the events comprising (the rest of) his action and persists throughout the series, so as to guide the agent's behaviour to completion. But the phenomenology does not present things this way. It does not present the agent as 'immanently' discharging some force (e.g.) and then allowing a series of 'transeunt' causes to take over and perform or complete the act on his behalf. Rather, the *sense* of immanent generation remains throughout the duration of an act, and this despite the fact the agent-cause has according to these theories already done its work: I seem directly to bring about my hand-waving at least as much as I seem to bring about whatever nameless cerebral event is supposed to make my hand wave, and I seem to be guiding my behaviour at least as much as my intentions seem to be doing the guiding for me. Yet if *its not seeming like* our actions are purely event-caused provides evidence that they are not, then it likewise provides evidence that whatever remains of our acts once we agent-cause their beginnings is not accomplished by any event-causes – whether cerebral or intentional – either. At no point, when we act, does it seem as though events within us are doing the actional work for us. Yet all sides agree that at least some degree of event-causation is nevertheless operative in any instance of agency.

This recognition underscores a significant point about the phenomenology of doing, especially as it relates to its veridicality conditions. That action is *not represented as being* event-caused is not to say that it is represented *as being not* event-caused.[14] If the latter were true then the phenomenology of doing would misrepresent its nature, assuming a naturalist stance. (Indeed, it would similarly undermine any theory specifying that action is in large measure constituted by event-causal processes; and so far as I know all agent-causation theories do.) But since the former is true, the phenomenology itself does not unambiguously support the familiar intuitions behind the thought that 'bringing things about' cannot consist in event-causation alone. And, intuitively, this isn't what we should expect the phenomenology to tell us in any case. Its representational function plausibly consists in providing 'feedback' to subjects: information that enables us to monitor, supervise and guide the direction of our activity, while alerting us to potential lapses in control and allowing for adjustments to behaviour as needed. But it is hard to see why the usefulness of such a feedback system should depend upon there being an irreducible agent-cause, or why its proper functioning would be compromised if agency consists in event-causes after all. Thus whereas we can affirm that the phenomenology of agency would be non-veridical (assuming naturalism) if it represented action *as being not* event-caused, we cannot infer the falsity of naturalism on the basis that action is *not represented as being* event-caused. For in this latter case the truth-value of naturalism about action is underdetermined by the phenomenological evidence; and to say that the phenomenology doesn't disclose the presence (or absence) of event-causation is not equivalent to affirming that the phenomenology is non-veridical if event-causation is present in action after all.

The approach I've put forward is clearly only a sketch, and as such it stands in need of development along several fronts. But it seems to me both promising and worthy of development. In any event, a sustained consideration of the phenomenology of agency as it relates to conceptual analyses of action is certainly overdue, and what analysis remains to be done from the third-person perspective will I think most fruitfully be done in interaction with it.

4   Natural free agency

In closing I want to briefly indicate how the approach sketched here impinges upon the topic of free will, particularly as concerns the viability of 'causal indeterminist' theories of libertarian freedom. These theories are libertarian inasmuch as they deny the compatibility of freedom and determinism while affirming the reality of freedom; and they are 'naturalistic' because they seek to construct a theory of free agency by employing only those resources available to naturalistic theorists of action.[15]

Since these approaches are naturalistic, they are impervious to the complaint that libertarianism requires the inclusion of naturalistically objectionable items in its ontological inventory – Cartesian souls, agent-causal powers and the like – and they are for that reason better placed to avoid a common accusation lodged against libertarian views. But according to libertarian critics of causal indeterminism, this gain in strategic posture is purchased at the cost of the theory's ability to deliver a genuinely libertarian account of free will. The worry is that an agency consisting in probabilistic event-causes results in 'basically a compatibilist strategy' for understanding human freedom, as Hasker (1999, p. 97) puts it. It fails to sufficiently enhance agential control, because if actions result from indeterministic event-causal processes they do not originate with agents themselves.

The assimilation of 'origination' with 'enhanced control' is widespread, and understandably so. Intuitively, unless an agent directly brings about one action as opposed to any other action he could have performed in those circumstances, he lacks the kind of control over his behaviour required for free will: and it seems he cannot bring his actions about in this manner without an agent-causal capacity. While I lack the space fully to defend this claim here, however, I contend that this assimilation of 'origination' and 'control' obfuscates two distinct issues. An agent 'controls' his behaviour in the most basic sense when he acts intentionally, or when he guides his behaviour in accordance with his reasons for acting so as to achieve the end(s) specified in the content of his intentions. The claim that such control can be captured in purely event-causal processes, irrespective of whether they operate deterministically or probabilistically, is something that contemporary agent-causalists (in contrast to some of their forebears) typically concede. This suggests that the payoff of introducing an agent-cause consists in establishing a strict or literal sense in which agents 'originate' their actions, but not in explaining how an agent's rational or voluntarily control may be more fully 'enhanced' by it.

What is striking about the stance of contemporary proponents of agent-causation is that, in opposition to Taylor, Nathan and (the early) Chisholm, they hold that an agent-causal capacity is needed only for *free* agency, and not for agency *as such:* thus 'agent causation should be seen as required for acting with free will, but not for acting,' according to Clarke (1993, p. 192).[16] But making this concession (so I claim) undercuts the need for an irreducible agent-cause at all, even in the case of free will. For if we concede that naturalistic theories of action do not turn 'actions' into 'mere happenings,' and are consistent with agents rationally and purposively bringing about what they do – and isn't this what it means to say that agent-causation is not needed for agency? – then it is unclear why the causal-indeterminist should be obliged to add an agent-cause to explain how agents 'originate' their actions in the indeterministic setting, or what it is such theorists are missing if they don't. If an agent-cause is needed at all, I suggest, it is needed for agency simpliciter – so as to secure the distinction between 'mere happenings' and 'bringing things about' – and it is needed for free agency only derivatively. Thus if it is not needed for agency simpliciter, then it is not required to explain how agents freely 'bring about' their behaviour either – granting the obvious, that the conditions for free agency may *otherwise* outstrip the conditions for agency itself. The debate about causal indeterminism therefore cannot be resolved in isolation from this more fundamental issue we have been considering.

I have argued that dissatisfaction with naturalistic theories stems from the appearance that the agent plays no role in originating his conduct; that this appearance may be diagnosed as being generated by the conceptual gap between first and third person perspectives on action; that this gap is itself explainable with reference to the phenomenal concepts we deploy when we consider agency from the interior perspective; and that the existence of this conceptual gap does not entail that 'bringing things about' cannot consist in suitably related event-causes. The dissatisfaction with naturalistic theories of libertarian freedom, I claim, should be understood and dealt with in a similar fashion. For the problem of 'bringing things about' is not created by causal-indeterminist theories specifically; and if it is answerable naturalistically at all it is answerable naturalistically for them, too.

Notes

1. E. J. Lowe (2008) has argued that agent-causation is continuous with causation throughout the rest of nature, because causation is a relation between

substances that produce changes in others. The proposal is interesting and worth a serious look, but I shall not evaluate it here.

2. Thus Melden: 'It is futile to attempt to explain conduct through the causal efficacy of desire – all *that* can explain is further happenings, not actions performed by agents. ... There is no place in this picture ... even for the conduct that was to be explained' (1961, pp. 128–9).
3. See Bishop (1983).
4. See Kim (1989).
5. See Ekstrom (1993, pp. 603–5).
6. I've excluded from this definition Ekstrom's libertarian specification that the inputs to the evaluative faculty 'cause but do not determine' the decisively formed preference.
7. See Ekstrom (1993, pp. 606–10).
8. Cf. Mele (2003, p. 220).
9. It is important to note that 'adding' such mental items to the mix here does not imply that what it's like to act has been successfully captured from the 'objective' standpoint. The claim is rather that affirming the existence and efficacy of such items does not help us to see how agency as we experience it from the internal perspective is compatible with event-causation (mental or physical) alone.
10. The phrase 'cognitive illusion' is Michael Tye's (2000).
11. See the essays in Alter and Walter (2006).
12. To clarify: it is consistent with my proposal that phenomenal concepts may not help explain consciousness naturalistically, for it's possible that the experience of agency is metaphysically irreducible *as a phenomenal state* even if the phenomenon it represents is naturalistically explicable.
13. A person can of course enjoy phenomenological experiences of agency while she is theorising about agency from the third-person standpoint, but it does not follow from this that the phenomenal content is itself contained within the third-person theoretic conceptualization of action.
14. Cf. Horgan et al. (p. 335).
15. See Kane's (1996) approach.
16. See for discussion and references O'Connor (2000, pp. 49–55) and Kane (1996, pp. 120–3).

Bibliography

Alter, T., and Sven W., (eds.) (2006), *Phenomenal Concepts and Phenomenal Knowledge: New Essays on Consciousness and Physicalism* (New York: Oxford University Press).

Bishop, J. (1989) *Natural Agency: An Essay on the Causal Theory of Action* (Cambridge: Cambridge University Press).

—— (1983), 'Agent-Causation,' *Mind* 92, 61–79.

Chisholm, R. (1966), 'Freedom and Action,' in Lehrer (ed.), *Freedom and Determinism* (New York: Random House).

—— (1964), '*Human Freedom and the Self*,' Lindley Lecture (Lawrence, Kans.).

Clarke, R. (1993), 'Toward a Credible Agent-Causal Account of Free Will,' *Noûs* 27, 191–203.

Ekstrom, L. W. (1993), 'A Coherence Theory of Autonomy,' *Philosophy and Phenomenological Research* 53, 599–616.

—— (2000), *Free Will: A Philosophical Study* (Boulder, CO: Westview Press).

Ginet, C. (1990), *On Action* (Cambridge: Cambridge University Press).

Hasker, W. (1999), *The Emergent Self* (Ithaca, NY: Cornell University Press).

Horgan, T., Tienson, J., and Graham, G. (2003), 'The Phenomenology of First-Person Agency,' in Walter and Heckmann (eds.), *Physicalism and Mental Causation: The Metaphysics of Mind and Action* (Imprint Academic).

Hornsby, J. (1993), 'Agency and Causal Explanation,' in Heil and Mele (eds.), *Mental Causation* (Oxford: Oxford University Press).

Kane, R. (1996), *The Significance of Free Will* (New York: Oxford University Press).

Kim, J. (1989), 'Mechanism, Purpose, and Explanatory Exclusion,' *Philosophical Perspectives* 3, 77–108.

Lowe, E. J. (2008), *Personal Agency: The Metaphysics of Mind and Action* (Oxford: Oxford University Press).

Melden, A. (1961), *Free Action* (London: Routledge and Kegan Paul).

Mele, A. (2003), *Motivation and Agency* (Oxford: Oxford University Press).

Nagel, T. (1986), *The View from Nowhere* (New York: Oxford University Press).

Nathan, N. M. L. (1975), 'Materialism and Action,' *Philosophy and Phenomenological Research* 35, 501–11.

O'Connor, T. (1995), 'Agent-Causation' in O'Connor (ed.), *Agents, Causes, and Events* (New York: Oxford University Press).

—— (2000), *Persons and Causes: The Metaphysics of Free Will* (New York: Oxford University Press).

Searle, J. (2001), *Rationality in Action* (Cambridge, MA.: MIT Press).

Shoemaker, S. and Swinburne, R. (1984), *Personal Identity* (Oxford: Blackwell).

Taylor, R. (1966), *Agent and Purpose* (Englewood Cliffs, NJ: Prentice Hall).

Tye, M. (2000), *Consciousness, Color, and Content* (Cambridge, MA: MIT Press).

Velleman, J. D. (1992), 'What Happens When Someone Acts?' *Mind* 101, 461–81.

—— (2000), *The Possibility of Practical Reason* (Oxford: Oxford University Press).

Hallward Library - Issue Receipt

Customer name: Loach, Emma Rachel

Title: New waves in metaphysics / edited by Allan Hazlett.
ID: 1006064971
Due: 04/12/2012 23:59

Total items: 1
09/10/2012 14:53

All items must be returned before the due date and time.

The Loan period may be shortened if the item is requested.

WWW.nottingham.ac.uk/is

6
Interpretation: Its Scope and Limits

Uriah Kriegel

According to interpretivism, all there is to having an intentional property is being best interpreted as having it. I present a regress-or-circularity argument against this. In Section 1, I elucidate interpretivism, and in Section 2, I present the argument against it.

1 Interpretivism

It is sometimes said that intentionality is a relation, though a special one, one that does not require the existence of all relata. In a pair of previous papers (Kriegel 2007, 2008a), I have argued that this is nonsense, akin to positing a special monadic property that can be instantiated even in the absence of something that instantiates it. Instead, I have argued for an adverbialist account of intentionality, according to which intentionality is a certain kind of intrinsic modification – a non-relational property of some mental states. What both adverbial and relational metaphysics of intentionality share is a certain objectivism about intentionality: the idea that there are objective facts of the matter about the correct assay of intentional properties. This assumption can be rejected, however. It is rejected, most notably, by interpretivist approaches to intentionality. It is therefore my goal, in this chapter, to argue against the viability of such interpretivism.

The term 'interpretivism' is used in a variety of different ways throughout the humanities. Here I will be concerned with the view of intentionality and content associated with Dennett and Davidson when they say such things as 'all there is to really and truly believing that *p* (for any proposition *p*) is being an intentional system for which *p* occurs as a belief in the best (most predictive) interpretation' (Dennett 1981, p. 72) and 'what a fully informed interpreter could know about what a speaker means is all there is to learn; the same goes for what the speaker believes' (Davidson 1986, p. 315). These quotes concern belief, but clearly Dennett and Davidson intend their claim to extend to all intentional states (presumably, they cite belief because they regard it as the paradigmatic intentional state). On their view, there is nothing more to a person's being in an intentional state, or to a state's having an intentional content, than the person being most profitably interpreted as being in that state, or the state being most profitably interpreted as having that content.[1]

1.1   Elucidating interpretivism

This kind of view of intentionality fits a general and somewhat familiar schema. According to secondary quality accounts of colour, for example, for something to be yellow just is for it to be such as to produce a yellowish experience in normal (or perhaps ideal) observers under normal (ideal) conditions. Similar views have been formulated for other perceptible properties, as well as for ethical properties, aesthetic properties, modal properties, and even causation and composition.[2] Such views are sometimes regimented via response-dependent biconditionals of the following form (Johnston 1989):

> (RD) x is F iff x is such as to produce an x-directed response R in a group of subjects S under conditions C.

The relevant kind of view is, or entails, that some such biconditional is true *a priori*, or at least necessarily.[3]

Interpretivism fits the schema. It is a sort of 'ideal interpreter theory' of intentionality: something has or is a belief that p just in case an ideal interpreter would, under ideal conditions, interpret it as having or being a belief that p.[4] Thus the following may be called *system-interpretivism:*

> (I1)   Necessarily, a system x is in intentional state S iff x is such as to produce in ideal interpreters under ideal conditions the response of interpreting x to be in S.

And the following would be *state-interpretivism:*

> (I2)   Necessarily, a state x has intentional content C iff x is such as to produce in ideal interpreters under ideal conditions the response of interpreting x to have C.

Thus, x has or is a belief that p iff x is such as to produce in ideal interpreters under ideal conditions the response of interpreting x to have or be the belief that p.

On the assumptions that (i) being in an intentional state is an intentional property of systems and (ii) having an intentional content is an intentional property of states, (I1) and (I2) can be subsumed under the following more general thesis (where x ranges over both systems and states):

> (Int) Necessarily, x instantiates intentional property P iff x is such as to produce in ideal interpreters under ideal conditions the response of interpreting x to be P.[5]

This is interpretivism *simpliciter*, if you will.[6] Some clarifications are in order.[7]

First, (Int) entails the thesis that *all intentional properties are response-dependent*. It is not *equivalent* to this thesis, because (Int) is more specific, as it narrows in on a specific response – interpretation. Thus (Int) entails also the following thesis: all intentional properties are interpretation-dependent.[8]

Second, (Int) admits of two readings, one where 'necessarily' denotes *metaphysical* modality and one where it denotes *epistemic* modality (i.e., aprioricity).[9] Accordingly, there are two versions of interpretivism, which we may label 'metaphInt' and 'epistInt'; the choice between them should not affect the discussion. It is of course common and genial to analyze both types of necessity in terms of possible worlds: metaphysical necessity is truth in every metaphysically possible world; epistemic necessity is truth in every epistemically possible world.[10]

Third, by 'intentional properties' we should hear not only the relevant properties of mental states and systems, but also linguistic meaning, pictorial content, and so on. Accordingly, (Int) entails (I1) and (I2), but it also entails more: that the intentional properties of linguistic expressions, paintings and photographs, traffic signs, and anything else are interpretation-dependent.[11] Interpretivism in these domains is much less controversial, and often widely accepted.

Fourth, the locution 'such as to produce' admits of at least three readings. On a *manifestational* reading, x is such as to produce y iff x does produce y. On a *dispositional* reading, x is such as to produce y iff x is *disposed* to produce y. On a *categorical* reading, x is such as to produce y iff x has the categorical property that *underlies* the disposition to produce y.[12] Accordingly, there are three versions of (Int), which we may label (MInt), (DInt), and (CInt). The choice between them will very much affect the discussion, as we will see in Section 2.

Fifth, there are legitimate questions surrounding how to construe the ideal interpreter. For starters, note that the business of interpreting systems is very different from that of interpreting states. Our ideal interpreter, however, may do *both* the best they can be done. But there is a question regarding the kind of knowledge the ideal interpreter brings to its task. It must be well-informed, but we cannot allow it to be omniscient, lest interpretivism be trivialized. I propose that we construe the ideal interpreter as a being who comes into the world possessed with (i) no knowledge of the intentional facts, (ii) complete knowledge of the non-intentional facts (i.e., knowledge of all instantiations of non-intentional properties), and (iii) the capacity to draw every valid deductive inference and every justifiable non-deductive inference from (i).[13] Thus the ideal interpreter is fully informed and a perfect reasoner, but initially has no knowledge of intentional facts whatsoever.[14,15]

Sixth, let a condition C be 'ideal' relative to a subject S and a task T just in case S can perform T ideally under C. Observe that against this background any condition is ideal relative to the ideal interpreter and the task of interpretation. For our ideal interpreter can perform its task ideally under any conditions.[16] So the qualifier 'in ideal conditions' is strictly speaking redundant.[17]

Seventh, in the present context we should construe interpretation as any act in which an intentional property is ascribed to something, and be as liberal as possible about which acts are like that. On one view, to interpret *x* is to judge that *x* means something, or represents something, or more generally has some intentional property. Another view allows interpretation to occur in purely perceptual, non-judicative states. Thus, it has been argued that we can directly perceive the semantic properties of text: when I look at English letters, but not at Cyrillic ones, I can *see* what (and that) they mean (Siegel 2006). A third view might construe interpretation as a *sui generis* propositional attitude.[18] These three views disagree on which acts involve the ascription of an intentional property, but they all agree that it is such acts that constitute interpretations.

1.2   Interpretivism, intentional realism, and original intentionality

I end this section with a discussion of two ways in which the above elucidation of interpretivism illuminates other ideas typically associated with interpretivists. None of this will affect the argument in Section 2; I discuss it merely by way of showing that (Int) indeed captures the spirit of interpretivism.

The first issue is the subtle relation of interpretivism to both *realist* and *irrealist* approaches to intentionality. The right characterization of intentional realism and irrealism is a contentious matter, but the general idea, put metaphorically, is that realists accept intentional ascriptions at metaphysical face value, whereas irrealists take them with a metaphysical grain of salt. Interpretivists – Dennett in particular – have often claimed to stake a middle ground. Just how they do so often remains unclear, but (Int) may help.

Consider first the realist aspect of the view. The bedrock of a realist view of certain properties is the thesis that the relevant properties *exist*. One way to show that a property exists is to show that it is *instantiated*. And at least the dispositional and categorical versions of (Int) lead to the result that intentional properties are instantiated routinely, since at least on these readings, many things are indeed such as to produce the responses mentioned in (Int). Thus, persons and states are in fact disposed to elicit interpretive responses. In general, most response-dependent accounts make room for the routine instantiation of the properties for which they attempt to account. Indeed, they offer a particular assay of the properties in question (as relational properties of a certain type). Perhaps because of this, such accounts often go by the name 'response-dependent realism.'

Consider next the irrealist aspect of the interpretivism. (Int) construes intentional properties as response-dependent. Since the relevant respondents (interpreters) are minds, (Int) implies that intentional properties are mind-dependent (and not only in the trivial sense that they are instantiated by minds).[19] Such mind-dependence is often taken to be the hallmark of irrealism across philosophy.[20] Perhaps because of this, Wright (1992) argues forcefully that the best way to cast the disagreement between realists and irrealists in any area of philosophy is in terms of response-dependent biconditionals. According to Wright, the irrealist holds that the relevant biconditional is true *a priori,* while the realist holds that it is true *a posteriori* if at all. It would follow that the best way to cast the disagreement between intentional realists and irrealists puts interpretivists in the latter camp.[21]

We need not take a position here on what the best delineation of the realist/irrealist divide is. The point is that on some reasonable delineations interpretivism is realist and on others it is irrealist, and this explains its affinity to both. Furthermore, (Int) may serve to illuminate the elusive role of 'real patterns' in interpretivism, which Dennett (1991) takes to underlie its realist component. Although it is not entirely transparent from Dennett's writings exactly what that role is, the idea may be that there are certain response-*independent* properties whose presence the ideal interpreter tracks when it responds in the relevant ways. After all, there is a question as to why the ideal interpreter would respond to x but not y. And the answer must be that there are certain response-independent features exhibited by x but not y that the ideal interpreter detects. These are the 'real patterns' that underlie intentionality but are not identical to it.[22]

The other central claim sometimes made in conjunction with interpretivism, and which is illuminated by (Int), is that all intentionality is *derivative* – none is *original* (Dennett 1988, 1990).[23] The distinction between derivative and non-derivative (or original) intentionality is due originally to Grice (1969), who argued that linguistic intentionality derives from mental intentionality: the concatenation of symbols c^a^t has no content in and of itself, but rather derives its content from the mental states of speakers, whereas those mental states do not derive their content from any other source, but rather have it in and of themselves. Dennett's claim is that in the relevant sense, nothing has its content in and of itself (mental states included). Everything contentful derives its content from some other source. Call this the 'no-original-intentionality' thesis, or (NOI).

My contention is that (NOI) is entailed by (Int). But to see this, we must formulate it more precisely. We can start by stating it as follows: for any item x and intentional property P, if x is P, then x is derivatively P. The question is how to explicate 'derivatively.'

One problem is that, as Horst (1996) notes, there are two ways to understand the derived/underived distinction. On one understanding, derived and underived intentionality are two different properties; on another, they are two different ways of acquiring, or having, one and the same property.[24] We can flag this by saying that 'x is derivatively intentional and y is underivatively intentional' may be read either as (i) 'x is derivatively-intentional and y is underivatively-intentional' or as (ii) 'x is-derivatively intentional and y is-underivatively intentional.'

The distinction relevant to (NOI) seems to be the latter. On this second understanding, when an intentional item has derivative intentionality, it derives it *from* some other intentional item. There could be different accounts of how this derivation occurs, but let us here use the label 'R' for whatever relation turns out to hold between a derivatively intentional item and that from which it derives its intentionality. We may then explicate derived intentionality as follows:

> (DI) Necessarily, for any item x and intentional property P, x is-derivatively P iff there is an item y and an intentional property P*, such that (i) x is P, (ii) y is P*, and (iii) x's being P bears R to y's being P*.[25,26]

The no-original-intentionality thesis can then be formulated thus:

> (NOI) There is a relation R, such that for any item x and intentional property P, if x is P, then there is an item y and an intentional property P*, such that (i) y is P* and (ii) x's being P bears R to y's being P*.

My contention is that (NOI) follows from (Int).

We can see this by noting that for (Int), R is the relation of being-interpreted-by, y is some interpretative act by the ideal interpreter, and P* is the property of having the content 'x is P.' We can thus derive (NOI) from (Int) in two steps. First, (Int) entails this:

> (*) For any item x and intentional property P, if x is P, then (i) there is an ideal interpretation with the content 'x is P' and (ii) x's being P bears the being-interpreted-by relation to this ideal interpretation.

Second, (*) entails (NOI).

In conclusion, (Int) is a useful gloss on interpretivism: it captures the intuitive idea while making interpretivism precise and illuminating its subtle relationship to intentional realism and irrealism and to the no-original-intentionality thesis.

2 Against interpretivism

In this section, I present an argument against (Int). The argument takes a regress-or-circularity form. I develop it in two stages: first I argue that the manifestational, dispositional, and categorical readings of (Int) all lead to an infinite regress; then I consider some options for stopping the regress and argue against them.[27]

(Before starting, an autobiographical remark: this general argumentative strategy has always struck me as the obvious first criticism to make against interpretivism, but a reasonably thorough survey of the literature has uncovered not only no sustained prosecution of this kind of argument, but virtually no passing mention of it either. I have found one exception to this – Slors 1996. But I propose to prosecute the argument more systematically and comprehensively here.[28])

2.1   Manifestational interpretivism

Recall that on the manifestational reading, 'such as to produce' is read as equivalent to 'produces.' The result is the following thesis:

> (MInt)   Necessarily, x instantiates intentional property P iff x produces in ideal interpreters (under ideal conditions) the response of interpreting x to be P.[29]

Now, (MInt) is immediately problematic, inasmuch as it entails that no intentional property is instantiated: since there *is* no ideal interpreter, nothing can produce in it any response, interpretive included.[30] But let us, for the sake of argument, adopt the supposition that there *is* an ideal interpreter: an interpreter god of sorts. Then according to (MInt), a person believes that p, say, just in case she produces in this interpreter god the response of interpreting her to believe that p. Even under this supposition, I contend, there is a fatal problem with (MInt).[31]

The problem is that (MInt) leads to a regress. This is because, first, the act of interpretation is itself intentional and contentful, and therefore, secondly, it must have its intentional content in virtue of some further act of interpretation. Let us consider the two parts of this.

First, on any remotely plausible construal, interpretation is itself an intentional state, a mental state endowed with intentional content: wherever there is interpretation, something is being interpreted.[32] In Section 1.1, I loosely characterized interpretation as a mental act in which an intentional property is ascribed to something. The 'in which' locution here must be read intentionally: a mental act in which an intentional property is ascribed to something is a mental act with an intentional content to the effect that some x has some intentional property F.[33] If so, when the interpreter god interprets a person as believing that p, the god is performing a mental act with the content 'this person believes that p.'[34] It thus performs a contentful mental act.

Secondly, since the scope of (Int) is universal, the interpreter god's intentional properties are also constituted by interpretation. What makes it the case that the intentional content of the interpreter god's interpretive act is 'this person believes that p' (and not 'that person desires that q,' say) is that the interpreter god produces in some ideal interpreter the response of interpreting it to interpret this person as believing that p (and not the response of interpreting it to interpret that person as desiring that q). This means that either (a) there is a second interpreter god interpreting the first, or (b) the interpreter god interprets itself. Either way, there must occur a second-order interpretive act, through which the first-order one acquires the content 'this person believes that p.' But the second-order interpretive act is itself intentional, and therefore requires the occurrence of a third-order interpretive act (with the content 'that mental act has a content to the effect that this person believes that p'). And so on *ad infinitum*.

2.2   Dispositional interpretivism

On the dispositional reading of (Int), 'such as to produce' is read as 'is disposed to produce.' The result is:

> (DInt)   Necessarily, x instantiates intentional property P iff x is disposed to produce in ideal interpreters (under ideal conditions) the response of interpreting x to be P.

For (DInt) it is *not* a problem that there is no ideal interpreter: the ideal interpreter's non-existence means that the disposition cited in (DInt) cannot be *manifested,* not that it cannot be *instantiated.*

The regress problem, however, persists. For the disposition cited is very specific: it is not the disposition to break, or to dissolve, but to produce certain interpretive acts in an ideal interpreter. But what makes the ideal interpreter's interpretive acts the intentional states they are is some further interpretive acts.

To see this more precisely, we would need to unpack the reference to dispositions. There are many different accounts of disposition, however, and space is limited. I will illustrate the central point with the *simple conditional analysis* of disposition (Ryle 1949; Quine 1960), because it is the first account that occurs to one when one reflects on the nature of dispositions. The point, however, should be the same on other accounts.[35]

According to the simple conditional analysis of disposition, x has the disposition to exhibit manifestation M under conditions C iff: if C were the case, x would exhibit M. Under this analysis, (DInt) is equivalent to:

> (DInt1)   Necessarily, x instantiates intentional property P iff: if there were an ideal interpreter (and conditions were ideal), x would produce in the ideal interpreter (under ideal conditions) the response of interpreting x to be P.

We can further unpack this by implementing Lewis's (1973) possible world semantics for counterfactual conditionals (again, only by way of illustration), with the following result:

> (DInt2)   Necessarily, x instantiates intentional property P iff: there is a possible world W, such that (i) in W there is an ideal interpreter (and conditions are ideal) and x produces in the ideal interpreter (under ideal conditions) the response of interpreting x to be P, and (ii) W is more similar to the actual world than any world in which there is an ideal interpreter (and conditions are ideal) but x does not produce in it the response of interpreting x to be P.[36]

We can readily appreciate the way the regress problem arises with (DInt2): the problem is essentially the same as with (MInt), except that the ideal interpreter lives in a different world. When a person in the actual world believes that p, there must be a world W, corresponding to the specifications in (DInt2), where the ideal interpreter performs an interpretive act with the content 'that person believes that p.' But something must make it the case that *that* is the content of the ideal interpreter's interpretive act in W. Given interpretivism, it must be that either (a) there is another world W*, which relates to W as W relates to the actual world, wherein a second ideal interpreter interprets the first ideal interpreter to perform an interpretive act with the content 'that person believes that p,' or (b) still in W, the local ideal interpreter interprets itself to perform an interpretive act with the content 'that person believes that p.' Either way, there must occur a second-order interpretive act, which in turn requires a third-order interpretive act, and so on *ad infinitum*.

This sort of trans-world regress, if you will, is just as vicious as the intra-world variety. What is vicious about the intra-world variety is not that too many things are intentional, but that there is no genuine account of intentionality. For until the regress is stopped, we do not yet grasp what constitutes the very first intentional fact. Compare: the problem with turtles all the way down is not that there are too many turtles, but that there is no genuine explanation of what keeps the world in place. Thus although a trans-world regress does not bloat the interpretivist's actual ontology, it does empty his or her account of any explanatory power.[37]

2.3   Categorical interpretivism

The categorical reading of (Int) is obtained by reading 'such as to produce' as denoting the categorical basis of the disposition to produce:

> (CInt)   Necessarily, x instantiates intentional property P iff x has the categorical property that underlies the disposition

to produce in ideal interpreters (under ideal conditions) the response of interpreting *x* to be P.

I want to suggest that (CInt) itself admits of two readings, one which is
not really a version of interpretivism and one which leads to the same
regress.[38]

On one reading, (CInt) adverts to the categorical property which actually underlies the relevant disposition. On another, it adverts to whichever categorical property turns out to underlie that disposition. The
difference is brought out when we consider the following possibility:
suppose that in the actual world, B is the categorical basis of D, but that
in some other world W, B is the basis of some other disposition D*, while
the basis of D is some other categorical property B*. The first reading of
(CInt) adverts to B in W, whereas the second reading adverts to B* in W.
This is, in effect, a distinction between reading (CInt) *de re* and reading
it *de dicto*. So we can disambiguate (CInt) in the usual manner:[39]

(rCInt)   There is a property F, such that (i) F is the categorical
basis of the disposition to produce in ideal interpreters
(under ideal conditions) the response of interpreting *x*
to be P, and (ii) necessarily, *x* instantiates intentional
property P iff *x* is F.

(dCInt)   Necessarily, *x* instantiates intentional property P iff
there is a property F, such that (i) F is the categorical
basis of the disposition to produce in ideal interpreters (under ideal conditions) the response of interpreting *x* to be P, and (ii) *x* is F.

(rCInt) is the first, *de re* reading, (dCInt) the second, *de dicto* one.

As this formulation makes plain, however, (rCInt) is not really a version of interpretivism. Because clause (i) is outside the scope of the modal
operator, (rCInt) creates no necessary connection between intentional
properties and interpretation. It creates a necessary connection between
intentional properties and some property F, but it is a contingent accident that F happens to be connected with interpretive responses. The
issue here is not merely terminological: whether we would like to dig-
nify the view with the label 'interpretivism.' The substantive point is
that according to (rCInt), intentionality is not interpretation-dependent
(though it happens to correlate with interpretation).

Only (dCInt) is a version of interpretivism. But for (dCInt) the regress
is exactly the same as for (DInt), since the relevant categorical property

is characterized precisely in terms of the interpretive responses it disposes its bearer to elicit. Thus the instantiation conditions of the categorical property F involve the disposition: we decide whether x is an instance of F by considering whether x has something that disposes it to elicit interpretive responses. Therefore, if the categorical property is instantiated, the dispositional one must be too. And as we saw above, if the dispositional property is *instantiated*, then in some possible world it is *manifested*, which means that in some possible world a contentful interpretive act occurs. The trans-world regress reappears.

We can bring this out again by adopting, again for the sake of exposition, the simple conditional analysis of dispositions and Lewis's semantics for counterfactual conditionals. The first adoption would result in something like this:

> (dCInt1)   Necessarily, x instantiates intentional property P iff there is a property F, such that (i) x is F, (ii) if there were an ideal interpreter (and conditions were ideal), x would produce in the ideal interpreter (under ideal conditions) the response of interpreting x to be P, and (iii) it is the case that (ii) because it is the case that (i).

Where the 'because' in the final clause denotes the kind of relationship that obtains between a disposition and its categorical basis (as in: 'the vase is fragile because it is made of thin glass,' 'the barrel is explosive because it contains potassium nitrate').[40] The second adoption then results in the following:

> (dCInt2)   Necessarily, x instantiates intentional property P iff there is a property F and a possible world W, such that (i) x is F, (ii) in W there is an ideal interpreter (and conditions are ideal) and x produces in the ideal interpreter (under the ideal conditions) the response of interpreting x to be P, (iii) W is more similar to the actual world than any world in which there is an ideal interpreter (and conditions are ideal) but x does not produce in the ideal interpreter (under the ideal conditions) the response of interpreting x to be P, and (iv) it is the case that (ii) and (iii) because it is the case that (i).

Clause (ii) generates the regress: when a person in the actual world believes that p, there must be a world W, corresponding to the above specifications, where the ideal interpreter performs an interpretive act with the content 'that person believes that *p*.' This leads to the same regress we saw in the discussion of (DInt).

It appears, then, that in all three readings (Int) leads to a vicious regress. This is not an unfamiliar predicament for certain response-dependent accounts. The view that yellow is the disposition to elicit yellow experiences, for example, is vulnerable to the same charge. For this reason, proponents of this kind of view have typically attempted to appeal to related but distinct properties, such as yellow' (Peacocke 1984). To avoid the regress, interpretivists would likewise have to appeal to something like interpretation', rather than interpretation. However, interpretation' would have to be construed in non-intentional terms if regress is to be avoided. Unfortunately, it is unclear what a non-intentional construal of interpretation' would look like, and what the resulting construe would be and what relation it would bear to interpretation.

This concludes the first stage of the argument: I have argued that (Int) leads to a vicious regress. I now turn to the second stage, where I consider some options for stopping the regress.

2.4 Stopping the regress

The first option is to convert the infinite series of interpretive acts into a wide circle of partially inter-interpreting ones. Consider a toy model with four interpretive acts with the following contents:[41]

I_1: this person believes that *p*.
I_2: I_1 has the content that this person believes that *p*.
I_3: I_2 has the content that I_1 has the content that this person believes that *p*.
I_4: I_3 has the content that I_2 has the content that I_1 has the content that this person believes that *p*.

Each I_i derives its content from I_{i+1}. Now let the loop 'close' by having I_4 be interpreted by I_1 rather than some I_5. The result is a kind of *coherentist interpretivism*, if you will, with no infinite regress of states.[42]

However, while this move stops the regress of *states*, it does nothing to stop the more pertinent regress, that of *contents*. For I_4 to derive its content from I_1, I_1 would have to carry a richer content than the one assigned to it above.[43] It would have to carry the following content:

I_1: this person believes that *p* & I_4 has the content that I_3 has the content that I_2 has the content that I_1 has the content that this person believes that *p*.

However, if I_1 is to have this content, I_2 cannot have the content assigned to it above either. It too requires a richer content, namely:

> I_2: I_1 has the content that this person believes that p & that I_4 has the content that I_3 has the content that I_2 has the content that I_1 has the content that this person believes that p.

For I_2 to have this content, however, I_3 would also require a richer content, and so we are off again on an infinite regress, this time of contents. The deeper point is again that the regress is vicious not because of the number of states it requires (which evidently need not be more than four!), but because until the regress stops there is no content at all. For the whole group of states (whether serial or circular) to acquire content, it must be anchored in some contentful act that does not acquire its content from interpretation. But according to interpretivism there is no such act. That is the real problem the regress brings out.[44]

A second option for stopping the regress is to posit self-interpreting states. In one version, these states carry two contents, one of which interprets the other. In another version, they carry a single conjunctive content, where one conjunct is an interpretation of the other. Thus, I_1 may have (in the first version) the first-order content 'this person believes that p' and the second-order content 'this very act has the content that this person believes that p' or (in the second version) the conjunctive content 'this person believes that p & this very act has the content that this person believes that p.'

Again, however, self-interpreting states offer no relief. In the first version, it is clear what endows I_1 with its first-order content, namely, its second-order content. But it is unclear what endows I_1 with its second-order content. According to (Int), for I_1 to have its second-order content, there must be some interpretive act with the content 'I_1 has the content that it itself has the content that this person believes that p.' Now, it may well be that it is I_1 itself that has this third-order content, but *something* must have it. And for something to have this third-order content, there would also have to be something that has the right fourth-order content – and so on and so forth. In the second version, the problem is basically the same: it is (perhaps) clear why I_1's content has its first-order conjunct (if you will), but unclear why it has its second-order conjunct.[45] The failure of the self-interpretation move should not be surprising: it is essentially just coherentist interpretivism with the smallest possible circle.

A third option is to recast interpretivism as a *non-reductive* account of intentionality. At the opening we stated that according to interpretivism, for a person or state to have an intentional property *just is* for that person or state to be most profitably interpreted as having that property. On this view, the interpretation of a person or state *constitutes* that their having an intentional property. But a milder kind of interpretivism might instead suggest that the interpretation and the intentional property somehow *go along*, without the former constituting the latter (see Child 1994). This is in effect to advance the response-dependent biconditional as metaphysically and/or epistemically *contingent* rather than necessary.[46] This milder, non-reductive interpretivism would not involve any infinite regress, since it could be combined with an independent account of what a person or state's having an intentional property actually consists in.

In response, I can only agree that non-reductive interpretivism does not lead to infinite regress nor circularity. In fact, I think it is true. But I also point out that it is *non-reductive*. That is, it does not really tell us what intentionality *is*. It merely makes a comment on intentionality: that it goes along with ideal interpretability. In short, the only thing I want to insist on here is that interpretivism as a theory of what (all) intentionality is is unviable. Other, less ambitious grades of interpretivism may well be viable. In any case, it is worth noting that the quotes I opened with from Dennett and Davidson sound very much reductive: it is clearly claimed that *all there is* to believing is being profitably interpreted as believing.

A fourth and final option is to offer an independent account of the intentionality of ideal interpreters. The idea is that while all other intentionality is based in ideal interpretation, the intentionality of ideal interpretation is grounded in something else.

For some purposes, this may well be a reasonable reaction, but note that it consists in capitulating to the regress argument rather than objecting to it. In essence, the move is to concede that interpretivism cannot be a theory of *all* intentionality, and some subset of intentional states must be intentional interpretation-*independently*. This is to stop the regress by introducing a kind of underived intentionality from which other intentionality can derive (via interpretation). Now, this is exactly the general reaction to the regress argument I would recommend. But that is precisely because it preserves the traditional, anti-interpretivist notion that there is a type of intentionality which is underived and for which we ought to be 'industrial-strength realists' (to use Dennett's expression) rather than interpretivists.

Once we adopt the general strategy of introducing an underived intentionality not based in interpretation, however, there are much more plausible candidates than the intentionality of ideal interpreters' interpretive acts. Most conspicuously, there are the theses (a) that mental intentionality (as opposed to linguistic or pictorial intentionality, say) is the underived intentionality, and (b) that conscious intentionality (excluding the intentionality of unconscious mental states) is the underived intentionality. Both are more antecedently plausible than the thesis (c) that (ideally) interpretive intentionality is the underived intentionality.[47] For *prima facie* there is not the kind of deep difference between interpretive and non-interpretive intentionality that there seems to be between mental and non-mental intentionality or between conscious and non-conscious intentionality. Moreover, since there actually *are* no ideal interpreters, it is unclear how designating ideal interpreters' intentionality as underived help derive all other intentionality (a problem that does not apply to mental and conscious intentionality).

2.5 The scope of interpretivism

The right procedure for choosing among (a)–(c) is to recall what the original motivation for interpretivism was and consider which type of intentionality that motivation is least compelling for. We cannot pursue this project here, but let me just state this. The motivation for interpretivism, both in Davidson and in Dennett, has to do with the normativity of intentional ascription, the fact that all intentional ascription is constitutively governed by the principle of charity. Whether such normativity would indeed support interpretivism I am not sure,[48] but elsewhere I have argued that in any case it is false of conscious intentionality: the ascription of some conscious intentional states is *not* constitutively governed by the principle of charity.[49]

If I am right about this, then we should choose (b), the thesis that conscious intentionality is the underived intentionality. We can still retain interpretivism for all non-conscious intentionality, including the intentionality of unconscious mental states and of non-mental items, such as photographs and linguistic expressions.[50] But conscious intentional states must be exempted. What would stop the interpretational regress is then the occurrence of *conscious interpretive acts*, whose underived intentionality would anchor the intentionality of that which is interpreted. We could therefore restate the interpretivist condition as requiring not the generic response of interpreting *x* to be P, but the more specific response of *consciously* interpreting *x* to be P. The upshot would be a kind of *limited interpretivism:*

> (LInt) Necessarily, *x* derivatively instantiates intentional property P iff *x* is such as to produce in ideal interpreters under ideal conditions the response of consciously interpreting *x* to be P.[51]

(LInt) is probably the best an interpretivist can hope for.[52] I have not argued for it here, since I have not argued for the truth of interpretivism for even the restricted domain of derived intentionality. In a way, I have argued that *at most* (LInt) is true, but not that *at least* it is true.

Nonetheless, (LInt) strikes me as antecedently plausible and worth pursuing. The overall picture of intentionality I would recommend offers a bifurcated account of intentionality, combining an interpretivist account of non-conscious intentionality with an independent account of conscious intentionality. Call this *hybrid interpretivism:*

> (HInt) Necessarily, *x* instantiates intentional property P iff: (i) if *x* is non-conscious, then *x* is such as to produce in ideal interpreters under ideal conditions the response of consciously interpreting *x* to be P, and (ii) if *x* is conscious, then _____

Filling the blank with an account of conscious intentionality would generate a comprehensive account of intentionality.

As with (LInt), I have not defended (HInt), though I find it antecedently attractive. One argumentative strategy we might pursue is to argue that (HInt) is favoured by the methodological principle that, other things being equal, one ought to be interpretivist about as much intentionality as possible, in some suitably articulated sense of 'possible.' The challenge for this strategy would be twofold: (a) to defend this principle, perhaps on the grounds that interpretivism is ontologically or metaphysically less committal than straightforward ('industrial-strength') realism; (b) to show that the principle supports (HInt), perhaps by showing that (HInt) is the most minimal yet non-artificial departure from the regress-plagued (Int). The result would be a non-demonstrative 'plausibility argument' for (HInt). I leave its pursuit to a future occasion.

3   Conclusion

The main purpose of this chapter has been to argue that interpretivism, properly understood, is unviable, inasmuch as it leads inevitably to a vicious regress. Subsidiary purposes have been to say how interpretivism is properly understood – that is, as (Int) – and sketch a kind of view of intentionality – that is, (HInt) – which I find plausible but have not defended here.

Notes

For comments on a previous draft, I would like to thank Michael Bruno, David Chalmers, and especially Allan Hazlett. I have also benefited from presenting the paper at the Pacific APA in April 2009; I am grateful to the audience there, in particular Ben Blumson, Josh Glasgow, Rae Langton, and Carolina Sartorio. This paper was written during a research fellowship at the University of Sydney, to which I am greatly indebted.

1. Two comments. First, I am interpreting Dennett and Davidson as making reductive claims about what belief *is*, not merely as making a comment on the contingent accompaniment of belief. More on this in Section 2.4. Second, the goals in the pursuit of which the interpretation would be profitable presumably have to do, in the first place, with the prediction and explanation of behaviour.
2. For such an account of colour, see Boghossian and Velleman 1989. Berkeley argued, of course, that all perceptible properties are 'secondary qualities.' For such an account of ethical properties, see McDowell 1985 and Wiggins 1987. The extension to esthetic properties (and arguably all normative properties) is relatively straightforward, and sketched in McDowell 1983. As for the more exotic accounts of the kind, proposed for modality, causation, and composition, see (respectively) Menzies 1998, Menzies and Price 1993, and Kriegel 2008b.
3. There is some debate on whether the biconditionals must be *a priori*, or could alternatively be allowed to be just necessary. Wright (1988) originally insisted that they must be *a priori*, but see Miscevic (1998) for dissent. None of this should matter for our present purposes, but more on this below.
4. I should note that neither Dennett nor Davidson anywhere bill their view as an 'ideal interpreter theory.' Rather, this is my own gloss.
5. It has been argued to me that (Int) does not capture interpretivism, because in addition to the equivalence between intentionality and interpretation, one must make an extra claim about the direction of constitution: that interpretation constitutes intentionality and not the other way round. However, all we need to ensure the direction of constitution we are interested in is to declare that we are offering (Int) as an account of intentionality, not of anything else.
6. Note that, since (Int) involves both modality and causation, and since there are response-dependent treatments of both, the one true version of (Int) might ultimately involve multiply embedded response-dependent biconditionals.
7. I will offer seven clarifications. The first is general, the other six explicate the main terms in (Int), since to understand (Int) we must understand 'necessarily,' 'intentional properties,' 'such as to produce,' 'ideal interpreter,' 'ideal conditions,' and 'the response of interpreting.'

8. *This* thesis (Int) may be equivalent to. This is so, however, only on the assumption that (RD) is the only acceptable gloss on response-dependence. Since I presented (RD) as stipulative, this is indeed the case.

9. As noted earlier, some might prefer to formulate such views as a priori rather than merely necessary in the metaphysical sense. I construe such apriority in terms of epistemic necessity, which is commonly seen as a formally well-behaved gloss on apriority (see Chalmers Ms).

10. It is a more controversial matter how to characterize metaphysically and epistemically possible worlds, but to a first approximation, a metaphysically possible world is a world in which no metaphysical truths obtain that do not obtain in the actual world, and an epistemically possible world is a world where there are no truths inconsistent with what the subject believes relative to whom the world is assessed as possible.

11. In other words, *x* in (Int) ranges not only over systems and states, but more. (Note well, though: this would count as 'more' only if linguistic expressions etc. are neither states nor systems. Otherwise, it will not count as 'more.') In any case, I am assuming here that the media enumerated in the text are intentional. It is certainly coherent to claim that paintings or photographs, for example, are non-intentional. If they are not, then (Int) will not apply to them.

12. For example, if we say that a vase V is such as to break, we could mean one of three things: (a) V breaks; (b) V is disposed to break; (c) V is made of a kind of material that disposes a thing to break.

13. What counts as a justifiable non-deductive inference is open to debate, but one should just plug here one's favourite view of the matter. For example, if one holds that all non-deductive inferences are to the best explanation and that the best explanation is always and everywhere that which maximizes unification, then one should construe the ideal interpreter as a being who infers the truth of the most unifying explanation of any non-intentional facts (in addition to making every valid deductive inference from those facts).

14. There are also ways to construe the ideal interpreter so that it is more continuous with real-life interpreters. For example, we might propose the following two-step elucidation: an interpreter who makes an ideal interpretation at *t* is an ideal interpreter at *t*; an ideal interpreter *simpliciter* is someone who is an ideal interpreter at *t* for any *t*.

15. Although it is somewhat premature to discuss this, let me point out that, in all probability, there *exist* no ideal interpreter so construed. So (Int) would be plausible only if it did not require *actual* responses on an ideal interpreter's part, but only counterfactual ones. It is hard to see how (MInt) could provide for this, but (DInt) and (CInt) probably do. More on this in the next section.

16. It may be thought that since the ideal interpreter is defined in terms of the *capacity* to draw inferences, and capacities can be inhibited, that there are some sub-ideal conditions for the ideal interpreter's execution of its interpretive function, namely, the conditions under which the relevant capacity is in fact inhibited. If so, we would need to specify in the response-dependent biconditional that the response is elicited in other conditions, conditions under which the interpreter's capacity to draw inferences is not inhibited.

17. It is an interesting question whether the point applies to every response-dependent conditional appealing to an ideal subject. The answer is that it depends on how the ideal subject is construed in each case. In any event, many response-dependent conditionals appeal to *normal* rather than *ideal* subject, so the citation of conditions is not redundant for them.

18. It may even be possible to hold that certain *behaviours* constitute interpretation. The following example is due to Michael Bruno: in a community of robots, it may be that whenever robots beep in a certain way covariantly with the presence of danger, so that when one robot beeps in a that way, all other robots flee the scene. The feeling behaviour may be taken to constitute an 'interpretation' of the beeping.

19. It has been observed that it is a non-trivial task to articulate the mind-dependence of mental phenomena. Since these phenomena occur in a mind, they are mind-dependence in an obvious way, and capturing the unobvious way is difficult. One option is to frame the issue in terms of observer-dependence instead of mind-dependence, though of course this would make it difficult to capture the sense in which observational phenomena might be observer-dependent in a non-trivial sense.

20. Thus, on this view, whether a creature is in an intentional state, such as believing that *p*, depends not only on how things are with the creature, but also on how things are with the interpreter. Clearly, this is quite a strong form of irrealism.

21. At least this is so if we interpret the modal operator in (Int) as denoting epistemic necessity – see the second clarification in Section 1.1.

22. The upshot is that construing interpretivism in terms of (Int) casts it as realist insofar as it makes room for the instantiation of intentional properties, as irrealists insofar as it makes those properties non-trivially mind-dependent, and realist again insofar as it finds a response- and mind-independent basis for them.

23. This claim is made more explicitly by Dennett. As for Davidson, it is natural to interpret him as actually holding that the intentionality of mental states derives from that of language, or as he would put it, the content of thought from the content of talk (see Davidson 1975).

24. As Horst puts it, there is 'conceptually derivative' intentionality and 'causally derivative' intentionality. The former involves a distinct property, the latter a distinct way to acquiring or coming to instantiate the same old property.

25. We can then say that *x* is-underivatively P iff it is not the case that *x* is-derivatively P.

26. I take the imperfect nominal '*x*'s being P' to denote a *state of affairs*, and so the relation R is defined over states of affairs. It is possible to formulate the third clause so that R is defined over propositions, but I prefer states of affairs to propositions.

27. I am assuming (what may not be so obvious) that if something causes *x*, then it is disposed to cause *x*, though the converse may not hold, and if something is disposed to cause *x*, then it has the categorical basis of that disposition (that is, that a categorical basis is a necessary but insufficient condition for a disposition and a disposition is a necessary but insufficient condition for a manifestation). If so, then the three varieties of interpretivism that I will consider are increasingly stronger.

28. There is the more general issue of how surprising or even interesting it is to make this kind of argument, given how obvious it is. I have nothing particularly illuminating to say on this subject, except that since the argument has not actually been suitably developed in the literature, it is worthwhile to try and formulate a cogent presentation of it. (After all, it is a familiar experience among philosophers, I take it, that what appears to be a promising argument in the abstract turns out not to work when the details are actually pursued.) Moreover, the critical discussion will help to bring out some of the logical geography of the interpretivist approach to intentionality.

29. In keeping with the fact that the restriction to ideal conditions is redundant, I parenthesize reference to ideal conditions here and in the sequels.

30. It is an interesting question whether this upshot should be construed as eliminativism about intentionality. In relevant discussions, it seems that the natural construal of eliminativism is as the view that there are no intentional properties. The view that no intentional properties are instantiated would entail the view that there are no intentional properties only under the assumption that there are no uninstantiated properties (Armstrong 1978). Since that assumption is not *logically* true, it is clear that the views that there are no intentional properties and that there are no intentional property instantiations are not logically equivalent.

31. (MInt) is admittedly *antecedently* implausible

32. Or at least something is putatively being interpreted, or it is putatively the case that something is being interpreted. There is a sense in which an interpretation can occur in the absence of anything interpreted, but that is so only in a way that establishes the contentfulness of interpretation: it shows that interpretation exhibits so-called intentional inexistence.

33. If interpretive acts are always judgments or beliefs, then they are propositional attitudes. If they can be perceptions or *sui generis* attitudes, they might be intentional states with non-propositional content. But either way they are intentional states.

34. Well, it does not have to be a content that picks out the target of interpretation indexically. The interpreter god could use a name or a definite description as well.

35. Many philosophers today reject the simple conditional analysis of dispositions, in favour of either a complicated conditional analysis (Lewis 1997), or a non-conditional analysis (Fara 2005), or a primitivist account (Molnar 1999). This is because of a number of counter-examples involving so-called finks, masks, and antidotes. This is not the place to discuss this literature, though it bears mentioning that the simple conditional analysis has been defended against these counter-examples (Choi 2006, 2008). In any case, as noted I contend that working with a different account of dispositions should not make much of a difference to the dialectical situation, even if it might complicate the *exposition* of the regress problem.

36. This is a special case of the following more general thesis: Necessarily, x instantiates intentional property P in a world ß iff: there is a possible world W, such that (i) in W there is an ideal interpreter (and conditions are ideal) and x produces in the ideal interpreter the response of interpreting x to be P, and (ii) W is more similar to ß than any world in which there is an ideal interpreter (and conditions are ideal) but x does not produce in any ideal

interpreter the response of interpreting *x* to be P. (DInt2) is the special case
in which ß is the actual world.

37. I am assuming, in the first part of this sentence, that we do not assay mere
possibilia as real concreta. A trans-world regress commits us not to many
things, but to many possible things. Only if possible things are things one
is ontologically committed to does this bloat one's ontology. If one is not
ontologically committed to merely possible things, then their duplication
does not add to one's ontology.

38. There can be many different versions of (CInt), corresponding to the different categorical properties one might wish to appeal to in further articulat-
ing the view. Perhaps the most natural version, for someone like Dennett, is
to take functional and/or behavioural properties to be the categorical basis
of the disposition to elicit interpretive acts. However, this way in which different versions of (CInt) would differ is orthogonal to the argument I want
to pursue against it.

39. Compare 'necessarily, the first black U.S. president is Barack Obama.' It is
important to distinguish the *de re* and *de dicto* readings of this statement,
since the former is true but the latter false. The standard way to formalize
the distinction is as follows: the *de re* reading is 'there is an x, such that x is
the first black U.S. president and necessarily, *x* is Barack Obama,' while the
de dicto reading is 'necessarily, there is an *x*, such that *x* is the first black U.S.
president and *x* is Barack Obama.'

40. There are different accounts of what that relation is, and I want to stay neutral among them. One classic view is that of Prior, Pargetter, and Jackson
(1982): a categorical basis of a disposition is any causally operative sufficient
condition for the manifestation of that disposition.

41. What appears before the colon designates the interpretive state, what
appears after the colon designates the content of that state.

42. I call this 'coherentist interpretivism' because it responds to the regress argument as coherentism about epistemic justification responds to a parallel
regress argument for foundationalism about justification. Foundationalists
often argue as follows: if every belief is only inferentially justified (i.e., justified by virtue of its inferential relations to other beliefs), then no belief is
justified, because there is an infinite regress of inferential justifications, so
therefore some beliefs must be non-inferentially justified (i.e., justified by
virtue of something other than their inferential relations to other beliefs).
In response, the coherentist maintains that all beliefs are inferentially justified, insisting that justification can arise from a wide enough web of suitably inferentially interrelated beliefs.

43. By 'richer' content here I merely mean a propositional content where the
relevant proposition is more complicated than we have supposed thus far.

44. It might be thought that a variant would do better in which the interrela-
tions among all the interpretive acts are characterized non-intentionally
(hence not in terms of interpretation). Perhaps there could be a web of
internal states with a certain broadly causal relation interconnecting them,
and when that causal relation obtains among them they all acquire content
at once, as it were. This amounts, however, to devising a new account of
intentionality, in terms of the relevant causal relation rather than in terms
of interpretation. I will discuss this move later on.

45. Things may actually be worse in this case, as it is not really all that clear how any conjunct could be part of a state's content before the state has its entire content.
46. That is to replace (Int) with (Int-): Contingently, x instantiates intentional property P iff x is such as to produce in ideal interpreters under ideal conditions the response of interpreting x to be P. As before, though, the contingency can be understood either as metaphysical or as epistemic, i.e., as a posteriori.
47. The view that mental intentionality is that underived one has been commonplace since Grice (1969); see also Cummins 1989. More recently, a number of authors have argued for, or at least suggested, a restriction of the domain of underived intentionality to conscious intentionality (McGinn 1988, Kriegel 2003, 2007, Strawson 2004, Georgalis 2006, Bourget forthcoming).
48. See Fodor and Lepore 1993 for a compelling argument that it would not.
49. These remarks are bound to be somewhat opaque in the present context. Clarifying them further would require, however, a discussion of Davidson and Dennett on the principle of charity that we cannot seriously undertake here.
50. If the interpretivist wants to keep the scope (Int) as broad as possible, that would be a reason to adopt (b) over (a), since conscious states are a proper subset of mental states.
51. As stated here, (LInt) is really a superposition of two theses. One is a limited interpretivism about derived intentionality, the other a limited interpretivism about non-conscious intentionality. We may formulate them as follows. (dLInt) would be the thesis that Necessarily, x derivatively instantiates intentional property P iff x is such as to produce in ideal interpreters under ideal conditions the response of non-derivatively interpreting x to be P. (nLInt) would be the thesis that Necessarily, x non-consciously instantiates intentional property P iff x is such as to produce in ideal interpreters under ideal conditions the response of consciously interpreting x to be P.
52. There is also the option of offering interpretivism as a *non-reductive* account of intentionality, that is, an account of intentionality that does not propose to account for the intentional in non-intentional terms. However, it is not clear in what sense the result would qualify as an *account* of intentionality, as opposed to just a statement about it.

Bibliography

Armstrong, D. M. (1978), *Nominalism and Realism: Universals and Scientific Realism,* vol. 1 (Cambridge: Cambridge University Press).

Boghossian, P. and Velleman, J. D. (1989), 'Colour as a Secondary Quality,' *Mind* 98, 81–103.

Bourget, D. (forthcoming), 'Consciousness is Underived Intentionality,' *Noûs.*

Chalmers, D. J. (manuscript), 'The Nature of Epistemic Space.'

Child, W. (1994), *Causality, Interpretation, and the Mind* (Oxford: Oxford University Press).

Choi, S. (2006), 'The Simple vs. Reformed Conditional Analysis of Dispositions,' *Synthese* 148, 369–79.

—— (2008), 'Dispositional Properties and Counterfactual Conditionals,' *Mind* 117, 795–841.

Cummins, R. C. (1989), *Meaning and Mental Representation* (Cambridge, MA: MIT Press).

Davidson, D. (1975), 'Thought and Talk,' in Guttenplan (ed.), *Mind and Language* (Oxford: Oxford University Press).

—— (1986), 'A Coherence Theory of Truth and Knowledge,' in Lepore (ed.), *Truth and Interpretation: Perspectives on the Philosophy of Donald Davidson* (Oxford: Blackwell).

Dennett, D. C. (1981), 'True Believers,' in Heath (ed.), *Scientific Explanation* (Oxford: Oxford University Press). Reprinted in Dennett 1987.

—— (1987), *The Intentional Stance* (Cambridge MA: MIT Press)

—— (1988), 'Evolution, Error, and Intentionality,' in Wilks and Partridge (eds.), *Sourcebook on the Foundations of Artificial Intelligence* (Albuquerque, N.M.: New Mexico University Press). Pre-printed in Dennett 1987.

—— (1990), 'The Myth of Original Intentionality,' in Mohyeldin et al. (eds.), *Modeling the Mind* (Oxford: Oxford University Press).

—— (1991), 'Real Patterns,' *Journal of Philosophy* 88, 27–51.

Fara, M. (2005), 'Dispositions and Habituals.' *Noûs* 39, 43–82.

Fodor, J. A. and Lepore, E. (1993), 'Is Intentional Ascription Intrinsically Normative?,' in Dahlbom (ed.), *Dennett and His Critics* (Oxford: Blackwell).

Georgalis, N. (2006), *The Primacy of the Subjective* (Cambridge, MA: MIT Press).

Grice, H. P. (1969), 'Utterer's Meaning and Intention,' *Philosophical Review* 68, 147–77.

Horst, S. W. (1996), *Symbols, Computation, and Intentionality* (Berkeley and Los Angeles: University of California Press).

Johnston, M. (1989), 'Dispositional Theories of Value,' *Proceedings of Aristotelian Society* 63, 139–74.

Kriegel, U. (2003), 'Is Intentionality Dependent upon Consciousness?,' *Philosophical Studies* 116, 271–307.

—— (2007), 'Intentional Inexistence and Phenomenal Intentionality,' *Philosophical Perspectives* 21, 307–40.

—— (2008a), 'The Dispensability of (Merely) Intentional Objects,' *Philosophical Studies* 141, 79–95.

—— (2008b), 'Composition as a Secondary Quality,' *Pacific Philosophical Quarterly* 89, 359–83.

Lewis, D. K. (1973), *Counterfactuals* (Oxford: Blackwell).

—— (1997), 'Finkish Dispositions,' *Philosophical Quarterly* 47, 143–58.

McDowell, J. (1983), 'Aesthetic Value, Objectivity, and the Fabric of the World,' in Schaper (ed.), *Pleasure, Preference and Value* (Cambridge: Cambridge University Press).

—— (1985), 'Values and Secondary Qualities,' in Honderich (ed.), *Morality and Objectivity: A Tribute to John Mackie* (London: Routledge and Kegan Paul).

McGinn, C. (1988), 'Consciousness and Content,' *Proceedings of the British Academy* 76, 219–39. Reprinted in Block, Flanagan, and Güzeldere (eds.), *The Nature of Consciousness: Philosophical Debates* (Cambridge, MA: MIT Press, 1997).

Menzies, P. (1998), 'Possibility and Conceivability: A Response-Dependent Account of Their Connection,' *European Review of Philosophy* 3, 255–77.

Menzies, P. and Price, H. (1998), 'Causation as a Secondary Quality,' *British Journal for the Philosophy of Science* 44, 187–203.

Miscevic, N. (1998), 'The Aposteriority of Response-Dependence,' *The Monist* 81, 69–84.

Molnar, G. (1999), 'Are Dispositions Reducible?,' *Philosophical Quarterly* 49, 1–17.

Peacocke, C. (1984), 'Colour Concepts and Colour Experience,' *Synthese* 58, 365–82.

Prior, E., Pargetter, R., and Jackson, F.C. (1982), 'Three Theses about Dispositions,' *American Philosophical Quarterly* 19, 251–57.

Quine, W. V. O. (1960), *Word and Object* (Cambridge, MA: MIT Press).

Ryle, G. (1949), *The Concept of Mind* (London: Hutchinson & Co.).

Siegel, S. (2006a), 'Which Properties Are Represented in Perception?,' in Gendler, Szabo, and Hawthorne (eds.), *Perceptual Experience* (Oxford: Oxford University Press).

Slors, M. (1996), 'Why Dennett Cannot Explain What It Is to Adopt the Intentional Stance,' *Philosophical Quarterly* 46, 93–8.

Strawson, G. (2004), 'Real Intentionality,' *Phenomenology and the Cognitive Sciences* 3, 287–313.

Wiggins, D. (1987), 'A Sensible Subjectivism?,' in his *Needs, Values and Truth* (Oxford: Clarendon).

Wright, C. (1988), 'Moral Values, Projection and Secondary Qualities,' *Proceedings of Aristotelian Society* 62, 1–26.

—— (1992), *Truth and Objectivity* (Cambridge, MA: Harvard University Press).

7
Empirical Analyses of Causation
Douglas Kutach

Imagine a psychologist who has formulated a theory of how people understand various interactions among physical stuff, that is, an account of the implicit folk theory of physics. His model incorporates parameters for characterizing contingent conditions like a value for how dense an object is represented as being or an implicit estimate of how quickly a certain object will return to rest after being set in motion. It includes hypotheses about variances among people and performance limitations that affect how people's understanding is applied in practice. Suppose all the psychologist's work is methodologically unimpeachable and that the model is stunningly successful given the criteria psychologists use for evaluating theories, for example, making precise and accurate predictions of people's responses to questions about physics and predictions about how they will behave when confronted with practical problems that test what they know about physics.

Now imagine the response our psychologist would receive if he suggested to the physics department that his psychological theory ought to be adopted as a constraint on their theories of force and energy and so forth. The physicist according to this program would be tasked with filling in the psychological theory's various parameters to arrive at a model that matches the structure of the external world. Or worse, imagine our psychologist arguing that regardless of any virtues the physicists' current theories have, they cannot concern genuine energy because in order for any theory to pertain to energy, its claims would need to avoid conflict with folk wisdom concerning energy, for example, that exercise increases a person's energy. Whether a psychology of folk physics serves as good constraint on theories of real world physics is of course ultimately an empirical question, but not only do we have independent reasons to reject this program as an extremely implausible strategy for improving physics, there is no reason to believe that a successful physics *must* obey the implicit logic of folk physics (or naive opinions about the use of physics terms) on pain of not really being a theory of physics.

Metaphysicians of causation routinely practice activities analogous to this hypothetical psychologist. All too frequently, theories designed to accommodate linguistic features of natural language are pressed into service as constraints on theories about the behaviour of the external world, with similar prospects for success. Metaphysical theories of causation are standardly required to concern the external world in the sense of being applicable to astronomy, ecology, and economics while at the same time vindicating the literal truth of folk intuitions about causes. The practice primarily stems from the routine use of a crippled form of conceptual analysis. While conceptual analysis of some sort is necessary for any useful intellectual investigation, malignant versions of it exert widespread influence over standard practices, including those of scholars who nominally disavow conceptual analysis.

The presence of the bad kind of conceptual analysis is at least understandable in philosophical disciplines having little relation to science. What is striking about the kind of conceptual analyses standardly presupposed in the philosophical literature on causation, though, is that an alternative form of conceptual analysis is readily available: empirical analysis. What empirical analysis consists in, I think, has not yet been adequately articulated, as demonstrated by continuing puzzlement over its aims, for example, Bontley (2006). The negative part of my task here is to expose that aspect of the orthodox metaphysics of causation which should be rejected by serious investigators of causation, and the positive part is to sketch a viable alternative to the orthodox methodology.

1 A case study

Nothing illustrates the odd character of the orthodox methodology better than David Lewis's (1979) theory of counterfactual asymmetry, which is tied to causation by way of his counterfactual accounts of causation (Lewis 1976, 2004). In the papers on causation, Lewis offers criteria to use in conjunction with his counterfactual logic (1973) in order to take some possible world including an event of interest e, and to determine whether a given event c is a cause of e in that world. The criteria discussed in the counterfactual asymmetry paper consist of a ranked list of respects in which two possible worlds can be compared to determine which is more similar to the actual world.

Ignoring whether the theory is successful on its own terms, it ought to strike anyone as a peculiar way to investigate causation. Lewis's grand argumentative structure involves first developing a logic of counterfactual conditionals by comparing the consequences of various axioms with suitably informed folk judgments about sample sentences and inferences; and second, examining the logic to find that it has a semantics involving a relation of comparative similarity among possible worlds. This is standard procedure in regimenting the logic and semantics of natural language and is by itself unproblematic. But in a curious third step, Lewis uses the semantic structure to concoct a system that generates truth values for the counterfactual conditionals relevant to the evaluation of causal claims. These counterfactuals are then fed into an account of causation to render judgments about instances of causation among ordinary events.

The success of the account, orthodox experts think, is to be judged by at least two crucial criteria. The first concerns how well it reproduces moderately refined folk judgments about specific cases of causation and general truths about causation, e.g., that effects never precede their causes (except perhaps in unusual environments). For every prominent account of causation *x*, the causation literature is replete with attacks on theory *x* of the form, 'In such and such scenario, *x*'s identification of the causes of *e* conflicts with a common sense identification of the causes.' It is possible for a successful account to oppose wildly popular judgments, but such disagreements are broadly presumed to count against the theory, not the intuitions. Accepting the theory in the face of clear counterexamples is generally considered a course of action to be taken only grudgingly as a last resort.

The second concerns how well the account provides a non-trivial systematization of claims about causation. A metaphysical theory of causation is not supposed to be an encyclopaedia of facts about causation nor a list of psychological heuristics that guide our identification of causes. Its purpose is to tell us about causation itself, especially what all instances of causation have in common. It should not merely fit the common sense intuitions in the way one draws a best fit curve through a graph of data points but should elucidate principles that connect causation to related concepts like laws, events, chance, time, as well as explain the reasonableness of our central beliefs concerning causation.

It is unclear what purpose is served by this methodology, especially its dismissal of accounts of causation that do not meet both standards. Some philosophers construe Lewis's project as an early *scientific* theory of causal influence.[1] So understood, the project audaciously proposes to uncover a theoretical structure that systematizes natural language, specifically our implicit counterfactual logic, and then to use that same structure to explain how causal influence in the external world operates. As illustrated by the psychologist who wants to impose his theory as a constraint on physics, such manoeuvres are fantastically implausible as guiding principles for a scientific program. Of course, the mere fact that a logical structure systematizes natural language does not by itself mean it is likely to be useless for science; propositional logic is handy for understanding fragments of ordinary language and for science as well. The implausibility comes from the counterfactual logic's ability to account for idiosyncratic features of natural language. That Lewis's own logic of counterfactuals is meant to explain features of human language that are unmotivated from a physical perspective is evident from, among other things, its use of the centring axiom (which results in a significant difference between the truth conditions when the antecedent is true versus when it is false), its treatment of the conditional as a variably-strict modal operator (which conflicts with a natural treatment of chancy influence), and its treatment of negation.[2] It is even more audacious to insist that a scientific theory of causal influence is defective if its model for evaluating 'what would have happened had things been otherwise' conflicts with the implicit logic of ordinary language counterfactuals.

An alternative interpretation of Lewis's counterfactual asymmetry paper tells us that it is an attempt to explicate the implicit psychology grounding our judgments of causal influence. The counterfactual logic is a constraint on theories of causation, the story would go, because one is hypothesizing that some cognitive module plays a role in our use of counterfactual language and also for causal reasoning. But, as Paul Horwich (1993) notes, Lewis's specific system is psychologically implausible because it employs facts about the amount of time two possible worlds are perfectly alike in their instantiation of properties and the spatial extent of miracles in these worlds (relative to laws of the actual world). Furthermore, construing Lewis's theory as merely teasing out an implicit psychology does not make sense of the fact that it is offered as an explanation of the causal asymmetry. One of Lewis's motivations for the theory is to avoid positing a fundamental temporal direction grounding the asymmetries of counterfactuals, influence, and causation, and instead to derive these asymmetries from facts about the contingent layout of historical fact. This makes sense if one is thinking about the account as part of a metaphysical or scientific project but not if it is just psychology. Given the psychological salience of temporal asymmetry, it is far more plausible that people simply judge causation and influence to be directed towards the future rather than continually deriving the causal direction from an estimation of durations of perfect match and sizes of miracles.

Lewis's theory is implausible as a theory of the science of causation and as a theory of the psychology of causation, but a third interpretation is that it is deliberately somewhere in between – a hybrid combining folk judgments of causation with what we know from science. This project, often known as 'conceptual analysis,' has been recently defended in general (e.g., Chalmers 1996; Jackson 1998; Chalmers and Jackson 2001), and specifically with regard to causation (e.g., Lewis 2004; Collins, Hall, and Paul 2004). Traditional versions of conceptual analysis were committed to the project of finding explicit definitions of folk concepts (e.g., Ducasse 1926), but contemporary defenders allow and usually advise regimentation and improvement of the concepts. I will call the contemporary version of conceptual analysis, 'orthodox analysis' because it is de rigueur in turn of the millennium philosophical circles.

It ought to be uncontroversial that some kind of conceptual analysis is a necessary component of any intellectual investigation, for without it, we would have no way to connect our theoretical terms to the folk terms they are intended to improve and the phenomena they are intended to describe. One needs to have a requirement in one's standards for theoretical adequacy so that, for example, a successful theory of planetary motion is not passed off as a successful theory of causation merely by attaching the label 'cause' to what we ordinarily think of as an orbit. But there are better and worse versions of conceptual analysis, and despite the improvements orthodox analysis provides to old-fashioned conceptual analysis, the resulting methodology is still defective.

2   Orthodox analysis

Food is important to our survival and flourishing, so we ought to know what things are food and what are not. This requires us to know the rules governing the extension of 'food.' In response to this challenge, a food scientist conducts a vast investigation into nutrition and finds out every detail concerning how various ingestible materials are related to creature health. The facts she uncovers, according to this fantasy, exhaustively identify every relation among every relevant variable food scientists care about. Upon completion of the scientific work, she says,

'Everything we wanted to know about food is subsumed by the nutrition relations I have found. Food is basically that which is nutritious.'

The orthodox analyst responds, 'Your analysis is either false or off topic. The goal was to find out what food is, and your theory of nutrition only identifies the extension of your newfangled concept "nutrient." For your theory to be of use in understanding food, you must solve the location problem (Jackson 1998), isolating (from the morass of nutrition relations your science has identified) some structure that well enough matches folk platitudes about food. Nutrition science alone does not show which substances count as food. It must be supplemented with a conceptual analysis that provides linkage between "nutrient" and our native food concept. To conduct such an analysis, one must compare what the theory says is nutritious with uncontroversial examples of food, as evinced from native informants or, even more efficiently, a few smart colleagues. When anyone examines your concept "nutrient," we find it does not match well with food. Your theory counts as nutrients tea, iron crowbars, human brains, and irradiated faeces, but we know a priori that tea is a beverage, a crowbar is inedible, etc. So, cheers for your theory of nutrition, but there still exists the very much unresolved project of understanding what food is.'

In defending the utility of orthodox analysis, philosophers have proposed amendments (or perhaps clarifications) to make conceptual analysis seem less like a parody. Jackson, for example, correctly emphasizes the following points:

1. One does not need to accommodate all the naive platitudes associated with the concept. One can dismiss some as mistakes or tangential aspects of the concept. Furthermore, if the full set of platitudes does not cohere, one can (presumably as a last resort) abandon enough platitudes to achieve coherence.
2. One does not need the sought-after a priori connections among concepts to take the form of an explicit definition. The conceptual analysis can handle cluster concepts by permitting somewhat handwaving connections among concepts that draw on people's native pattern-recognition ability.

I agree that these two principles should be adopted for conceptual analysis, but they pose a problem for orthodox analysis because they appear to weaken the standards for adequate analysis so much that it becomes indistinguishable from the kind of conceptual analysis common in science, where little attention is paid to disagreements with folk opinion. An examination of the actual practices of orthodox analysts reveals that their intended form of analysis is more restrictive by insisting on the importance of rendering folk platitudes literally true. Collins, Hall, and Paul (2004, p. 31) attempt to ward off an overly permissive form of conceptual analysis by stating 'although the account can selectively diverge from these intuitions, provided there are principled reasons for doing so, it should not diverge from them wholesale.' Depending on one's standards for 'principled' and 'wholesale divergence,' orthodox analysis could still be interpreted as allowing the kind of revisionary conceptual precisifications common in science, but I take their claim to be an attempt to disallow such a weak construal of the standards of adequacy. What the orthodoxy must defend – in order to be distinguishable from the empirically oriented version of conceptual analysis I will soon clarify – is its practice of imposing a heavy burden of explanation on any proponent to account for why we should reject obvious truths that conflict with her proposal.

According to official doctrine, the orthodoxy insists in general that folk intuitions and platitudes about X be taken as touchstones for judging the adequacy of analyses of X in the sense that the analysis must make them come out as strict truths and not as strictly false but entirely reasonable simplifications of reality. But in practice, the doctrine is applied in a biased fashion to accord with popular opinion. In cases like the relation between 'nutrient' and 'food,' where a strict implementation of the orthodox methodology would reveal itself as preposterous, the common sense intuitions are brushed aside as pedantic niceties. In practice, that is, orthodox analysts accept the food scientist's claims about nutrients as informing us about food despite the lack of explicit explanations of all the discrepancies between 'nutrient' and 'food.'

However, in cases where orthodox analysis serves as a useful shield for the analyst's prejudices or the status quo, the folk intuitions are held up as definitive standards, obvious truths to be abandoned only as a last resort under the force of weighty reasons.

Specifically with regard to causation, the orthodox analyst is insistent that central folk intuitions be strictly respected. Every orthodox analyst demands that an adequate account of causation must respect the principles that (1) events do not cause themselves, (2) effects do not cause their causes, and (3) pre-empted would-be causes are not genuine causes.[3] Contradicting any of these obvious truths about causation counts as grounds for dismissal, unless a convincing explanation is provided for why the violated principle should be abandoned. For example, a symmetric theory of causation holds that anytime c causes e, e

also causes c. One counterexample that is taken seriously by the orthodox theorist as sufficient grounds for rejecting the symmetric theory is the common sense observation that an ordinary instance of thunder is not a cause of the previous lightning. Attempts to brush off the alleged counterexample by claiming that our disinclination to identify it as a genuine cause is just a result of pragmatic factors – for example, that we often conflate the more practically useful future-directed causation with causation simplicter – are not taken seriously without extensive explanation.

But what marks the difference between discrepancies that are so easily explained away that they hardly demand explicit discussion from discrepancies where a heavy burden is placed on the proponent? The de facto standard is that an explanatory burden exists if and only if most experts find the account's claim counterintuitive. But this rule is ipso facto incapable of distinguishing misguided intuitions shared by the bulk of the expert community from intuitions that are essential for the analysis to be correct and on topic. The crux of the problem with orthodox analysis is simply this: An orthodox analysis of X has no *principled* means for distinguishing between (1) platitudes one must accommodate because to dispense with them would guarantee either that the account is false or that it is not an analysis of X, and (2) platitudes that are misguided but strongly believed as strictly true because we humans are simple minded, easily indoctrinated, or genetically predisposed. This deficiency prevents a successful analysis whenever people share strongly held intuitions, some of which are crucial for isolating the subject of discussion and others of which are bogus beliefs due to widespread ignorance or failure to recognize the ridiculousness of prevailing doctrines, etc. In those cases, any attempt at orthodox analysis will necessarily be crippled by its obligation to vindicate the literal truth of the bogus intuitions. Once accepted as among the platitudes that concern the meaning of X, an orthodox analysis of X has no mechanism to expunge the cognitive dreck without facing the damning charge of having changed topic or having claimed something patently false. At best, an orthodox analysis can grudgingly come to accept an imperfect fit with the folk intuitions once it has become clear enough that no perfect analysis is forthcoming.

Orthodox analysis thus provides no *structured* means of escaping a conceptual trap, defined as any situation where our native concept of X includes platitudes that are in fact strictly false (or are strictly false according to some ideal account of X that we would all recognize as the best account if we were suitably informed). The orthodoxy's only means for avoiding conceptual traps is to permit some platitudes to be abandoned if there are 'principled arguments for doing so.' But because typically there are multiple ways to imperfectly vindicate the full set of platitudes, and orthodox analysis provides no guidance beyond gut feeling for how to prefer one platitude over another or how to balance degree of systematization against degree of platitude fit, the acceptance of orthodox analysis as the way to conduct philosophical disputes often results in fruitless squabbles over whose imperfect analysis should count as the unique best analysis.[4] By contrast, empirical analysis provides a methodology for escaping conceptual traps.

3   Empirical analysis

A small fraction of the literature on causation is directed towards a somewhat different goal from that of orthodox analysis. Though the general idea has been presented under various names, I will follow Phil Dowe by labelling the alternative approach the 'empirical analysis' of causation. The first chapter of Phil Dowe's (2000) *Physical Causation* marks an advance in clarifying this different kind of investigation of causation. In this section, I will distinguish my version of empirical analysis, using Dowe's as a reference point. My differences with Dowe should be read not so much as criticism of his project but as an attempt to push his key idea much further to make a cleaner break from orthodox analysis.

Dowe characterizes the empirical analysis of causation in several ways. Its task is 'to discover what causation is in the objective world' (p. 1). It 'aims to map the objective world, not our concepts' (p. 3). Dowe argues that it is a mistake to demand empirical analyses account for all the ways we talk about causation, or to demand that empirical analysis 'hold good for all logically possible worlds.' (p. 6). Thus, it is in the business of discovering 'what causation is as a contingent fact' (p. 4). Dowe contrasts it with the old-fashioned conceptual analysis espoused by Ducasse (1926).

I agree with Dowe as far as he goes, but he does not go nearly far enough to distinguish what makes empirical analysis a better way to conduct conceptual analysis. The key question Dowe does not answer is, 'What distinguishes those intuitions the analysis needs to accommodate from those that it can set aside?' Like orthodox analysis, Dowe's explicit characterization of empirical analysis provides no guidance, and his own empirical analysis of causation, his conserved quantity account, does not provide many clues as to what the answer would be. On some occasions (p. 110), he emphasizes that his account does not need to accommodate all folk intuitions about causation, but on other occasions, he appeals to everyday causal talk to criticize other accounts (pp. 24, 40) and to motivate significant extensions to his own theory (p. 148). What is missing is a scheme to unpack the operational meaning of 'what causation is.'

Here is my attempt to characterize empirical analysis.

> An *empirical analysis* of X is a conceptual structure designed to optimize explanations of whatever empirical phenomena make X a concept worth having.

There is obviously a lot of vagueness in this definition and a threat of vacuity, but it is not fruitful to pretend that this statement or some more precise version of it should count as a set of informative necessary and sufficient conditions that will stake out a clear boundary between empirical analysis and orthodox analysis. Instead, one acquires the thrust of empirical analysis by abstracting from the kind of conceptual analysis done in exemplary sciences. Empirical analysis is a cluster concept, best identified as any conceptual analysis that comes close enough to paradigmatic examples of the kinds of analysis done in science. In addition to the already mentioned example from food science, I will discuss two exemplars that illustrate different features of empirical analysis. Many other sciences exhibit excellent conceptual design, but two examples should be enough to convey the basic idea. Then, we can make the methodology a bit more precise by formulating an algorithm for how to hack through any bogus platitudes that hold us in a conceptual trap.

Conducting an empirical analysis is not the investigation of some concept that we take as a pre-existing object of inquiry but rather as a task of conceptual engineering. Classical physics, for example, distinguishes three kinds of mass: Inertial mass is a body's degree of resistance to external forces. Gravitational source mass quantifies how strong of a gravitational field that body produces. Gravitational coupling mass quantifies how much that body is affected by the gravitational field at its location. Because all three aspects can be represented without loss of content by the same variable, classical physics treats them all as aspects of a single mass property. In the standard interpretation of general relativity (GR), the three notions come apart. Inertial mass retains its classical role, but the coupling mass drops out of the theory entirely because gravity is no longer really a force, and the gravitational source mass is replaced with a ten-component tensor. If one were conducting an orthodox analysis (working under the fiction that GR represents the final scientific story about mass) the question to be asked, according to the defender of orthodox analysis, would be, 'Which structure in GR best plays the naive mass role?' The physicist rightly does not much care about such a question. The important work was getting the theory of gravity right and clarifying what structures are needed to play each role. Of course, some conceptual relation must exist between the various mass-like theoretical concepts and what we intuitively take to be masses, but an acceptable connection comes from the totality of GR's concepts through the explanations it provides. The reason for having our naive mass concept is that it allows us to think in simple terms and still get a practical theory of motion and gravity. But to the extent we are satisfied with GR's explanations, we should automatically be satisfied about the utility of the naive mass concept without needing to find which unique structure in the internals of GR best corresponds to the totality of roles we associate with mass. In an empirical analysis, it is not obligatory to solve Jackson's (1998) location problem, at least as he conceives of it.

Another illustration of empirical analysis exists in the famous debate over whether space is a substance. In classical physics, there is a clear enough distinction between two opposing camps. Anti-substantivalists believe space is merely a fiction useful for describing facts that are fundamentally about distance relations among material bodies. Substantivalists believe space exists as something in its own right, despite its being unusual (for a substance) by not acting on or reacting to other substances by way of forces. GR alters the debate by providing an empirically superior account of the physics where the distinction between matter and space (or, from here on, spacetime) becomes blurrier. Given how it handles the concept of mass, one might think empirical analysis should avoid taking sides on whether the best account of spacetime in GR is a substance: that so long as GR is a good empirical guide, whether its spacetime is substantival is a mere labelling issue. But that would be incorrect because what is philosophically important is whether the motivation in the classical debate for caring about whether space (or spacetime) is substantival is satisfied by GR. It is clear enough that the classical anti-substantivalist wanted to explain the motion of particles without taking ontologically seriously this allegedly metaphysically problematic spatial structure and to account for its conceptual utility by recovering putative facts about space from a fundamental metaphysics that is paradigmatically material. So when it turns out in GR that the spacetime structure needed to explain the motion of matter is not derivable from relations among paradigmatically material entities, it arguably posits a structure that is ontologically more than just an aspect of matter. Thus, whether spacetime is a substance is not a verbal dispute. Rather, GR vindicates substantivalism because the scientific motivation for being a substantivalist about space is that it takes more than just spatial relations among paradigmatically material things to account for motion. There remains some controversy among experts about whether this is the correct lesson to draw from GR, but my purpose here is to illustrate how empirical analysis is not merely a disguised form of instrumentalism. There are genuine debates about what structures are to be taken metaphysically seriously, debates that are to be settled where possible by careful examination of which metaphysical system best accounts for the empirical phenomena.

The method suggested by these examples is that we begin an empirical analysis of X by assembling all our common sense intuitions about X and platitudes about the constitutive roles associated with X. Then we try to figure out which empirical facts make this collection useful, preferably by formulating experiments that characterize the core empirical facts. Then, we seek scientific explanations for these experiments, optimizing our concepts to improve these explanations. The advocated methodology does not require that we find a unique correct empirical fact that corresponds to the concept. One should just examine what seem like prima facie interesting empirical questions that motivate us in believing something roughly resembling the initial collection of platitudes. Conducting the analysis might motivate reconsideration of what is important or a revision in exactly what the core issue is, as happened in the change from caring about whether space is a substance to whether spacetime is a substance. Also, because there is no way to think about empirical facts without conceiving of these facts in some way, there is always some extent to which intuitions and naive beliefs about reality inescapably affect one's conceptual analysis. Finally, it is important that empirical analysis be understood in a way that does not require a sharp distinction between what is empirical and what is conceptual because such a distinction cannot be made precise for the intended notion of 'empirical' and the success of science in general does not depend on it. For example, we might think, 'Does spacetime exist?' is an empirical question in the sense that we can empirically assess the relative prospects of spacetime theories versus competitors that posit no spacetime. But we could also think of the existence of spacetime as not being an empirical issue for a variety of reasons. Science might result in two equally acceptable, ideally adequate fundamental theories, one of which treats spacetime structure as a fiction and the other of which treats it ontologically seriously. If so, our inability to experimentally check whether spacetime exists casts no serious doubt on the quality of the explanations the two theories provide, and thus no doubt on the utility of the concepts honed to improve these explanations.

Almost always, the initial platitudes concerning X will cluster into two core groups: those associated with X itself (as something out there in the real world) and those associated with our psychology of X. For example, our initial platitudes about food might include that it is the kind of thing that (1) we require for survival, (2) share with guests, (3) is not gaseous, and (4) typically provokes a 'Yes' response by English speakers who are asked, 'Is this food?' When we think of why we care about food, it is obvious enough that its role in our survival and proper physiological development is of primary importance and its role in facilitating social bonds is parasitic on its utility for survival. The experiments clarifying the empirical phenomena are obvious: People who eat the normal amount of paradigmatic foods survive better than people who ingest similar amounts of paradigmatic non-foods like rubber or wood. The correct skeletal explanation – that food is composed of molecules that promote survival – motivates us to use a regimented concept of food, which we then optimize to fit better with facts that we did not initially include as part of the food platitudes. Oxygen molecules promote survival too, and so does iron, which might motivate us to count them as nutrients. But as we optimize 'food' towards 'nutrient,' we generate greater discrepancy with platitudes like (2), (3), and (4). For orthodox analyses, such discrepancies put pressure on us either to say a block of iron is not food or that nutrients are not (near enough) the same thing as food. For empirical analyses, we treat such platitudes as irrelevant to the explanation of what was really important about food, and instead delegate them to a psychological study of our native food concept. Where orthodox analysis indiscriminately mixes platitudes about X and about the psychology of X, the empirical approach instructs us to segregate the platitudes into these two groups and to systematize each group separately using an empirical analysis.

4   The empirical analysis of causation

So much for empirical analysis in general. What are its implications for the metaphysics of causation? The goal of inquiry into the metaphysics of causation is to find scientific explanations for whatever empirical phenomena make causation a concept worth having. An empirical analysis of causation is just the collection of concepts optimized for such explanations. To conduct an empirical analysis, one should isolate whatever phenomena vindicate our use of causal concepts, and then try to extract some characterization of those phenomena in terms of stuff whose empirical status is not controversial.

Rather than survey the full space of possibilities, it is useful for illustrating the power of empirical analysis that we just examine one commonly mentioned reason for believing in causal structure: that there exist 'effective strategies,' in Nancy Cartwright's (1979) phrase, for influencing the world. Creatures like us, who behave in paradigmatically agential ways, are able to manipulate events, including what we directly control and what we indirectly influence. For this to be true, there needs to be at least some regular structure in how various bits of the world are generally correlated with our actions. But in what sense is that backed by something empirical? Suppose we have a bunch of nearly identical experimental setups instantiating an agent embedded in an environment. Let S be the event type representing what is common in such setups. Half of the setups involve the agent performing an action of type A_1 and the other half A_2. The empirical import of 'effective strategies' can be interpreted as the fact that there exist a vast number of event types S, E, A_1, and A_2 such that E happens more often when things start with $S + A_1$ than with $S + A_2$. There is a lot of fuzziness concerning what kinds of event types are being claimed to exist. While there is no need for great precision, enough of them need to be epistemically identifiable and expressible using human concepts, so that the types are not generally gerrymandered in a way that trivializes the existence of effective strategies.

So far, we have identified a fact that is prima facie empirical, but characterizing effective strategies in terms of agency might raise a worry that the employed notion of agency incorporates something non-empirical into our explanandum. If the invoked notion requires some epistemically inaccessible aspect of reality, we would have failed to distill the 'effective strategies' idea into a satisfactory basis for empirical analysis. To ensure that agency is empirically kosher, one should show that agency can be construed in a way that is no more mysterious than any ordinary physical functionality. One argument involves demonstrating that along a continuum as one considers entities that are less and less agential, the features about agency that appear in the characterization of effective strategies degrades gracefully. Even if one wants to designate a precise boundary between agents and non-agents for the purposes of logic or semantics or ethics, one would still like it to be the case that the empirical behaviour of a pair of very nearly identical entities – one just barely an agent, the other just barely a non-agent – differs only because of their material constitution, not because the evolution of the material world treats agency itself as significant. To check whether agency degrades gracefully, we can consider agents so crude that they hardly deserve to be called agents, and see what 'effective strategies' means for them. For example, although volcanoes do not literally formulate and execute strategies, it is still true that there is some objective structure in the world such that the action of volcanoes makes a difference in whether lava is spread around. Examine a lot of volcanoes that are similar except for whether they are erupting. The empirical upshot of the volcanoes' 'ability' to spread lava consists in the fact that the erupting group of volcanoes is followed shortly by more lava having been spread around than in the non-erupting group. This captures the essence of the 'effective strategies' idea without invoking any suspicious kind of agency.

One should continue unpacking the content of any seemingly empirically dubious element, thoroughly rooting them out until one gets to a basis that is scientifically uncontroversial. This does not require settling on some specific type of empirically fundamental entity. One just uses whatever standards are scientifically acceptable, and any disputes are delegated to epistemology or the theory of perception. For this brief illustration, I will assume the empirical content of causation can be stripped down to some facts about the layout of paradigmatically material stuff, including some laws of nature.

With the basic structure in place, one can review other aspects of causation to see whether there is a corresponding collection of empirical phenomena motivating it. In the case of the asymmetry of causation, there is an obvious family of possibilities to explore, which is that while some effective strategies exist for influencing the future, apparently there are none for influencing the past. To flesh out this idea one should try to formulate an experiment that reveals the facts to be explained. For a simplified example, imagine some event-kind E and a bunch of agents randomly assigned either the goal of having E occur or the goal of having E not occur. A plausible candidate for the empirical upshot of the causal asymmetry is that (1) for many event-kinds E in the future, E occurs reliably more often for agents trying to accomplish E than for agents who are trying to avoid E; and (2) for any E located towards the past, E happens just as often when the agent's goal is E as when the agent's goal is not-E.[5] I will not argue here that this is the best way to think about the asymmetry of causation but merely point out that characterizing such experiments is crucial to a proper empirical analysis.

Empirical analysis offers us a significant advantage over orthodox analysis in understanding causal asymmetry. If we take every common sense intuition seriously as a touchstone, that requires an analysis to make literally true such parcels of wisdom as, 'Effects never precede their causes,' or 'Present facts do not causally influence the past.'[6] With empirical analysis, we do not need to assume these naive intuitions are strictly true. We only need to make sense of the phenomena that make these claims seemingly reasonable things to believe if you haven't bothered to think deeply about the issues involved. This helps to explain how a causal asymmetry among macroscopic stuff is compatible with determinism without positing a fundamental direction of causation. One could argue (e.g., Kutach 2010) that we routinely influence the past, but because such influence is unexploitable for accomplishing goals, it is cognitively convenient and mostly harmless to think of the past as immune to influence.

For another example of how empirical analysis leads us away from the orthodoxy's demand to validate naive intuitions about test cases, we need only consider what empirical phenomenon grounds cases of pre-emption. Pre-emption occurs when there are two potential causes, C_1 and C_2, of a single effect E, and one of them, say C_2, stops C_1 from causing E. For concreteness, suppose at some initial time there is an event C_1, a slow moving rock on a trajectory that it is initially 90% likely to break a certain window. Shortly thereafter, C_2 occurs: someone throws a rock that is very fast and has only a 1% chance of breaking the window. As chance has it, the second rock succeeds in breaking the window quickly, thus making the first rock pass through the broken window without touching any glass. Folk intuition dictates that C_1 is not among the causes of the breakage, and the orthodoxy insists that any successful theory of causation make that folk intuition come out literally true.

Suppose everyone grants the following two classes of facts as among those which are empirically accessible.

1. There are the fully detailed singular facts about the rocks, window, and the environment, that is, the full microscopic history.
2. There are also general facts about what the laws entail for any hypothetical setup, including any chances that the laws fix for future events.

The first is empirical in the ordinary scientific sense where every actual chunk of physics is individually epistemically accessible in principle. The second is empirical in the sense that we can learn about the laws of nature, and we can learn about what they entail for given initial conditions by running multiple trials with the same initial conditions, and inferring the chances from the outcome frequencies. Of course, there are limitations in our ability to establish desired initial conditions and to correctly infer chances from frequencies, but such limitations are routine in science and so do not threaten the kind of epistemic accessibility we need for empirical analysis.

Notice that the pre-emption example presumes that C_1 is a cause in the very weak sense that it instantiates something that plays a part in the overall physical development of nature towards E. It is also a probability-raiser of E because the presence of C_1 (rather than no rock at that location) makes the probability of E be roughly 91% (rather than 1%). When the orthodox metaphysician of causation says that C_1 is not a cause, he does not mean that it plays absolutely no role in E's coming about, for it exerts a gravitational influence if nothing else and it uncontroversially affects the chance of E. The orthodox analyst is claiming that C_1 is not a cause in the pertinent sense. Now the question to ask is whether there is anything empirical to C_1's alleged status as a non-cause that goes beyond the singular fact that it played a role in the development of reality towards E and general facts about chances, that broken windows are more likely when a slow but accurate throw is made than in situations that are identical except without the throw.

It is certainly an empirically testable fact that if you present people with the description of the pre-emption example, they will identify C_1 as not being a cause of E, so there exist empirical facts that need to be accounted for. But these are the proper subject of a psychology of causation. The metaphysically relevant issue is whether there is something in the external world that verifies the folk claim that C_1 is not a cause of E beyond just making it generally reasonable for folk to have the kind of rough and ready notion of singular causation that includes intuitions about pre-emption. The method of empirical analysis tells us that the way to figure out whether there is a metaphysical fact of the matter that C_1 is not a cause is to figure out whether we can explain the existence and general character of effective strategies just using the two classes of facts listed earlier, that is, without using or implying additional facts about which events were genuine causes of E. If so, the intuition that C_1 was pre-empted does not correspond to anything in the metaphysics but is just a psychological artefact. This illustrates skeletally how empirical analysis provides a principled methodology for getting out of the conceptual trap. If we determine that facts about pre-emption play no role in explaining the empirical phenomena that give us a reason to think in causal terms, we can set aside platitudes about pre-emption as metaphysically irrelevant. That makes it much easier to figure out what causation is 'in the objective world.'

Orthodox analysis in the metaphysics of causation sets for itself the task of satisfying platitudes concerning our somewhat folksy identification of causes as well as platitudes concerning the relation of causation to time and laws and other things that are uncontroversially part of metaphysics. The method of empirical analysis suggests we should break apart the set of platitudes into those that concern our psychology of causation and those that concern the metaphysics of causation. By using two empirical analyses, one of causation and another of the psychology of causation, a more optimal conceptual design can be achieved. Because the metaphysically oriented concepts are not held captive to naive intuitions about singular causes among ordinary events, one gets a cleaner account of how determination and probability-raising explains the existence and character of effective strategies. Because the psychologically oriented concepts do not need to do any metaphysical work, they can be treated in a more hand-waving fashion, without demanding that such intuitions be ultimately coherent.

5   Conclusion

Returning to the food analogy, there is one respectable project of uncovering that which is nutritious. Another respectable project is to figure out people's psychology of food, i.e., why they categorize certain items as food and others as non-food. Whatever that story is, it almost certainly is going to involve as a first approximation that our food concept roughly tracks that which is nutritious. At a second order approximation, facts about perception, culture, the need for cognitive efficiency, and a whole bunch of other factors irrelevant to nutrition are going to come into play to explain why 'what is food' is not precisely the same as 'what is nutritious.'

Analogously, one respectable project is to find out how the external world is structured such that some events serve as good means for bringing about other events. That constitutes the metaphysics of causation. Another respectable project is to figure out people's psychology of causation, why they categorize certain happenings as causes and others as non-causes. Whatever that story is, it almost certainly will involve a first approximation that the causation concept roughly tracks whatever is responsible for the existence of effective strategies and general facts about them, e.g., that effective strategies are temporally asymmetric. At a second order approximation, facts about perception, our need to learn about causal regularities without running controlled experimental trials, cognitive efficiency, and perhaps even culture are all going to come into play to explain why 'what was the cause' is not equivalent to 'what was driving the world's temporal evolution.'

Notes

1. I have in mind specifically David Albert's address at the 2002 Philosophy of Science Association meeting but such an interpretation also seems to be implicitly assumed by scientifically sophisticated criticisms by Elga (2001), and other similar literature that attacks Lewis's theory with technical physics.
2. I discuss these issues elsewhere, but one can find criticisms along these lines in Pruss 2003, Gunderson 2004, and Hawthorne 2005.
3. Pre-empted events are by definition not causes of that which they were going to cause. What I mean is the non-trivial claim, 'Those events people standardly identify as having been pre-empted from causing *E* are not genuine causes of *E*.' Also, the orthodox analyst is free to allow that the asymmetry of causation might be violated in exceptional circumstances.
4. See (Hitchcock 2003) for a list of such pseudo-debates in the causation literature.
5. Of course, many actual distributions will reveals a difference due to do ordinary statistical error. My prediction is that we will only find as many correlations as our theory of statistical error indicates.
6. Again, the orthodoxy can permit exceptions for unusual circumstances where these principles are violated, like in the presence of space-time wormholes or time travel machines.

Bibliography

Bontley, T. (2006), 'What is an Empirical Analysis of Causation?,' *Synthese* 151, 177–200.

Cartwright, N. (1979), 'Causal Laws and Effective Strategies,' *Noûs* 13, 419–37. Reprinted in N. Cartwright (ed.) (1983), *How the Laws of Physics Lie* (Oxford: Clarendon Press), pp. 21–43.

Chalmers, D. (1996), *The Conscious Mind: In Search of a Fundamental Theory* (Oxford: Oxford University Press).

Chalmers, D. and Jackson, F. (2001), 'Conceptual Analysis and Reductive Explanation,' *The Philosophical Review* 110 (3), 315–60.

Collins, J., Hall, N., and Paul, L. A. (2004), *Causation and Counterfactuals* (Cambridge, MA: MIT Press).

Dowe, P. (2000), *Physical Causation* (Cambridge: Cambridge University Press).

Elga, A. (2001), 'Statistical Mechanics and the Asymmetry of Counterfactual Dependence,' *Philosophy of Science* 68 (3), Supplement: Proceedings of the 2000 Biennial Meeting of the Philosophy of Science Association, Part I: Contributed Papers, S313–24.

Gunderson, L. B. (2004), 'Outline of a New Semantics for Counterfactuals,' *Pacific Philosophical Quarterly* 85, 1–20.

Hawthorne, J. (2005), 'Chance and Counterfactuals,' *Philosophy and Phenomenological Research* 70 (2), 396–405.

Hitchcock, C. (2003), 'Of Humean Bondage,' *British Journal for the Philosophy of Science* 54, 1–25.

Horwich, P. (1993), 'Lewis's Programme,' in *Causation*, E. Sosa and M. Tooley (eds.) (Oxford: Oxford University Press).

Jackson, F. (1998), *From Metaphysics to Ethics: A Defence of Conceptual Analysis* (Oxford: Oxford University Press).

Kutach, D. (2010), 'The Asymmetry of Influence,' in *The Oxford Handbook of Time* (Oxford: Oxford University Press).

Lewis, D. (1973), *Counterfactuals* (Oxford: Blackwell).

—— (1976), 'Causation,' *The Journal of Philosophy* 70, 556–67.

—— (1979), 'Counterfactual Dependence and Time's Arrow,' *Noûs* 13, 455–76. Reprinted in his *Philosophical Papers*, vol. 2 (Oxford: Oxford University Press, 1986).

—— (2004), 'Causation as Influence,' in *Causation and Counterfactuals*, J. Collins, N. Hall and L.A. Paul (eds.) (Cambridge, MA: MIT Press).

Pruss, A. (2003), 'David Lewis's Counterfactual Arrow of Time,' *Noûs* 37 (4), 606–37.

8
Ghosts in the World Machine? Humility and Its Alternatives

Rae Langton and Christopher Robichaud

1 Humility

1.1 Background

At the heart of being lies a mystery, according to Kant: we have 'no insight whatsoever into the intrinsic nature of things.' Some people complain, but their complaints are misguided.

> If the complaints that 'we have no insight whatsoever into the intrinsic nature of things' are supposed to mean that we cannot grasp by pure understanding what the things which appear to us may be in themselves, they are completely unreasonable and stupid. What is wanted is that we should to be able to be acquainted with things without senses! (Kant 1781/1787, A277/B333)

The complainers cherish a hope that our minds should grasp how the things that appear to us may be 'in themselves.' But this is 'completely unreasonable and stupid.' And why? It amounts to a hope 'that we should be able to be acquainted with things without senses' – a foolish hope that

> we should have a faculty of knowledge completely different from the human, not just in degree ... but also in kind – in other words, that we should be, not human beings, but beings of whom we cannot even say whether they are possible, still less how they are constituted. (A277/B333)

Given that we are human beings, not gods, we are receptive creatures who find out about the world by sensing it: our knowledge of the world depends on our being affected by it. This fact of receptivity destines us to ignorance of an intrinsic aspect of the world (Langton 1998).

Kant's pessimism is shared by a number of more recent philosophers. Bertrand Russell said that science gives us knowledge of the structure of the world, but that 'we know nothing of the intrinsic quality of the physical world' (1927, p. 264). Grover Maxwell said that science leaves us 'completely ignorant as to what [the] intrinsic properties are' (1978, p. 9). David Armstrong says,

> if we look at the properties of physical objects that physicists are prepared to allow them such as mass, electric charge, or momentum, these show a distressing tendency to dissolve into relations that one object has to another. What, then, are the things that have these relations to each other? Must they not have a non-relational nature if they are to sustain relations? But what is this nature? (1968, pp. 74–5.)

Frank Jackson says,

> I think we should acknowledge as a possible, interesting position one we might call Kantian physicalism. It holds that a large part (possibly all) of the intrinsic nature of our world is irretrievably beyond our reach, but that all the nature we know about supervenes on the causal cum relational nature that the physical sciences tell us about. (1998, p. 24)

Most recently, David Lewis has agreed with Kant (or Langton's version of Kant). We are ignorant –

> of the intrinsic properties of substances. The substances that bear these intrinsic properties are the very same unhidden substances that do indeed affect us perceptually. But they affect us, and they affect other things that in turn affect us, in virtue of their causal powers, which are among their relational properties. Thereby we find out about these substances as bearers of causal powers, but we find out nothing about them as they are in themselves.

This opinion is, he says, 'true' – 'or at least something very like it is' (Lewis 2009, p. 203).

According to Humility, we can in principle learn about everything in the world that physics describes; nothing in the great machine of the world is beyond us. But we are missing out on certain intrinsic properties, which we should not, perhaps, call 'physical' – first, for the minimal reason that physics cannot capture them; second, for the more troubling reason that they may, for all we know, be mental. Jackson describes the view as 'Kantian physicalism': but it is hardly physicalism, if the fundamental properties 'irretrievably beyond our reach' are not what 'the physical sciences tell us about.' The early mechanists posited something 'incorporeal' that would 'pervade and support the universal machine of the world' (Gassendi 1649, I.IV.8), and they supposed it to be divine. Without going as far as that, it seems there may indeed be ghosts in the world machine, properties that are in some sense non-physical, and hidden from view.

Let us call this ignorance 'Humility.' We shall not dwell unduly on its ghostly aspects, though we do return to this theme at the end. Our plan, in this essay, is to explain Humility and defend it, bringing out three ambiguities that are sometimes ignored. We shall compare some varieties of Humility. And we shall cast a critical eye on five responses to Humility. Some say the argument is incoherent. Some prefer a causal-structuralist alternative. Some offer an anti-sceptical response. Some offer a pan-psychist response, which embraces the troubling possibility that Humility admits. And some, finally, respond with a ghost-busting shrug of the shoulders: 'Humility – who cares?'

These responses, we shall suggest, are no better than the problem they aim to fix. The argument for Humility is not incoherent. Attempts by causal structuralists to do away with these intrinsic properties face their own version of Humility. Attempts to save knowledge of such properties are wrong when they say Humility is scepticism, extravagant when they embrace pan-psychism. And as for the shrug? Humility is not a trivial thesis, so let's face up to it. We're ignorant of the intrinsic natures of things, and have to make the best of it.

1.2   Humility: the thesis, and an argument template

The thesis of Humility is straightforward enough. There is a fundamental, intrinsic aspect of the world, and it is beyond us. There are certain properties, intrinsic properties, that escape our cognitive grasp. Let us say provisionally that a thing's intrinsic properties are solely a matter of how that thing is, in itself; the intrinsic properties don't depend on anything external to the thing; the intrinsic properties of a thing are compatible with isolation or 'loneliness'; the intrinsic properties of a thing are shared by duplicates of the thing. The idea of an intrinsic property is thus a metaphysical idea, about a certain class of properties. (We don't do justice to the literature, but see, e.g., Kim 1982, Lewis 1983, Dunn

1990, Humberstone 1992, Vallentyne 1997, Langton and Lewis 1998, Yablo 1999, Marshall and Parsons 2001, and Weatherson 2001.)

Humility is not scepticism. It is compatible with our knowing a great deal about familiar observable physical objects of common sense – hands and dressing gowns, paper, and heating stoves. It is compatible with our knowing a great deal about less familiar, unobservable physical objects of science – quarks and gluons, fields and electrons. For the same reasons, Humility is not idealism. It is a kind of epistemic modesty, hence the label. There may be many aspects of the world that are wholly within our grasp, and they may be as real as you like: but they are not the whole deal. Something else is there, but we cannot reach it. There are thus two dimensions to –

Humility: the Thesis

Existence: Fundamental intrinsic properties exist;

Ignorance: We don't know what the fundamental intrinsic properties are.

Some may find this formulation a little odd. Don't all properties 'exist,' in Plato's Heaven, or its equivalent, if not here? Perhaps the point about existence could be better put as a point about instantiation, or about facts. The point is that the fundamental properties instantiated in our actual world are intrinsic properties; there are facts about how fundamental intrinsic properties are instantiated. For reasons partly to do with the Kantian heritage of the idea, for present purposes we prefer the formulation given in Existence above, but we would be happy for readers to substitute their own favoured paraphrase. So much for the thesis of Humility.

Now the argument for Humility. This can take a number of different forms. If we were to sketch a common pattern, it might look like this:

Humility: an Argument Template

P1. *Epistemic Restriction to the Relational:* the most fundamental properties discoverable by experience are relational.

P2. *Metaphysical Commitment to the Intrinsic:* the most fundamental properties that exist are intrinsic.

C. *Humility:* the most fundamental properties that exist are intrinsic properties, not discoverable by experience.

That conclusion is, near enough, the thesis of Humility just outlined. It conjoins Existence and Ignorance: it says that fundamental intrinsic properties exist, and that we are ignorant of them – or at any rate, that we are ignorant of them, so far as *experience* can teach us. A bridge to the full thesis of Humility is strictly speaking made only if it is further allowed that experience is the *only* way we could find out which particular properties are instantiated in the world. We take this is as given; so having noted this caveat, we'll leave it behind for present purposes, and regard the conclusion of this template as, effectively, the thesis of Humility.

Let us look now at those premises. There will be different interpretations of, and reasons for, the Restriction in the first premise. For Kant, the Restriction is there because of *receptivity*. Having receptive senses means, he thinks, that we can gain access only to relational, causal powers. For more recent philosophers, the Restriction is there because of *science*. Through science we discover the fundamental properties of the world, and we find that they are in fact (or: must be in principle) relational, dispositional properties. Note that the Restriction on its own does not imply that we are missing out on anything. For all the Restriction shows, what there is and what we could discover may be in perfect harmony: the most fundamental properties we can discover are relational – and if those just *are* the most fundamental properties, no problem. It is only with the next premise that Humility gets going.

The next premise brings a metaphysical Commitment to intrinsic properties. There will be different interpretations of, and reasons for, this premise, too. For Kant, the Commitment comes from a metaphysical intuition that substances, being substances, must have intrinsic properties. For more recent philosophers, the Commitment comes from a metaphysical intuition that dispositional properties, being dispositional, require intrinsic, categorical grounds.

These different versions of the second premise yield different versions of the conclusion, Humility. Perhaps the conclusion is that we are ignorant of the intrinsic properties of substances. Perhaps the conclusion is that we are ignorant of the categorical bases of dispositions. There is sufficient similarity, however, for us to speak here of a family of arguments, yielding some version of the conclusion that we are ignorant of certain intrinsic properties – some version of Humility.

Since the thesis of Humility involves both Existence and Ignorance, it can be seen as a species of a wider genus of Humility theses, consisting of similar Existence-plus-Ignorance conjunctions, about a variety of possible domains. Some Humility theses will look substantive. Consider, for example, Theistic Humility, which has an illustrious pedigree.

> *Existence:* God exists
> *Ignorance:* We don't know what (most of) his or her properties are.

Perhaps God's Existence is supported by arguments about God as a first cause. Perhaps Ignorance is supported by arguments about the ineffability of the divine nature. Whatever the grounds, believers in Theistic Humility think we are missing out on something that matters. By comparison, some Humility theses will look trivial. Consider, for example, Paleoformic Humility, which has no pedigree, illustrious or otherwise:

> *Existence:* Many ants existed at determinate locations a million years ago.
> *Ignorance:* We don't know what (most of) those determinate locations were.

An elementary grasp of the evolutionary history of ants will be enough to yield Existence. An elementary understanding of the limits of paleontological investigation will be enough to yield Ignorance. Yet this sort of Humility is unlikely to keep us awake at night. For Kant Humility is substantive; he thinks we are missing out on something. In this respect Humility is like Theistic Humility, and unlike Paleoformic Humility. We yearn for knowledge of things in themselves, in a way we do not yearn for the precise pre-historic location facts about ants. When it comes to things in themselves, we have an 'inextinguishable desire to find firm footing somewhere beyond the bounds of experience' (A796/B824); but our aspirations, alas, are doomed. (See Langton 1998, ch. 1; *pace* Allison 1983.)

2 Three ambiguities in Humility

The Argument for Humility says the most fundamental properties 'discoverable by experience' are relational. This makes one wonder about the status of the Restriction to the Relational: is it supposed to be an empirical matter? The Argument also has a metaphysical Commitment to the Intrinsic, clearly an *a priori* matter: but how should we understand the 'intrinsic' to which it is committed? These questions raise three ambiguities, which we want to draw out and comment upon, if not wholly resolve.

2.1 Restriction to the relational: a priori or a posteriori?

Sometimes the claim that we are restricted to relational properties looks like an empirical discovery. Armstrong cites the authority of physics: he says 'the properties of physical objects that physicists are prepared

to allow them...show a distressing tendency to dissolve into relations.'
Brian Ellis and Caroline Lierse offer what they call –

> ...the argument from Science. With few exceptions, the most fun-
> damental properties that we know about are all dispositional.
> They are of the nature of powers, capacities, and propensities.
> (1994, p. 32)

Humility's recent discussants often cite science in its support (Russell
1927; Blackburn 1993; Hawthorne 2001; Ney 2007). Physics has discovered the falsity of long-held metaphysical views about causal determinism; likewise physics discovers the falsity of long-held metaphysical
views about physical intrinsic properties. On this way of thinking, the
philosopher, humble handmaid of science, willingly alters her steps to
dance to the physicist's new tune.

This impression, we suggest, is misleading. The Restriction is an
a priori matter, whether for Kantian or contemporary versions of
Humility. It is *a priori* that we cannot discover these intrinsic properties through experience. The Restriction is a claim about what experience cannot reach, given *a priori* facts about the receptive nature of
our knowledge, or about the nature of scientific theorizing, as we
shall see as we go on.

2.2 'Relational' and 'intrinsic': conceptual or metaphysical?

This Commitment to 'intrinsic' properties, this epistemic Restriction
to 'relational' properties – are these claims about concepts or properties? Is Armstrong worried that the concept of 'charge' cannot be
captured without talking about relations; or that charge is an extrinsic property? A distinction between concepts and properties is not
always observed, and we ourselves speak loosely of 'relational properties' without adequately marking it. But relational concepts don't
always match up to extrinsic properties. Your nose may be shaped
like Julius Caesar's. Having that shape is an intrinsic property of your
nose; having a nose with that shape is an intrinsic property of you. By
any standard test for intrinsicness, the property of having a nose with
that shape is an intrinsic property. You could have it, in the absence
of other things. You could have it in a possible world where nothing
else exists – not even Julius Caesar. Your duplicates have it. But there
is something relational about it. Lloyd Humberstone suggests using
the labels 'non-relational/relational' for a distinction operating at the
level of concepts; and 'intrinsic/extrinsic' for a distinction operating

at the level of metaphysically robust properties (1996). The distinction is not always easy to apply, but it has potential to yield different varieties of Humility (Allais 2007, Langton 2007, Ney 2007). Perhaps we are ignorant of the 'intrinsic' because our concepts of fundamental physical properties are relational. Or perhaps we are ignorant of the 'intrinsic' because the most fundamental properties we can access are extrinsic.

2.3   Commitment to the 'intrinsic': intrinsic or categorical?

Kant's commitment to intrinsic properties is based on the idea that relational properties require substantial bearers, which must have some intrinsic properties or other. In like vein, apparently, Gareth Evans argues that there must be intrinsic, primary quality grounds for dispositional, secondary qualities (1980). But Kant's substantiality requirement is not the same as Evans's categoricity requirement: Kant demands some intrinsic properties or other, Evans demands categorical bases for dispositions. Evans's opinion belongs to a contemporary orthodoxy about the metaphysics of dispositions (Jackson et al. 1982; Prior 1985). So here we have two rather different routes to a Commitment to 'intrinsic' properties.

Naturally this has implications for our interpretation of Humility. Is Armstrong worried that a fundamental property like charge is not intrinsic, or that it is not categorical? The fear appears to be that charge is merely dispositional. Similar misgivings are expressed by P. F. Strawson, in responding to Evans:

> It seems that our search for the properties of the categorical base must finally lead us to the undeniably theoretical properties which physics assigns to the ultimate constituents of matter – perhaps force, mass, impenetrability, electric charge. But these properties themselves seem to be thoroughly dispositional in character....[T]he categorical base is still to seek. (1980, p. 280)

And by Simon Blackburn:

> [A]ny conceivable improvement in science will give us only a better pattern of dispositions and powers. That's the way physics works...[the intrinsic ground of these powers] will remain, therefore, entirely beyond our ken, a something-we-know-not-what identified only by the powers and dispositions it supports. (1993, p. 256)

Dispositional properties are traditionally contrasted with 'categorical' properties, a contrast which has been much debated. Dispositions, unlike categorical properties, are thought to support counterfactuals about their manifestations (Jackson et al. 1982; Prior 1985; Mumford 1998; Holton 1999). But not always: witness the possibility of 'finkish' and other inconvenient dispositions, which render counterfactuals false (Martin 1994; Bird 1998). And not only: witness the possibility of categorical properties likewise supporting counterfactuals (Mellor 1983). But what about a contrast between dispositions and *intrinsic* properties?

Dispositional properties are often brought under the 'relational' side of a distinction between intrinsic and relational properties, a practice we find reasonable enough. Typically, if a property like charge is understood as a disposition, it will be conceptually relational: it's part of the concept of charge that something has it just in case it would relate to other things in certain ways. Perhaps that's what Armstrong means when he worries that charge will dissolve into 'relations.' Many dispositional properties are, then, conceptually relational. (Not all: think of a time bomb's disposition to explode.)

That's not to say dispositions are extrinsic, for as we have noted, these are not the same. Are they extrinsic, too? Some philosophers think dispositions are intrinsic, so a possible view is that while a dispositional concept is relational, the property is intrinsic. After all, my glass can be fragile, even if it's the only thing in the universe. Fragility is compatible with isolation or 'loneliness.' My glass can be fragile, independently of anything outside it – though to be sure, its fragility implies much about how it *would* relate to other things in certain circumstances. Fragility is shared by duplicates – at least in worlds that have the same laws of nature. This latter caveat, however, is significant. If we apply a duplicate test more strictly, fragility is not after all intrinsic: in worlds with different laws, my glass will simply bounce. If we apply an isolation test more strictly, fragility is not intrinsic: fragility is not compatible with isolation *and lawlessness* (Langton and Lewis 1998, Langton 1998). By these stricter standards, then, dispositional properties are extrinsic.

To sum up, dispositional properties can be regarded as 'relational' in two ways: first, their concepts typically involve relations to other things; second, on strict standards of metaphysical intrinsicness, they typically count as extrinsic properties. So ignorance of 'intrinsic' properties may result from a Restriction to relational, extrinsic, dispositional properties.

3   Kantian and Ramseyan Humility

3.1   Kantian Humility

Kant's famous epistemological conclusion is drawn against a less famous metaphysical backdrop: so ignorance of 'things in themselves' is really ignorance of intrinsic properties (Kant 1781/1787; Langton 1998). This is admittedly a controversial interpretation of Kant (Falkenstein 2001; van Cleve 2002; Ameriks 2003, ch. 5; Strawson 2003; Allison 2004, ch. 1; Breitenbach 2004; Allais 2007). But we shall assume rather than defend it here. This metaphysical backdrop, with its distinction between classes of properties, supplies one premise of our template argument for Humility:

> *Metaphysical Commitment to the Intrinsic:* The most fundamental properties that exist are intrinsic properties.

Here is early expression of it, with its philosophical motivation.

> Besides external presence, i.e. relational determinations of substance, there are other, intrinsic, determinations, without which the relational determinations would not be, because there would be no subject in which they inhered. (Kant 1756)

Kant envisions a 'physical monadology,' positing non-extended substances, or monads, whose 'relational determinations' – elsewhere described as physical forces of attraction and repulsion – interactively constitute the physical world. Kant here expresses the substantiality requirement just described. Relational properties or forces must be ascribed to a substance, namely, the monad, since they require a bearer. The substance in turn must have some other properties, *intrinsic* properties, since otherwise it wouldn't be a substance. If a substance is independent of other things, it needs properties independent of other things.

A general inference to intrinsic properties appears again at different points in the *Critique of Pure Reason:*

> The understanding, when it entitles an object in a relation mere phenomenon, at the same time forms, apart from that relation, a representation of an object in itself. (B307)

> Concepts of relation presuppose things which are absolutely [i.e., independently] given, and without these are impossible. (A284/B340)

> Substances in general must have some intrinsic nature, which is therefore free from all external relations. (A274/B330)

These passages express the same Commitment to intrinsic properties. They point to a conception of substance as a bearer of intrinsic properties, and infer the existence of intrinsic properties via the thought that substances need properties appropriate to their independent nature. Note that the contrast between 'phenomenon' and 'in itself' is made to match up with a contrast between 'relational' and 'intrinsic.' Since Kant famously thinks we have knowledge only of 'phenomena,' this brings us to the other premise in our template Argument for Humility.

> *Epistemic Restriction to the Relational:* the most fundamental properties discoverable by experience are relational.

We have knowledge only of phenomena – things 'in a relation.' Are phenomena 'relational' in the sense of conceptually relational, or metaphysically extrinsic? They are at least the former; and there may be room for both interpretations (see Allais 2007; Langton 2007; Ney 2007). Given Kant's isolation thought experiment, we take it that they are also the latter: phenomenal properties are extrinsic.

It is an on-going theme in Kant that the realm of phenomena consists entirely of 'relations':

> It is certainly startling to hear that a thing is to be taken as consisting wholly of relations. Such a thing is, however, mere appearance. (A285/B341)

> Matter is *substantia phaenomenon.* I search for that which belongs to it intrinsically in all parts of the space which it occupies, and in all the actions it performs....I have nothing that is absolutely intrinsic, but only what is comparatively intrinsic, and that is itself again constituted by external relations.... The transcendental object which may be the ground of this appearance that we call matter is a mere something... (A277/B333)

Kant thinks we can discover through experience (including scientific investigation) a great deal about phenomenal substance, or matter; but that phenomenal substance, namely matter, is 'constituted by relations.'

It seems likely that Kant's version of this Restriction is actually stronger than stated above: it's not just that *fundamental* phenomenal properties are extrinsic, but *all* phenomenal properties are extrinsic. We ordinarily take familiar shape properties to be intrinsic, but Kant thinks that, being part-dependent, they are not (A339/A283) (see Langton 1998, ch. 2, for the relevant notion of intrinsicness). The phenomenal world is, for Kant, relational all the way down.

We have noted that for Kant the Restriction has its source in the receptivity of the senses; but there is more to the story. Kant, like many philosophers, is persuaded of the contingency of the connection between intrinsic properties and causal powers. He argues in an early paper that it is possible for God to create an isolated substance, with its intrinsic properties, without thereby creating any causal powers at all. Intrinsic properties, on their own, do not entail causal power. He says God needs to 'add' something to a substance, with its intrinsic properties, if that substance is to have the power to interact with other substances. He draws from these reflections about contingency a conclusion that many philosophers would reject, namely that the intrinsic properties are causally inert:

> A substance never has the power through its own intrinsic properties to determine others different from itself, as has been proven. (1756, p. 415)

A path to Kantian Humility is now plain. A Commitment to the Intrinsic is already in place: given that there must be substances, there must be bearers of intrinsic properties. A Restriction to the Relational is also in place, based, as we see, on considerations that are wholly *a priori*. We are receptive creatures, who must be affected by something if we are to have knowledge of it. Iff we are not affected by intrinsic properties because they are inert, then we can have no knowledge of intrinsic properties. Intrinsic properties exist; but we don't know what they are. 'The substantial is the thing in itself and unknown' (R5292); 'we have no insight whatsoever into the intrinsic [nature] of things' (A277/B333). This, we propose, is Kant's route to Humility.

3.2 Ramseyan Humility

Whether Kantian Humility is right as an account of Kant, something like it is just plain right, according to Lewis. Many of us will reject Kant's thought that the intrinsic properties are causally inert, but even so we must confront the news, sad or otherwise, that we are ignorant of things in themselves:

> Being the ground of a certain disposition is only one case among many of role occupancy. There are a variety of occupied roles,

among them nomological roles and others as well. Quite generally, to the extent that we know of the properties of things only as role-occupants, we have not yet identified those properties. No amount of knowledge about what roles are occupied will tell us which properties occupy which roles. (2009, p. 204)

Lewis's idea clearly has much in common with the earlier quoted opinions of Russell, Maxwell, Armstrong, Evans, Strawson, and Blackburn. The background metaphysics here distinguishes between dispositions and categorical properties, between roles and realizers, and this supplies Lewis's version of the metaphysical premise:

> *Metaphysical Commitment to the Intrinsic:* The most fundamental properties that exist are intrinsic, or categorical, properties.

Given that there are roles, there must be something to realize those roles; given that there are dispositional properties, there must categorical bases to those dispositions.

An argument about Ramsification then yields Lewis's version of the key epistemological premise.

> *Epistemic Restriction to the Relational:* the most fundamental properties discoverable by experience are relational.

This Restriction follows in an entirely *a priori* way from the nature of theorizing itself. We have here a philosophical argument about science, not an empirical argument from science. The idea is this. We find out about the fundamental properties of the world via our scientific theories. Suppose we had a grand, final theory which names our fundamental active properties. Such a theory will specify how each thing causally relates to everything else our theory talks about. Call our grand theory 'T.' And suppose we have a language, 'O,' rich enough to express our observations. The Ramsey sentence of T will replace names in T with existentially quantified variables; it will say that T has at least one actual realization; and it will imply the O-language sentences that are theorems of T. Predictive success for T will be predictive success for the Ramsey sentence. And here comes the crunch. *If* our theory T has more than one possible realization, observation won't tell us which realization is actual. Humility follows from this. We don't know what the realizer properties are.

Does the theory have more than one possible realization? Yes, because of the contingent connection between causal role properties, and realizer properties. Lewis offers a 'permutation argument' for this possibility. Suppose our theory names two fundamental intrinsic properties, F1 and F2. Given the fact of contingency, there is a possible world where these two properties are swapped around. The laws governing F1 there are the same as the laws governing F2 here, and *vice versa*. This yields one different possible realization of T. He offers an additional 'replacement argument' for the possibility. Our grand theory will leave out 'idler' properties (if any), namely instantiated but inactive properties; it will leave out 'alien' properties, uninstantiated in the actual world. There will be a possible world like ours, except the fundamental properties F1 and F2 that are T's actual realization are replaced by properties that to us are idlers, or aliens. This yields another different possible realization of T.

Lewis's argument goes much further than this, in directions we can't take up here; and questions remain about whether, on this account, the fundamental properties to which we have access are conceptually relational, or extrinsic (Ney 2007). But for readers with reservations about dark eighteenth-century metaphysics, Lewis's argument may at least show that Humility is closer than you think.

4   Five responses to Humility

If we accept some version of the argument for Humility, we must accept that there are intrinsic aspects to the world that are forever beyond our grasp. Suppose one does not wish to accept this uncomfortable conclusion. How should one react? We are going to outline five possible responses. (For some other helpful efforts to outline options, see Schaffer 2005; Hawthorne 2001; Ney 2007; Locke 2009.) Most are interesting, some are extravagant; but none, we suggest, is more attractive than Humility itself.

4.1   An accusation of incoherence

According to Alyssa Ney, there is a deep tension in the argument for Humility. To put her point in a nutshell: the argument affirms a strong and optimistic physicalism, and denies it at the very same time. Her paper offers a refreshingly clear and robust critique, but it is, we shall argue, mistaken. She captures the argument for Kantian Humility in the following terms. We add our labels, in order to bring out the relationship to the argument template proposed here.

> *Restriction to the Relational.* (a) We learn from current science that all fundamental properties are extrinsic. (b) There is no scientific

reason to posit intrinsic properties that would serve as the grounds of these properties.

Commitment to the Intrinsic. But substances do have intrinsic properties, since it is part of their nature that they must.

Humility. There are intrinsic properties of which we cannot have knowledge.

The argument for Humility first says that science discovers the most fundamental properties, and finds that they happen to be relational, or (better) extrinsic. It then says that metaphysics discovers there must be other fundamental properties, and finds that they must be intrinsic. The first step says the fundamental properties are extrinsic, because science says so. The next step says the fundamental properties are intrinsic, because metaphysics says so. The first step assumes a strong and optimistic physicalism, according to which science discovers the fundamental properties, on which all other properties supervene. The second step denies that optimism, and pulls the rug out from under the feet of the first. The argument is, she concludes, incoherent.

But Ney is mistaken. The argument does indeed depend on a Restriction to relational properties, which says the most fundamental properties we can know about, via experience, are relational, or extrinsic, properties. But this is not a strong and optimistic physicalism. First, as we have seen, it needn't be a point about *science* at all. For Kant, the Restriction follows from some abstract facts about the *receptivity* of our knowledge of the world. Second, even if we do make science the starting point, it is still going to be an *a priori* matter about what science can in principle discover, not (as Ney suggests) a matter of what 'current science' in fact turns up. Finally, and most importantly, it needn't say that the fundamental properties posited by science are the fundamental properties *tout court*. It is only this reading which creates a conflict with the Commitment to intrinsic properties.

See how very strong Ney's physicalism is. Science (a) tells us what the fundamental properties of science are; (b) says that they are relational, or extrinsic; *and* (c) says the fundamental properties of science are the fundamental properties, *tout court*. It is the third clause which makes it so ambitious, and creates the conflict with the next, metaphysical, step of the argument. But we needn't assert the third clause – needn't say that the fundamental properties described by science just *are* the fundamental properties. The idea is not that 'we learn from current science that all fundamental properties are extrinsic,' as Ney puts it. The idea is rather that 'all the fundamental properties we in principle learn about from science are extrinsic.' In short, then, despite its great interest, Ney's critique fails. She finds a contradiction in the argument, only because she put it there.

4.2   A causal structuralist alternative

You might reject the argument for Humility by denying the metaphysical Commitment to intrinsic properties. In so doing, you would deny the thesis of Humility by denying Existence: there simply *are no* fundamental intrinsic properties – at least, no fundamental intrinsic properties that are *distinct* from the relational properties. It is possible to find a version of this response in certain (though not all) developments of causal structuralism, by Sydney Shoemaker (1980), Alexander Bird (2007), John Hawthorne (2001), James Ladyman (2002), and Ann Whittle (2006), among others.

We saw that there can be different philosophical motivations for the Commitment: Kant's requirement that substances have some intrinsic properties or other; Evans' requirement that dispositions have categorical bases; Lewis's requirement that role properties have realizers. Might one remain unmoved by these metaphysical considerations? That is what the causal structuralist has to do.

Perhaps it is possible. It's worth noting that Kant's own theory of physical force was adapted in just this direction by pioneers of field theory. Kant's physical forces were ascribed to monads, endowed with intrinsic properties. Why not liberate forces from substances, and posit simply the 'relational determinations' or forces, existing without any 'intrinsic determinations'? Michael Faraday, influenced by Kantian natural philosophy, seems to have done just this (Faraday 1844, pp. 290–1; for Kant's influence, see Williams 1965). Suppose, he said, we distinguish a substantial particle *a*, from its powers or forces *m*. What we empirically encounter must be simply –

> the properties or forces of the *m*, not of the *a*, which, without the forces, is conceived of as having no powers. But then surely the *m* is the *matter*....To my mind...the *a* or nucleus vanishes, and the substance consists of the powers, or *m*; and indeed what notion can we form of the nucleus independent of its powers: what thought remains on which to hang the imagination of an *a* independent of

the acknowledged forces? Why then assume the existence of that of which we are ignorant, which we cannot conceive, and for which there is no philosophical necessity? (pp. 290–1)

What is Faraday doing here? He accepts the epistemological Restriction to relational powers, and takes it as a reason to retreat from any Commitment to fundamental intrinsic properties. The only fundamental properties we know about through experience are the relational, or extrinsic, ones: so that's what there are. More recently John Hawthorne has unconsciously echoed Faraday's strategy and his final ringing words:

> Science seems to offer no conception of negative charge as something over and above 'the thing that plays the charge role.' If there were a quiddity that were, so to speak, the role filler, it would not be something that science had any direct cognitive access to, except via the reference fixer 'the quiddity that actually plays the charge role.' Why invoke what you don't need? (2001, p. 368)

Faraday's denial of a substantial 'nucleus' underlying powers might not be quite the same thing as Hawthorne's denial of a 'role filler,' but the line of thinking is similar. Hawthorne, for his part, is not inventing field theory, but taking seriously Shoemaker's proposal that there is, in some sense, nothing more to a property than its causal profile – no essence or 'quiddity' of the property independent of its causal profile (Shoemaker 1980). And adopting this approach has some promise of enabling one to deny there must be categorical properties distinct from dispositional properties; and hence deny this version of the Commitment to intrinsic properties.

There are many ways to understand the causal-structuralist project, to which we cannot do justice here (see Bird 2007; Ladyman 2002; Ellis and Lierse 1984; Schaffer 2005; Whittle 2006). But the causal-structuralist project is widely advertised as offering epistemological advantages (Shoemaker 1980; Hawthorne 2001; Schaffer 2005; Whittle 2006; Ney 2007). Does it indeed present a way to avoid Humility?

Not entirely. Suppose we distinguish a thin and a thick causal structuralism. A thin structuralism might claim that there are no fundamental intrinsic properties, because the fundamental properties are bare dispositions. This avoids Humility – but is open to traditional objections to bare dispositions (Blackburn 1993; but see Holton 1999). A thick structuralism might claim that the fundamental property is intrinsic and categorical, but essentially associated with a particular causal role.

Suppose we can make sense of this proposal. (Tests for intrinsicness are hard to apply here, as defenders allow: see Whittle 2006). Would this thick causal structuralism avoid Humility?

No, for it has its own version of the Commitment to intrinsic properties, which is what provides the step to Humility. To be sure, Lewis's permutation argument for Humility will not go through, since there is no possible world where we have *this* intrinsic, categorical property associated with a *different* relational disposition, or *vice versa*. But there remains an unknowable something, all the same. There is something there, that is intrinsic, and categorical, but we do not know what it is. Telling us that it is essentially connected to a causal role does not tell us what it is in itself. An analogy: suppose it is essential to A that her parents are B and C. Have I told you who A is, in herself, when I have told you that her parents are B and C? It seems not. Likewise, it seems, for the causal-structuralist account of properties. Much more needs to be said here: but for now let us rest with the thought that causal structuralism might well face its own version of Humility.

4.3   An anti-sceptical alternative

Humility is about ignorance, so it is tempting to compare it to scepticism. Suppose you treat ignorance of intrinsic properties as if it were just a kind of scepticism, and respond as you respond to the sceptic: we know these intrinsic properties in the same way we know any other properties. You deny the argument for Humility, by rejecting the epistemic Restriction to relational properties. In so doing, you would deny the thesis of Humility by denying Ignorance: there are fundamental intrinsic properties, and we *can know* after all what they are. We find this response most prominently in the work of Jonathan Schaffer (2005); it is taken seriously, at least as *ad hominem,* by Langton (2004).

On this way of thinking, the direct realist should say she directly perceives the fundamental intrinsic properties; the contextualist should say she 'properly ignores' the possibilities cited by Lewis in 'Ramseyan Humility'; and in general, for each favourite response to the sceptic there will be a favourite response to Humility. We cannot assess this approach adequately here, though we are dubious (see Robichaud, manuscript). But we want to insist that even if Humility has something in common with scepticism, it is not scepticism. Ordinary life is incompatible with a literal commitment to scepticism; it is not incompatible with a literal commitment to Humility. We can believe Humility, and get on with life without resort to Humean 'carelessness and inattention.'

We've seen how the anti-sceptical response tries to block the argument for Humility by rejecting the epistemic Restriction to relational properties; and to deny Humility by rejecting Ignorance. Let's turn now to another, more adventurous attempt to achieve the same result.

4.4   A pan-psychist alternative

Suppose you concede we don't have knowledge of these intrinsic properties in the usual way, via our theories, but we know about them a different way. We know them the way we know mental, or experiential, properties – because *that's what they are*. We have immediate acquaintance with psychic properties, and we take properties like those to be the fundamental ones. This route leads to *pan-psychism,* near enough.

Kant himself dabbled with pan-psychism, speculating at one point that the intrinsic properties of the world are mental:

> It could ... be that the something which lies at the ground of external appearances, which affects our sense so that our sense receives representations of space, matter, shape, and so on – it could be that this something ... is at the same time the subject of thoughts. (A358)

Having taken this Leibnizian pan-psychism seriously, Kant then distances himself, retreating to a more cautious Humility:

> Without allowing these hypotheses, however, one can note the following general point: [...] if we compare the thinking 'I' not with matter but with the intelligible which lies at the ground of the external appearance we call matter, we cannot say that the soul is intrinsically any different from it, since we know nothing at all of it. (A360)

Pan-psychism is no mere historical curiosity. It is receiving something of a revival (Russell 1927; Maxwell 1978; Foster 1982; Chalmers 2003; G. Strawson 2006; Stoljar 2001, 2006). Its proponents needn't believe that the properties at the fundamental level are mental in the full, conscious way that applies to our own minds. But the properties are supposed to be psychological, or 'proto-psychic,' all the same – comparable in some respects, perhaps, to the 'petite perceptions' posited by Leibniz as being among the intrinsic properties of monads. Pan-psychism is welcomed as offering a solution not just to the problem of Humility, but to the problem of consciousness. Ascribing ghosts to the world machine is thought to help us understand how conscious beings can be ghosts in bodily machines.

According to Humility, there are fundamental properties which are, in a minimal sense, not physical, given that physics cannot reach them; if we work with a 'theory-based' notion of 'physical,' such properties are non-physical (Stoljar 2001). (We take Stoljar's contrasting 'object-based' concept of 'physical' is too liberal, since it would count Berkeley and Leibniz as physicalists; there is admittedly a large debate here about the meaning of 'physical.') Pan-psychism goes beyond this minimal sense of 'non-physical': the fundamental properties are non-physical because they are literally psychological. It is often assumed that psychological properties are 'intrinsic': philosophers discuss the 'intrinsic' quality of experience and wonder whether there is a place for it in functional and physical accounts of the mind. If such properties are intrinsic (there is room for doubt here), then there are some fundamental intrinsic qualities with which we have acquaintance. So the pan-psychist's strategy can look appealing: why not let these properties, or something like them, do the job we need intrinsic properties to do? Thus do qualia shift their shape, moving from the guise of thorny problem for philosophy of mind, to surprising solution to the problem of Humility.

The pan-psychist alternative presents an exciting proposal – rather too exciting, we think. Evaluating it properly would take us too far afield, but for now we want to say that it seems as extravagant as anything Leibniz thought up; and we doubt it can greatly help the philosophy of mind, though this is altogether another issue. To admit the theoretical possibility of pan-psychism is one thing, and Humility admits this; to embrace it with open arms is quite another.

4.5 The shrug: Humility – who cares?

You might accept that Humility is true, and say it doesn't matter. We are ignorant of fundamental intrinsic properties – and *so what?* There is nothing 'ominous' about such ignorance. There are many things we can't know about: perhaps we can't know exactly where all the ants were standing, exactly 30 million years ago; perhaps we can't know what the fundamental intrinsic properties of things really are. But why worry? (Lewis 2009 denies Humility is 'ominous'; see also Whittle 2006; Hawthorne 2001; Schaffer 2005; Ney 2007; Locke 2009).

Many discussions of Humility proceed on an assumption that it makes us ignorant of trivial properties, comparable to the haecceities of individuals: we are ignorant of a property's identity tag, so to speak, which it keeps from world to possible world, regardless of the dispositions it is associated with it. We suggest on the contrary that Kant is right on this question, and the shruggers are wrong. If there are fundamental intrinsic properties, and we don't know what they are, then we don't know that they are only trivial, identity-involving properties. All that we know is that they are intrinsic, or categorical. Kant says we cannot rule out the possibility that the fundamental intrinsic properties are thoughts; Humility cannot rule out pan-psychism, though it does not embrace it. But 'not knowing what the properties are' means, not knowing what they are.

So, to conclude, we admit ghosts in the world machine, properties that are non-physical, in the minimal sense that physics cannot find them; and we can't rule out their being non-physical in the more troubling sense that pan-psychists embrace. Humility is not to be shrugged off; but we can live with it.

Bibliography

Allais, L. (2007), 'Intrinsic Natures: A Critique of Langton on Kant,' *Philosophy and Phenomenological Research* 73, 144–69.

Allison, H. (2004), *Kant's Transcendental Idealism: An Interpretation and Defense, Revised and Enlarged Edition* (New Haven, CT: Yale University Press).

Ameriks, K. (2003), *Interpreting Kant's Critiques* (Oxford: Oxford University Press).

Armstrong, D. (1968), *A Materialist Theory of Mind* (London: Routledge and Kegan Paul).

Bird, A. (2007), *Nature's Metaphysics: Laws and Properties* (Oxford: Oxford University Press).

—— (1998), 'Dispositions and Antidotes,' *The Philosophical Quarterly* 48, 227–34.

Blackburn, S. (1993), 'Filling In Space,' reprinted in his *Essays in Quasi-realism* (Oxford: Oxford University Press).

Breitenbach, A. (2004), 'Langton on Things in Themselves: A Critique of Kantian Humility,' *Studies in History and Philosophy of Science* 35, 137–48.

Chalmers, D. (2003), 'Consciousness and its Place in Nature,' in Stich and Warfield (eds.), *The Blackwell Guide to Philosophy of Mind* (Cambridge, MA:Blackwell).

Dunn, J. M. (1990), 'Relevant Predication 2: Intrinsic Properties and Internal Relations,' *Philosophical Studies* 60, 177–206.

Ellis, B., and Lierse, C. (1994), 'Dispositional Essentialism,' *Australasian Journal of Philosophy* 72, 27–45.

Evans, G. (1980), 'Things without the Mind,' in van Straaten (ed.), *Philosophical Subjects: Essays Presented to P.F. Strawson* (Oxford: Oxford University Press), pp. 76–116.

Falkenstein, L. (2001), 'Langton on Things in Themselves: A Critique of *Kantian Humility,*' *Kantian Review* 5, 49–64.

Freeman, A. (ed.) (2006), *Consciousness and Its Place in Nature: Does Physicalism Entail Pan-Psychism?* (Exeter, UK: Imprint Academic).

Faraday, M. (1844), 'A Speculation Touching Electric Conduction and the Nature of Matter,' in *Experimental Researches in Electricity,* vol. 2 (London: Richard and John Edward Taylor).

Foster, J. (1982), *The Case for Idealism* (London: Routledge and Kegan Paul).

Hawthorne, J. (2001), 'Causal Structuralism,' *Philosophical Perspectives* 15, 361–78.

Holton, R. (1999), 'Dispositions All the Way Round,' *Analysis* 59, 9–14.

Humberstone, I. L. (1996), 'Intrinsic/Extrinsic,' *Synthese* 108, 205–67.

Jackson, F. (1988), *From Metaphysics to Ethics: A Defense of Conceptual Analysis* (Oxford: Clarendon Press).

Jackson, F., Pargetter, R., and Prior, E. (1982), 'Three Theses about Dispositions,' *American Philosophical Quarterly* 19, 251–7.

Kant, I. (1922), *Gesammelte Schriften*, ed. Königlich Preussischen Akademie der Wissenschaften (Berlin and Leipzig: de Gruyter); abbreviated *Ak*.

—— *Principiorum primorum cognitionis metaphysicae nova dilucidatio* (1755), *Ak.* Vol. 1. English translation: 'A New Exposition of the First Principles of Metaphysical Knowledge,' in L. W. Beck et al., eds., *Kant's Latin Writings: Translations, Commentaries and Notes* (New York: P. Lang, 1986).

—— *Monadologia physica* (1756), *Ak.* Vol. 1. English translation: 'Physical Monadology,' in L. W. Beck et al. (eds.), *Kant's Latin Writings: Translations, Commentaries and Notes* (New York: P. Lang, 1986).

—— *Kritik der reinen Vernunft* (1781/1787), *Ak.* Vol. 4. The customary practice of citing the pagination of the 1781 (A) edition and/or the 1787 (B) edition is followed. English translation: *Critique of Pure Reason,* tr. Norman Kemp Smith (London: Macmillan, 1929). Translations adapted by Langton.

Kim, J. (1982), 'Psychophysical Supervenience,' *Philosophical Studies* 41, 51–70.

Ladyman, J. (2002), 'Science, Metaphysics and Structural Realism,' *Philosophica* 67, 57–76

Langsam, H. (1994), 'Kant, Hume, and Our Ordinary Concept of Causation,' *Philosophy and Phenomenological Research* 54, 625–47.

Langton, R. (1998), *Kantian Humility: Our Ignorance of Things in Themselves* (Oxford: Clarendon Press).

—— (2004), 'Elusive Knowledge of Things in Themselves,' *Australasian Journal of Philosophy* 82, 129–36.

—— (2006), 'Kant's Phenomena: Extrinsic or Relational Properties? A Reply to Allais,' *Philosophy and Phenomenological Research* 73, 170–85.

Langton, R. and Lewis, D. (1998), 'Defining "Intrinsic,"' *Philosophy and Phenomenological Research* 58, 333–45; reprinted in Lewis (1999), pp. 116–32.

Lewis, D. (1983), 'Extrinsic Properties,' *Philosophical Studies* 44, 197-200.

—— (1999), *Papers in Metaphysics and Epistemology* (Cambridge: Cambridge University Press).

—— (2009), 'Ramseyan Humility,' in Braddon-Mitchell and Nola (eds.), *Conceptual Analysis and Philosophical Naturalism* (Cambridge, MA.: MIT Press), pp. 203–22.

Locke, D. (2009), 'A Partial Defense of Ramseyan Humility,' in Braddon-Mitchell and Nola (eds.), *Conceptual Analysis and Philosophical Naturalism* (Cambridge, MA.: MIT Press), pp. 223–41.

Locke, J. (1975), *Essay Concerning Human Understanding* (1689), P. Nidditch (ed.) (Oxford: Oxford University Press).

Marshall, D. and Josh P. (2001), 'Langton and Lewis on "Intrinsic,"' *Philosophy and Phenomenological Research* 63, 347–51.

Martin, C. B. (1994), 'Dispositions and Conditionals,' *The Philosophical Quarterly* 44, 1–8.

Maxwell, G. (1978), 'Rigid Designators and Mind-Brain Identity,' *Minnesota Studies in the Philosophy of Science*, pp. 365–403.

Mellor, D. H. (1974), 'In Defense of Dispositions,' *The Philosophical Review* 83, 157–81.

Mumford, S. (1988), *Dispositions* (Oxford: Oxford University Press).

Ney, A. (2007), 'Physicalism and our Knowledge of Intrinsic Properties,' *Australasian Journal of Philosophy* 85, 41–60.

Prior, E. (1985), *Dispositions* (Aberdeen: Aberdeen University Press).

Robichaud, C. (manuscript), 'What Lies Beneath: Defending the Ominous Aspects of Humility.'

Russell, B. (1927), *The Analysis of Matter* (London: Allen and Unwin).

Schaffer, J. (2005), 'Quiddistic Knowledge,' *Philosophical Studies* 123, 1–32.

Shoemaker, S. (1980), 'Causality and Properties,' in van Inwagen (ed.), *Time and Cause* (Dordrecht: Reidel), pp. 109–35.

Strawson, G. (2006), 'Realistic Monism: Why Physicalism Entails Pan-Psychism,' *Journal for Consciousness Studies* 13.

Strawson, P. F. (1980), 'Reply to Evans,' in van Straaten (ed.), *Philosophical Subjects: Essays Presented to P. F. Strawson* (Oxford: Oxford University Press), pp. 273-82.

—— (2003), 'A Bit of Intellectual Autobiography,' in Glock (ed.), *Strawson and Kant* (Oxford: Oxford University Press), pp. 7–13.

Stoljar, D. (2006), *Ignorance and Imagination: The Epistemic Origin of the Problem of Consciousness* (New York: Oxford University Press).

—— (2001), 'Two Conceptions of the Physical,' *Philosophy and Phenomenological Research* 62, 253–81.

Swoyer, C. (1982), 'The Nature of Natural Laws,' *Australasian Journal of Philosophy* 60, 203–23.

Vallentyne, P. (1997), 'Intrinsic Properties Defined,' *Philosophical Studies* 88, 209–19.

Van Cleve, J. (2002), 'Receptivity and Our Knowledge of Intrinsic Properties,' *Philosophy and Phenomenological Research* 65, 218–37.

Weatherson, B. (2001), 'Intrinsic Properties and Combinatorial Principles,' *Philosophy and Phenomenological Research* 63, 365–80.

Williams, L.P. (1965), *Michael Faraday: A Biography* (London: Chapman and Hall).

Whittle, A. (2006), 'On an Argument for Humility,' *Philosophical Studies* 130, 461–97.

Yablo, S. (1999), 'Intrinsicness,' *Philosophical Topics* 26, 479–505.

9
Is Everything Relative? Anti-Realism, Truth, and Feminism

Mari Mikkola

I do believe in truth, and I have *never* understood why people concerned with justice have given it such a bad rap. Surely one of the goals of feminism is to *tell the truth* about women's lives and women's experience.... What in the world else could we be doing when we talk about [the reality of oppression], *other* than asserting that the world actually *is* a certain way? (Antony 2002, pp. 115–16)

[T]ruth is a social construct used to uphold patriarchal interests. (Weedon 1987, p. 99)

1 Introduction

This chapter takes issue with feminist views that eschew objectivity: minimally, the view that there is an objective gap between what *is* the case and what we *take to be* the case. As I see it, doing so is politically worrying and philosophically unfounded. Imagine that a company CEO claims it is an acceptable part of normal working life to ask junior staff sexual favours in return for promotions (they are explicitly condoning quid pro quo sexual harassment).[1] To the best of my knowledge, every feminist disagrees with the CEO. But following some feminist philosophical positions we cannot say that the CEO's claim is simply *false*. Such positions are (in my terms) anti-realist about objectivity. One such well-known position is Catherine MacKinnon's: for her, truth is relative being 'produced in the interests of those with power to shape reality' (1989, p. 118).[2] There is no 'ungendered' reality (MacKinnon holds) that adjudicates between what is the case and what we think is the case because there is no 'ungendered' Archimedean perspective from which such reality can be described and inspected. Actually, those who are socially powerful can shape reality so that what they *think* is the case *becomes* the case.

MacKinnon's metaphysical position has significant political implications. First, her anti-realism implies that there are different perspective dependent realities. It is true (relative to the CEO's worldview) that it is acceptable to ask for sexual favours in exchange for promotions; and it is true (relative to a feminist worldview) that it is not. This is not so only with evaluative judgements; all claims about reality are true or false relative to some perspective and conceptual scheme. Call this 'the relativist implication.' Second, MacKinnon's metaphysics implies that reality just is the enforced projection of the powerful group's needs and desires. So, if the powerful group constructs a reality where it is *in fact* acceptable to condone quid pro quo sexual harassment, the feminist claim that it is not turns out to be *in fact* false. Call this 'the quietist implication.'

As a fellow feminist, as someone who thinks that unjust social arrangements disadvantaging women should be eradicated, I find these implications unnerving. Following the relativist implication, it is not possible to say that anti-feminist claims are just false; and following the quietist implication, feminist claims about reality end up being false. These consequences are politically worrying. If we allow anti-feminist perspectives to have a claim to truth, how can feminists justify their claim that some ways of treating women are just wrong? And if feminist claims about reality come out as false, how can feminists critique the way the world is? Now, MacKinnon does not intend her anti-realism to have these implications. Although she thinks that what is true of reality depends on one's perspective, MacKinnon does not intend to endorse 'anything goes' relativism: for her, a feminist reality is unequivocally better than an anti-feminist one. Further, she certainly does not intend to be quietist about gender oppression. Is there, then, a way to avoid these implications while retaining anti-realism about objectivity?[3] I see no possible way to reconcile the quietist implication with feminist political goals: it is time to give up one's metaphysics, if it leads to such a quietist take on oppression. But, the situation is less straightforward with respect to the relativist implication. Some non-feminist philosophers, notably Hilary Putnam, have argued that it is possible to block radical relativism while endorsing worldview pluralism. Putnam's 'internal realism' takes there to be a plurality of conceptual schemes between which we cannot adjudicate by appealing to some scheme independent reality; nonetheless, we can rule out some schemes as being rationally unacceptable. Perhaps Putnam's position, then, enables MacKinnon to retain her anti-realism about objectivity without problematic relativism.

While many of Putnam's insights are attractive, I will nonetheless argue, they cannot save feminist anti-realism from relativism. Putnam's conception of objectivity simply isn't objectivist enough for feminist purposes. My discussion will take the following shape. A large bulk of this chapter deals with the claim that anti-realism is politically problematic. In Section 2, I will look at MacKinnon's anti-realism and its metaphysical implications. Since I hold that the quietist implication is a non-starter for feminism, I will leave it to one side and consider whether the relativist implication can be reconciled with feminist goals. With this in mind, I will explore whether Putnam's internal realism can dispel my relativist worries. In Section 3, I will outline Putnam's view in more detail. However, in Section 4, I go on to argue that it cannot sufficiently undercut the relativism that anti-realist feminism implies. Finally, in Section 5, I will discuss why feminist anti-realism is philosophically unfounded claiming that the reasons given for why one should eschew objectivity are not good.

2 MacKinnon and male reality

The feminist suspicion of objectivity is often generated by scepticism about a particular epistemic position (for more, see Haslanger 1995). Metaphysical objectivity supposedly requires occupying an epistemically objective 'view from nowhere' from which we can say as a matter of fact what is the case; but there is no objective epistemic standpoint; so (the argument goes), there cannot be metaphysical objectivity either. Its existence is an illusion. Instead, what we take to be the case is (or becomes) the case. Reality is a *product* of our practices and conventions; it is our *making*. MacKinnon's argument takes this shape. She takes metaphysical objectivity to require epistemic objectivity. But 'there is no ungendered reality or ungendered perspective' (MacKinnon 1989, p. 114) – this would require an Archimedean standpoint that does not exist. Rather, those who are socially powerful can make it seem *as if* their perspective *is* the Archimedean perspective. And since men as a group are socially powerful, they 'are their own Archimedean point,' which is 'not very Archimedean' (1989, p. 117). We falsely, then, take the male perspective to be the epistemically objective perspective. But, the latter does not exist; after all, it is just the concealed male perspective. And since metaphysical objectivity requires that a genuinely objective epistemic viewpoint exists, metaphysical objectivity does not exist.[4]

MacKinnon makes a further claim about the construction of reality: 'objectivity – the nonsituated, universal standpoint... tacitly participates in constructing reality from the dominant point of view' (1989, p. 114). Reality is always constructed from the dominant perspective and, since males are the dominant social group, it is constructed from *their* perspective – reality is male. Further, the mechanism of construction is objectification: male power has the ability to create 'the world in its own image, the image of its desires' (MacKinnon 1989, p. 118) through women's objectification. The idea is something like the following. Pornography falsely portrays women as being sexually submissive, and this conditions male desire to find dominance and submission 'sexy.' As a result,

(a) Men *view* and *treat* women as objects of male sexual desire;
(b) Men *desire* women to be submissive and object-like and *force* them to submit;
(c) Men *believe* that women are in fact submissive and object-like;
(d) Men believe that women are in fact submissive and object-like *by nature*. (Papadaki 2008, p. 240)

So, the male perspective desires women to be submissive and since this is the perspective of the dominant group, men have the power to project and enforce their perspective onto the world (make their desires 'real' in the world). The male perspective, then, believes women *in fact* to be submissive: it is believed that sexual submissiveness is an independently existing fact about women's 'nature.' And treating women accordingly makes it the case that women become submissive in patriarchal societies.[5]

Now, MacKinnon's political position aims to undercut this by showing that being sexually submissive is just a contingent fact about women; women are not essentially submissive. But, since she rejects the existence of a perspective independent reality, MacKinnon cannot do so by appealing to some supposedly true reality hidden and covered up by the male reality. Rather, a new feminist reality must be constructed to replace the male one. It is possible to construct any reality provided that one has enough social power to do so. Haslanger describes MacKinnon's view as follows:

> [For MacKinnon] different points of view generate competing realities, and to decide between them is to take a moral stand. MacKinnon's own moral stand is unequivocal; she proposes that we stop acting

on the basis of what is real *to men* and instead begin to take seriously what is real *to women*. (1995, pp. 123–4)

A feminist reality is better than the male reality. As a result, feminists (and women generally) must gain enough social power to project and make real their conception of reality to replace male reality. What makes the feminist reality better is that the male reality oppresses women. MacKinnon denies the view that women's oppression is just 'in the head'; in fact, the male reality literally hits women in the face (1987, p. 57). So, even though our choice of realities is a moral decision, MacKinnon still thinks that our moral judgements rest on some facts about reality: after all, because the male reality *in fact* oppresses women, there is a moral obligation to choose the feminist reality and start taking seriously what is 'real' to women.

Unfortunately, MacKinnon's metaphysics undercuts her powerful political message. First, the relativist implication: there are different perspective dependent accounts of what is the case or what the facts are. After all, MacKinnon seems to be committed to there being (at least) two perspectives on reality: the feminist and anti-feminist ones. The implication is that a statement like 'It is acceptable to ask sexual favours in exchange for promotions' is true from the male perspective, and its negation is true from the feminist perspective. Now, I take it that MacKinnon would want to say that the former claim is just false because the anti-feminist perspective gets things wrong. But, if truth is relative to one's perspective, this move is unavailable: the statement, while being false for feminists, is true for anti-feminists. And without a perspective independent reality, we cannot adjudicate between the two. The anti-feminist perspective is afforded a claim to truth.

Second, the quietist implication: MacKinnon claims that by treating women in submissive ways, women become submissive – they become 'walking embodiments of men's projected needs' (1989, p. 119). But, then the feminist claim that women are not in fact submissive comes out as being *false*. A number of *prima facie* oppressive phenomena turn out not really to exist: for instance, as long as sex-for-promotions is seen as part of everyday working life, being defined as such from the male perspective, quid pro quo sexual harassment simply doesn't exist. If sexual harassment is not real to men and if they have the power to construct reality so that what is real in general just reflects what is real to them, sexual harassment turns out not to be real. Problematically, it seems that this is what MacKinnon has in mind when she claims, 'the reality of women's oppression is, finally, neither demonstrable nor

refutable empirically' (1989, p. 124). And, if the male perspective constructs reality, the implication is that the feminist perspective does not
describe or capture reality as it is – feminists are crying abuse when
there is none. This undercuts feminist claims about oppression, as these
claims simply won't capture reality *as it is*.

These implications concede politically too much to the anti-
feminist perspective. Actually, the quietist implication makes feminism impossible. And given that MacKinnon thinks feminism is
possible, I think we should bracket off her radically constructivist
claims and focus on the claims that have the relativist implications.
So, MacKinnon holds that there is no ungendered reality or perspective that adjudicates between different realities. She also holds that
a feminist reality just is better than an anti-feminist one. My worry
is this: given her metaphysical claims, I cannot see how MacKinnon
can justify her political/moral claims and avoid conceding too much
to the anti-feminist position. In Section 4, I will consider whether
Putnam's internal realism enables this. Before that, let's outline
Putnam's view in more detail.

3   Putnam's anti-realism

Internal realism has two components: conceptual relativity and (a kind
of) objectivity about truth. First conceptual relativity. Putnam rejects
metaphysical realism, on which

> the world consists of some fixed totality of mind-independent
> objects. There is exactly one true and complete description of 'the
> way the world is.' Truth involves some sort of correspondence rela-
> tion between words ... and external things ... its favorite point of view
> is a God's-Eye point of view. (1981, p. 49)

By contrast, Putnam's internal realism takes

> *what objects does the world consist of?* [as] a question that it only makes
> sense to ask *within* a theory or description ... there is more than one
> 'true' theory or description of the world. 'Truth' ... is some sort of
> (idealized) rational acceptability – some sort of ideal coherence of
> our beliefs with each other and with our experiences *as those experi-
> ences are themselves represented in our belief system.* ... [It is] not corres-
> pondence with mind-independent or discourse-independent 'states
> of affairs.' (1981, pp. 49–50)[6]

For Putnam, there is no conceptual scheme independent reality: '"Objects" do not exist independently of conceptual schemes. *We* cut up the world into objects when we introduce one or another scheme of description' (1981, p. 52).[7] There is no fact about which conceptual scheme is 'really true'; each scheme will contain bits that 'are right and wrong *by the standards appropriate to the scheme itself* – but the question "which kind of "true" is really Truth" is one that internal realism rejects' (Putnam 1990, p. 96).

Consider Putnam's example to clarify (1996b, p. 24). A commonsense realist and a mereologist encounter three entities: x1, x2, and x3. How many objects are there? For the former, there are just three. But for the latter, there are seven: in addition to those mentioned, there are the mereological sums x1+x2, x2+x3, x1+x3, x1+x2+x3. Now, one is probably tempted to ask: how many objects are there *really,* or which conceptual scheme is *the true* one? For Putnam, these questions cannot be answered. Doing so would require a perspective on reality from which we look 'in' while standing outside; this 'God's Eye' perspective would require surveying reality from 'outside our own skins' that is impossible (Putnam 1990, p. 17). So, *'either way of describing [the world] is equally "true"'* and to think that there is some scheme independent way of counting objects is 'an illusion' (Putnam 1996a, p. 188).

In a sense, then, internal realism enables us to describe the 'same' reality in many equally true ways. For instance, consider the chair one is sitting on:

> From the molecular point of view, it is an enormous collection of molecules…. From the point of view of wave equations in physics, there is no chair, but only wave forms. From a human point of view, it is a single object. [And] whether the chair is a particular object…or a bunch of molecules or a wave form is not a question that has a unique correct answer. All the answers can be correct, but correct within different conceptual schemes. (Lakoff 1987, p. 262)

For Putnam, this demonstrates that a sharp fact/value distinction is an illusion: in choosing some scheme of description, I am already wearing my value commitments on my sleeve. If I describe chairs from the physicist perspective, I am already demonstrating that (for me) this scheme is more appropriate/relevant than, say, the commonsense scheme. Which 'picture of the world' we take to be 'true (or true by our present lights, or "as true as anything is"),' Putnam writes, 'rests on and reveals our total system of value commitments' (1981, p. 201). The same goes for our criteria of relevance, which questions we pose, which concepts we use, how we classify things and how we describe those things we have classified.

Putnam also holds that internal realism does not lead to 'anything goes' relativism whereby every conceptual scheme is 'just as good as every other' (1981, p. 54). To block this Putnam claims to hold an objectivist conception of truth where (briefly put) 'truth comes to no more than idealized rational acceptability' (1990, p. 41). *Prima facie,* some schemes are ruled out, not because they fail to correspond to some conceptual scheme independent reality, but because they are (in some sense) rationally unacceptable. Still, although we cannot adjudicate between (say) the commonsense realist and the physicist schemes, they are both rationally acceptable and this makes them equally true descriptions of reality. By combining conceptual relativity with an objectivist conception of truth Putnam aims to have a genuine plurality of equally true conceptual schemes without having to concede that all schemes are equally true.

4   Can internal realism undercut relativism?

My contention is that the relativist implication of MacKinnon's metaphysics concedes politically too much to the anti-feminist perspective. Can Putnam's internal realism provide a way to block this? The answer hinges on Putnam's conception of truth. For him, truth is idealized rational acceptability. Tentatively this means that (1) truth is 'independent of justification here and now, but not independent of *all* justification. To claim a statement is true is to claim it could be justified'; (2) truth is 'stable or "convergent"' (Putnam 1981, p. 56). Truth cannot be just what is rationally acceptable since a 'statement can be rationally acceptable *at a time* but not *true*' (1981, p. x). 'The Earth is flat' was rationally acceptable once, but no more. Yet we cannot say that the statement was true then and false now, because either 'that would mean that the earth has changed its shape' or that truth is non-convergent; and since the Earth's shape has not changed and truth is 'a property of a statement that cannot be lost', truth must be 'an *idealization* of rational acceptability' (Putnam 1981, p. 55).

This characterization of Putnam's conception of truth is still very vague. Actually there is no straightforward detailed way to characterize it since Putnam provides a number of different, more specific, formulations. Consider first (what I will call) the 'Idealised Epistemic Conditions' formulation or IEC: truth is what we are justified in rationally accepting under ideal epistemic conditions (Putnam 1981, p.55). What makes for such conditions? Putnam explains:

> If I say 'There is a chair in my study,' an ideal epistemic situation would be to be in my study with the lights on or with daylight streaming through the window, with nothing wrong with my eyesight, with an unfocused mind, without having taken drugs or been subjected to hypnosis, and so forth, and to look and see if there is a chair there. (1990, p. vii)

Think back to the feminist case. Following Putnam, I would be justified in accepting that 'It is unacceptable to ask sexual favours in exchange for promotions' is true, provided that I were under ideal epistemic conditions. And it is very tempting to say that the anti-feminists, who take the statement to be false, are simply under epistemically non-ideal conditions. Were the anti-feminists to view the world under epistemically ideal conditions, they would see that the statement is true. Feminists would be able to say that their claims *are* true whether or not the anti-feminists take them to be true since they are viewing the world under ideal epistemic conditions. But, think about what makes for such conditions: if not being drunk, not having taken drugs and having the usual sensory abilities make for ideal epistemic conditions, can we say that the anti-feminist is under *non-*ideal conditions? It is not obvious that we can. Let me clarify: I think that the anti-feminist *is* under non-ideal epistemic conditions, but not for the reasons Putnam cites. Rather, their apparent sexist biases make the epistemic conditions non-ideal. What renders the epistemic conditions non-ideal, thus preventing the anti-feminist from seeing what is the case, is the anti-feminist's *prejudices* instead of impaired sensory capacities or drunkenness.

This does not yet show that the IEC formulation is unacceptable, although it leaves much to be desired. Perhaps by including lack of biases and prejudices to the list of ideal epistemic conditions, it could handle my worries. However, this would make the story quite a bit more complicated. Many feminist epistemologists have claimed that ridding oneself of all biases is neither possible nor something that makes for ideal epistemic conditions (for an overview, see Saul 2003, ch. 8). Some biases are needed (if you like) to see clearly. Feminist biases are a particularly good example: because of their prior feminist beliefs, those political activists who campaigned for women's vote could see that withholding women political rights was a grave injustice. So, biases are not all on a par and some are beneficial for 'looking and seeing' what is the case. For the IEC formulation to be helpful for feminist purposes, we must expand the list of conditions under which justification is epistemically ideal, be able to discriminate between good and bad biases, and only include the former. This is no easy feat and opens up yet another host of questions about what makes for goodness and badness of biases (see Antony 2002 for an interesting discussion). At the very least, the IEC formulation *as Putnam puts it* is not objectivist enough for feminist purposes. Actually, Putnam's own remarks suggest that it never could be: he claims that we can never *really* attain ideal epistemic conditions (1981, p. 55), and that such talk is only meant to serve as a metaphor (1990, p. viii). Feminists, however, need more than metaphors to avoid the relativist implication that gives anti-feminism a claim to truth.

Consider next (what I will call) the 'Idealised Rational Acceptability' formulation or IRA. Putnam offers two different ways to understand IRA.

> (IRA*): 'the only criterion for what is a fact is what it is *rational* to accept' where 'our notion of rationality is, at bottom, just one part of our conception of human flourishing, our idea of the good.' (1981, p. x)

> (IRA**): truth is idealised rational acceptability that is a 'sort of ideal coherence of our beliefs with each other and with our experiences.' (1981, p. 50)[8]

First, take IRA*. On this conception, truth 'depends for its content on our standards of rational acceptability, and these in turn rest on and presuppose our values...theory of truth presupposes theory of rationality which in turn presupposes our theory of the good' (Putnam 1981, p. 215). But, not all ideas of the good or conceptions of human flourishing are equally acceptable; some are wrong, infantile, sick and one-sided (Putnam 1981, p. 148). So, if our theory of rationality is grounded in a bad conception of flourishing, it won't yield truth. Now, IRA* would appear to rule out the anti-feminist perspective as having a morally degenerate conception of human flourishing; so, the anti-feminist does not act rationally because their conception of the good is unacceptable. And feminists can say that 'It is unacceptable to ask sexual favours in exchange for promotions' is true because they are rationally justified in accepting this claim insofar as their rationality is grounded in a good theory of the good.

I think Putnam is in many ways right: some conceptions of human flourishing simply are morally degenerate and we want to rule them out as leading to an unacceptable and non-rational take on reality. But, Putnam denies that there is a 'given, ahistorical, set of "moral principles" which define once and for all what human flourishing consists in' (1981, p. xi). And this seriously undermines his case. He has simply shifted the locus of the relativist concern: if there is no conceptual scheme independent notion of human good, how can we adjudicate between *different* conceptions of the good clearly ruling out the morally corrupt ones?[9] We want to rule out conceptual schemes that are based on 'bad' conceptions of human flourishing; but what is the criterion for distinguishing good conceptions from those that we falsely think are good? Putnam provides no such criterion. Instead, he claims that when debates about conflicting conceptions of the good are 'intelligently conducted on both sides' with the use of *prima facie* good arguments, perhaps 'all that can happen is that one sensitively diagnoses and delineates the source of the disagreement' (1981, p. 164). So, we must agree to disagree, if my anti-feminist opponent is sufficiently glib at philosophical debate. This is clearly not enough for feminist purposes, and it fails to rule out the anti-feminist perspective as rationally unacceptable.[10]

Can IRA** fare any better? I think not. This formulation is about how coherent one's beliefs are and how well they fit experiential evidence. For instance, if one's conceptual scheme included the belief that one can fly, experiential input gained from acting on that belief would quickly lead one to revise one's beliefs (Putnam 1981, p. 50). It would not be rational to endorse the set that contained this belief. Now, Putnam also holds that our descriptions of reality reflect our interests and values: in choosing one conceptual scheme over another I am wearing my value commitments on my sleeve. Further, the experiential input that shapes our conceptual schemes is also shaped by our schemes: there are no experiential inputs '*which are not themselves to some extent shaped by our concepts,* by the vocabulary we use to report and describe them, or any inputs *which admit of only one description, independent of all conceptual choices*' (Putnam 1981, p. 54). Our experiential inputs inform us about what *is* the case – what it is rational for us to believe. These experiential inputs, however, are shaped by our conceptual schemes: our comprehension of our experiences (of what *is* the case) depends on our conceptual choices (on what we *take to be* the case). So, what we take to be the case shapes what, for us, is the case. And as long as what we take to be the case (all our beliefs) constitutes an internally coherent set and as long as our experiences fit this set, *this* is what it is rational for us to believe.

Clearly IRA** cannot give feminists what they need. Imagine that one's conceptual scheme is made up of a perfectly coherent set of anti-feminist beliefs. Now, since our conceptual schemes shape how we comprehend our experiences, there is no guarantee that experiential input would lead one to modify one's beliefs or to reject the conceptual scheme as rationally unacceptable. This is because our prior beliefs (in a sense) colour our experiences. Take my anti-feminist opponent who has such internally coherent set of anti-feminist beliefs. Two things can happen when they are faced with (say) a sexual harassment complaint. Either the anti-feminist modifies their beliefs about the acceptability of asking sex-for-promotions when faced with experiential input that appears to suggest the contrary. Or they interpret the *prima facie* contrary experiential input so that it fits the anti-feminist's conceptual scheme concluding that nothing unacceptable is going on. The anti-feminist may hold that they need not revise their conceptual scheme; it is the conceptual scheme of the complainant that is in need of revision. The anti-feminist's experiential input, or what for the anti-feminist is the case, is shaped by what they take to be the case. Further, this can make the experiential input entirely consistent with the anti-feminist's set of (anti-feminist) beliefs. So, following Putnam, my opponent can *rationally* accept that the claim 'It is unacceptable to ask sexual favours in exchange for promotions' is false. This formulation of truth does not deliver what feminists need: if it is rational to accept what is the case and if what is the case depends on how we interpret experiences given our conceptual schemes (given what we *think* is the case), then we may have to conclude that it is rational to accept (as Putnam puts it) morally wrong and sick schemes provided that they are internally coherent and fit one's experiences. One may have to conclude that it is rational to accept an anti-feminist scheme, which is precisely what feminists should seek to undermine. As I see it, Putnam's three formulations of truth do not enable feminists to rule out anti-feminist conceptual schemes and perspectives. Not being able to do so, then, grants too much to the anti-feminist and fails to dispel my relativist worries about feminist anti-realism.[11]

5   Why is anti-realism philosophically problematic?

My contention is not just that anti-realism about objectivity is politically problematic; it is also philosophically unfounded.[12] Objectivity is not the philosophical bugbear some take it to be and it is not susceptible to the charges levelled against it. Some anti-realists (like MacKinnon and Putnam) understand metaphysical objectivity as follows:

(a) It requires epistemic objectivity (a 'God's-Eye' perspective).
(b) It requires the existence of a conceptual scheme independent reality, and that such reality can be described conceptual scheme independently.
(c) It implies a conception of truth whereby our claims about reality are true if they correspond to the way the world is, and false if they do not.

Those sceptical of metaphysical objectivity usually seek to undermine it holding instead that:

(a*) Epistemic objectivity is impossible since we can never occupy a God's Eye perspective.
(b*) There is no conceptual scheme independent way to describe reality and, so, no scheme independent reality.
(c*) The conception of truth metaphysical objectivity buys into is problematic implying that there is some single, unique 'way the world is.' But, (i) there isn't; (ii) thinking that there is falsely presupposes the existence of 'absolute truth' along with (iii) the rejection of indeterminacy.[13]

However, metaphysical objectivity does not presuppose what anti-realists take it to presuppose.

(a**) It does not require epistemic objectivity understood as a God's Eye perspective.
(b**) Although our descriptions of reality are scheme dependent, it does not follow that reality (what our descriptions are *about*) is also scheme dependent.
(c**) Metaphysical objectivity need not presuppose a problematic conception of truth.

Scepticism about metaphysical objectivity is misplaced. Due to this, I see no reason to eschew it. Consider (a**)–(c**) in more detail.

5.1 Metaphysical objectivity does not require epistemic objectivity

We need not posit some 'view from nowhere' in order to maintain the objectivist gap between how reality is and how we think it is. Many everyday examples demonstrate this. For instance, on a minimalist conception of truth, the statement 'Today is sunny' is true if and only if today is sunny. And I need not occupy some special Archimedean perspective in order to see that it either is or is not sunny. In fact, quite often seeing what is the case requires that we occupy a *particular situated* standpoint or perspective. Consider Putnam's example that in order to see whether 'There is a chair in [Hilary Putnam's] office' is true, we must be in a position to 'look and see' whether this is the case. In order to do so, we must occupy a *specific* perspective; among other things, we must be in a position to see inside Hilary Putnam's office. In order to distinguish what is the case (whether there is a chair in the office) from what we think is the case (whether we just suspect that there is one), we need *not* occupy a God's Eye view or step outside our skins. The impossibility of this sort of epistemic objectivity, then, does not undermine metaphysical objectivity.

One might claim that the feminist/anti-feminist situation is different though. Perhaps in order to say definitively whether something is the case with respect to (say) quid pro quo sexual harassment, I need to occupy some non-situated perspective. After all, our social situations and circumstances are not always clear-cut. Given the complexities of particular situations, one cannot easily (if at all) determine whether sexual harassment took place. So, (the argument goes) in order to say *for certain* what is the case, epistemic objectivity in this case is required. It seems to me that we cannot always determine for certain whether some behaviour counts as sexual harassment. But this simply demonstrates that sometimes what is the case is indeterminate. Metaphysical objectivity has not, however, been undermined; the example just shows that our ability to say definitively what is the case in all situations is limited. If one's metaphysics has the result that we cannot rule out anti-feminist perspectives that accept sex-for-promotions to be a normal part of everyday work life, *because* we cannot always determine for certain whether sexual harassment has taken place, one is throwing the baby out with the bathwater.

5.2   Metaphysical objectivity is not undermined by our descriptions of reality being conceptual scheme dependent

MacKinnon and Putnam deny the existence of a conceptual scheme independent reality since this would require a 'God's-Eye' view or an Archimedean perspective. Now, what I claimed above already undermines this move. I agree that epistemic objectivity as *they* see it is unachievable; but since it is not required for metaphysical objectivity, its impossibility is metaphysically speaking benign. However, there is another way in which we can see that metaphysical objectivity is not threatened by the claim that we can never describe reality scheme independently. My thought is this: Putnam is right in claiming that we can never *describe* reality conceptual scheme independently. So, in this sense, it is impossible to say what is the case independently of all conceptual choices. But, this does not mean that *reality* is conceptual scheme dependent: although my description of some x depends on my conceptual choices, it does not follow that what I am describing (x) also depends on them. Take Lakoff's example of the chair (1987, p. 262) that I mentioned earlier. We can describe the chair as a collection of molecules or a wave form. Both are equally true descriptions of the chair (both are true relative to a conceptual scheme). But, even in this example that is meant to support Putnam, what I am describing (the chair) does not undergo change relative to a scheme; *the object* I am describing remains the same, only my *description of it* differs relative to a scheme. Metaphysical objectivity has not yet been undermined: although our descriptions of what is the case are always scheme dependent, this does not mean that what is the case simply changes relative to a scheme. So, the existence of a gap between what is and what we think is the case has not been undermined.

5.3 Metaphysical objectivity need not presuppose a problematic conception of truth

Metaphysical objectivity apparently requires that there is some way the world is. And the idea of there being some way the world is allegedly commits us to the existence of absolute truth and lack of indeterminacy. But, the argument goes, because we cannot say whether feminist claims well and truly correspond to the way the world is (to some absolute truth that admits of no indeterminacy), we must eschew metaphysical objectivity. That is, metaphysical objectivity presupposes a problematic conception of truth. This line of argument is apparent in the following passage:

> [Feminists should reject metaphysical objectivity because it is not possible to] uncover the Truth of the whole once and for all. Such an absolute truth (e.g., the explanation for all gender arrangements at all times is X ...) would require the existence of an 'Archimedes point' outside of the whole and beyond our embeddedness in it from which we could see (and represent) the whole. (Flax 1987, p. 631)

Now, consider the following: it is the case that I am 151cm tall. This fact, then, is part of the way the world is. Does it presuppose the existence of absolute truth? Well, if we take absolute truth to be just the way the world is, the fact about my height is part of it. But, this isn't particularly problematic. We can quite easily accept all sorts of facts about what is true absolutely, if this just means what is true of the way the world is. If there is some special problem with claims that appeal to absolute truth, then these claims cannot simply be about the way the world is. And in this case we are owed some explanation of what is meant by 'absolute truth,' why metaphysical objectivity supposedly presupposes it and why this is problematic. In any case, I fail to see why metaphysical objectivity would or should presuppose some mysterious conception of 'absolute truth,' and the pull of this objection.

Next, consider indeterminacy and explanatory claims about gender oppression. There are many ways in which women are disadvantaged; and these ways depend on a whole host of factors having to do with one's social position, race, ethnicity, nationality, ability, class and so forth. Given this, it is extremely implausible to think that one could provide an explanation of all gender arrangements for all times and even more implausible to think that one could do so in some simple manner. But to say that *as a result* feminists should eschew metaphysical objectivity (again) throws the baby out with the bath water: although many feminist explanatory claims may not clearly and neatly correspond to the way the world is because the world is not neat and simple, this does not prevent feminists from making numerous factual claims that do correspond to the way the world is. For instance, those who endorse metaphysical objectivity hold that the claim 'Many female primary caretakers of small children find it hard to combine work and family lives' is true only if empirical evidence suggests they *do* find it hard (only if the claim corresponds to some facts). Further, accepting this does not mean one must reject indeterminacy. Our statements may have indeterminate truth conditions because they contain vague predicates or because of the complexity of issues involved. The truth conditions of 'My brother is tall' and 'Domestic abuse stems from a desire to control one's partner due to a traumatic childhood event' are (it seems to me) indeterminate. In the former case, this is because 'is tall' is a vague predicate; in the latter case, because determining the causes of domestic abuse is a hugely complex issue. Accepting metaphysical objectivity does not mean we can always distinguish what is the case from what we think is the case. Quite simply: the world is too complex for us always to be able to do so and facts do not come neatly packaged so that we can always easily (or at all) reduce the explanandum to some explanans. Still, indeterminacy does not count against metaphysical objectivity; and metaphysical objectivity does not deny the existence of indeterminacy.

Finally, consider the claim that there is no single unique way the world is. Actually, it is far from clear what this means. If it means that there is only one way in which things in fact contingently are, the claim seems innocuous. Either it is sunny just now or it isn't. Depending on what is the case, we accept one of these descriptions as describing *the way the world is*. But I have not yet committed myself to any metaphysically problematic claim. Now, if the claim about reality's uniqueness is about how reality necessarily is, the claim is much more contention. So, on this reading the claim is: it is currently sunny and *things could not be otherwise*. But, now we simply end up saying something false and something metaphysical objectivity is not committed to. Just because there is a gap between it being sunny and my thinking that it is sunny, this does not entail that if it is sunny, this is *necessarily* so. So, depending on how we cash out the claim about reality's singular uniqueness, we either end up saying something that is utterly unproblematic, or we end up saying something that metaphysical objectivity simply is not committed to.

6   Concluding remarks

I have argued that feminists should not eschew metaphysical objectivity. Those feminists who fear it fear something that need not be feared. And those who endorse anti-realism about objectivity grant too much to anti-feminist views doing feminism a serious political disfavour. As I see it, feminist metaphysical positions must not grant anti-feminist perspectives a claim to truth – otherwise, what would be the point of feminism as a political movement? What would be the point of a political movement that aims to do away with unjust gender oppression, if *that movement's own metaphysics* suggests that the existence of unjust gender oppression is somehow in doubt? I see no better way for feminists to undermine their own claims about the reality of oppression. This is why objectivity should be retained: it is needed to make good crucial feminist political claims.

Notes

I have presented earlier versions of this chapter at the Universities of Lancaster and Nottingham, and at the Pacific APA meeting in Vancouver, April 2009. I am very grateful to all those present for their insightful comments and constructive advice on how to develop the paper further. A particular thanks goes to Allan Hazlett for his extremely detailed, interesting, and helpful comments.

1. Many countries nowadays have legislation against quid pro quo sexual harassment. Prior to such legislation, it was seen as perhaps unfortunate, even by some as immoral, but not a matter for the courts (Crouch 2001). For the sake of the example, imagine that the CEO's claims are made prior to sexual harassment legislation being in place. So the CEO is not condoning anything that is illegal.

2. MacKinnon is not alone in holding such a position; see also Harding 1991.

3. Actually, the quietist implication undercuts the relativist implication: if the anti-feminist perspective fixes what is the case due to which feminist claims end up being false, there is no relativism (anti-feminist claims are just true, feminist claims are just false). However, MacKinnon clearly thinks that there are different perspective dependent realities. So, her metaphysical position ends up having incompatible implications, which raises questions about its coherence. I won't focus on this issue here; my concern is with her metaphysical position being *politically* unacceptable and how this warrants the rejection of her metaphysics.

4. Note that the male perspective is *not* the perspective of all males. It is a perspective that takes maleness as 'the standard' (MacKinnon 1987, p. 52). For example, much of our language use is conducted from a male perspective, like the convention of using the pronoun 'he' when talking about a person whose sex is unknown or when attempting to speak gender-neutrally. But, of course, this does not entail that all men employ language in this fashion and that no women do. Further, having social power is not the same as having political power. So, one need not occupy some powerful institutional position to be socially powerful. This is akin to white people being more socially powerful than non-whites in white supremacist societies: such societies are structured in ways that benefit and reflect the needs of the former often to the detriment of the latter. Men as a group, then, are socially powerful in patriarchal societies in the same way as white people as a group are socially powerful in white supremacist societies.

5. I won't consider whether MacKinnon can plausibly maintain the link between objectivity and objectification; I recommend Sally Haslanger's (2002) illuminating discussion on the issue.

6. A quick clarification: I have characterized Putnam's view as anti-realist, although his position is explicitly called 'internal realism.' Putnam holds that his view is realist insofar as it takes reality 'at face value' (1996b, p. 23). But Putnam is an anti-realist in that he rejects some privileged conception of what exists and how reality is to be described. So, for Putnam, although idealism is false, external reality is not individuated mind-independently.

7. Here Putnam appears to be saying that *literally* there are no objects prior to our conceptual schemes picking them out, which seems implausible. Consider stars. Surely we didn't *bring* them into existence when we devised conceptual schemes that pick them out? Some take Putnam to hold this view. Elder claims that for Putnam 'the objects we consider real are partly of our own making: we carve them out of the world' (2005, p. 41). Due to this, 'carving' is metaphysically prior to the existence of objects. And, Elder (2006) argues,

this makes Putnam's view internally contradictory: how can we carve out x, if x does not exist prior to us carving it? Others disagree: for instance, Devitt claims that Putnam's talk of constructing objects 'can be nothing but a metaphor' (1984, p. 192; see also Lakoff [1987, p. 262]). It is a moot point just how constructivist Putnam is. Undermining Devitt's claim, he writes: 'as I maintain, "objects" themselves are as much made as discovered, as much products of our conceptual invention as of the "objective" factor in experience' (1981, p. 54). And yet elsewhere Putnam claims that we didn't make (e.g.) Sirius a star, although we did create the concept *star* (1996a, pp. 182–3). However, nothing hangs on this for my purposes.

8. It is far from obvious how these different formulations are meant to hang together. In fact, commentators often focus on just one as being *the* conception Putnam endorses. For instance, Folina (1995) takes this to be the IEC formulation.

9. Putnam does write that male chauvinism and slavery simply are wrong (1990, p. 183). However, the passage in which he does so is ambiguous: it is not clear whether Putnam is expounding his own views, or whether he is describing views that many currently accept.

10. Douglas Rasmussen writes that Putnam's conception of human flourishing is too agent-neutral: Putnam's approach is too impersonal, which means 'it does not matter ethically speaking whose human flourishing' we are talking about (2008, pp. 80–1). And, since human flourishing is always flourishing '*for* some person or other,' Putnam's conception is problematic (p. 81). That is, Rasmussen's complaint appears to be that Putnam's conception of human flourishing is not relative enough, whereas my complaint is that it is too relative.

11. I am not claiming that this shows Putnam's conception of truth is altogether unacceptable. My point is merely that his conception is unsuitable for feminist purposes.

12. Earlier I claimed that MacKinnon's anti-realist metaphysics appears incoherent. My claim here is different: it is not about the coherence of one's anti-realist alternative, but about one's reasons for thinking that such an alternative is needed to being with.

13. Here I am talking about anti-realists more broadly and not just about MacKinnon and Putnam. For instance, Putnam holds that (c) is problematic (among other things) because of (i) but not because of (ii) or (iii).

Bibliography

Antony, L. (2002), 'Quine as a Feminist,' in Antony and Witt (eds.), *A Mind of One's Own* (Boulder, CO.: Westview Press).

Crouch, M. A. (2001), *Thinking About Sexual Harassment: A Guide for the Perplexed* (Oxford: Oxford University Press).

Devitt, M. (1984), *Realism and Truth* (Oxford: Blackwell).

Elder, C. (2005), 'Undercutting the Idea of Carving Reality,' *Southern Journal of Philosophy*, 43, 41–59.

—— (2006), 'Conventionalism and Realism-Imitating Counterfactuals,' *The Philosophical Quarterly* 56 (222), 1–15.

Flax, J. (1987), 'Postmodernism and Gender Relations in Feminist Theory,' *Signs* 12(4), 621–43.

Folina, J. (1995), 'Putnam, Realism and Truth,' *Synthese* 103, 141–52.

Harding, S. (1991), *Whose Science? Whose Knowledge?* (Milton Keynes, UK: Open University Press).

Haslanger, S. (1995), 'Ontology and Social Construction,' *Philosophical Topics,* 23 (2), 95–125.

—— (2002), 'On Being Objective and Being Objectified,' in Antony and Witt (eds.), *A Mind of One's Own* (Boulder, CO.: Westview Press).

Lakoff, G. (1987), *Women, Fire and Dangerous Things* (Chicago: University of Chicago Press).

MacKinnon, C. (1987), *Feminism Unmodified* (Cambridge, MA: Harvard University Press).

—— (1989), *Toward a Feminist Theory of State* (Cambridge, MA: Harvard University Press).

Papadaki, L. (2008), 'Women's Objectification and the Norm of Assumed Objectivity,' *Episteme,* 5 (2), 239–50.

Putnam, H. (1981), *Reason, Truth and History* (Cambridge: Cambridge University Press).

—— (1990), *Realism with a Human Face* (Cambridge, MA: Harvard University Press).

—— (1996a), 'Irrealism and Deconstruction,' in McCormick (ed.), *Starmaking* (Cambridge, MA: MIT Press).

—— (1996b), 'Is There Still Anything to Say about Reality and Truth?,' in McCormick (ed.), *Starmaking* (Cambridge, MA: MIT Press).

Rasmussen, D.B. (2008), 'The Importance of Metaphysical Realism for Ethical Knowledge,' *Social Philosophy and Policy,* 25 (1), 56–99.

Saul, J. (2003), *Feminism: Issues and Arguments* (Oxford: Oxford University Press).

Weedon, C. (1987), *Feminist Practice and Poststructuralist Theory* (Oxford, OK: Basil Blackwell).

10
The Nature of Mathematical Objects: Minimalism and Modality

Kristie Miller

1   Introduction

There are two influential schools of thought within the philosophy of maths. One of these, championed by Bob Hale and Crispin Wright, follows in the tradition of Fregean logicism. Within this tradition we find a common argument for the conclusion that we should be necessitarian Platonists: we should think that abstract mathematical objects exist, and necessarily so. A different school, championed by, among others, Hartry Field and Mark Colyvan, follows in the tradition of Quinean empiricism. Within this tradition we find a common argument for the conclusion that we should be contingent Platonists (or contingent fictionalists): we should think that mathematical objects exist in some, but not other worlds.

Hale, Wright, Field, and Colyvan agree about some things. They agree that mathematical discourse is truth apt, and that it is true only if the entities that it quantifies over, namely mathematical objects, exist. And they agree that if mathematical objects exist, then, necessarily, they are abstracta: they agree, for instance, that non-error-theoretic brands of nominalism, such as those that identify mathematical objects with sets of concreta, are false. Hale, Wright, and Field agree about something else. Each is, broadly speaking, a minimalist about truth, though a minimalist of a somewhat different stripe. Field is a minimalist of the Quinean disquotationalist variety. Hale and Wright endorse a more Fregean style minimalism. But they agree that truth is not a substantial property and that sentences are not true in virtue of corresponding in the appropriate way to the way the world is. While, like Field, Colyvan is working within a broadly Quinean paradigm, he is best thought of as a maximalist about truth. This difference will turn out to be important.

This chapter is interested in how disagreement about the nature of abstract mathematical objects, and about the modal status of those objects, can be traced to adoption of one or the other of the neo-Fregean or Quinean frameworks. The chapter explores the *relationship* between three arguments for the existence of mathematical objects that issue from these paradigms, it explores the *nature* of the mathematical objects that those arguments yield, and it explores the *modal status* of those objects. The three arguments in question are the argument from singular referring terms (from the neo-Fregean paradigm) the *original* indispensability argument (from the Quinean paradigm) and the *new* indispensability argument (in part from the Quinean paradigm).

This chapter seeks to show that the argument from singular referring terms and the original indispensability argument yield what we might think of as *minimal mathematical object*s: they yield a commitment to mathematical objects whose nature is ontologically thin because it is exhausted either by the totality of true sentences that jointly make up scientific theory, or by the identity conditions used to stipulatively introduce those objects via an abstraction principle. It follows then, that for a wide range of properties mathematical objects neither have, nor lack, those properties.

If successful, the argument from singular referring terms and the original indispensability argument yield apparently Platonist conclusions (at least with respect to some worlds). But in each case we might reasonably ask whether the entities to which we end up committed as so minimal that anything like true Platonism is really vindicated.

Section 2 introduces the original indispensability argument and shows why it yields the conclusion that minimal mathematical objects exist contingently. Though it is not the primary focus of the chapter, along the way I point out some of the more problematic aspects of the Quinean framework that underpins this argument. In Section 2.1, I explicate the new indispensability argument and argue that, despite its proponents' claims, the modal force of its conclusion is unclear. The new indispensability argument rejects some of the minimalist assumptions of the original Quinean framework, and ultimately, I argue, its proponents are faced with a dilemma. Either they must accept the strong naturalism that is part of the Quinean paradigm, or they must reject that claim. If they reject strong naturalism they almost entirely jettison the Quinean framework, and in doing so concede that we must in part look to metaphysics to discern our ontological commitments. As I see it, the view would then collapse into the common view that our ontology should be guided by our metaphysical commitments, and would no longer count as an indispensability argument. Given this, I take it that proponents of the new indispensability argument must endorse strong naturalism. But if they do so, I argue, they must distribute their credences between the view that mathematical objects are minimal entities, and the view that they are non-minimal entities whose nature we can in principle never come to know, and can never have reason to suppose is one way rather than another. Either our ontology, or our epistemology, then, is thin.

Section 3 outlines the neo-Fregean framework and shows why it yields a commitment to necessarily existing minimal mathematical objects. Finally, in Section 4, I explore the relationship between the neo-Fregean framework and the mathematical objects that issue from it, and the Quinean framework and the mathematical objects that issue from it. I suggest that there is a good deal in common between the two frameworks, and that this is what accounts for the fact that what we get, at the end, are minimal objects and that those who are predisposed towards Platonism have good reason to be suspicious that such objects are too minimal for the views that posit them to count as Platonist at all.

2 The Quinean framework and the indispensability argument

Mark Colyvan and Hartry Field work within a broadly Quinean framework, according to which a theory, suitably regimented into first order classical logic, is committed to all and only the entities to which the bound variables of the theory must be capable of referring in order that the claims made in the theory are true (Quine 1953, pp. 114–15). What has become known as the indispensability argument moves from the Quinean claim that we should be committed to all and only the entities quantified over by our best suitably regimented scientific theories via the claim that mathematical objects are quantified over by our best suitably regimented scientific theories, to the conclusion that we should be committed to the existence of mathematical objects (Colyvan 1998a, 1998b).[1]

It is in virtue of their commitment to the indispensability argument that Colyvan and Field embrace contingentism about the existence of mathematical objects (Colyvan 2000, Field 1993). They hold that it is contingent whether mathematical objects are dispensable to best theory in part because it is likely that our best scientific theories are, if true, contingently true. Call the totality of consistent best scientific theories of a world a *complete* scientific theory. Call any world in which mathematical objects are indispensable to complete best theory a *mathematically indispensable world,* and call any world in which mathematical objects are dispensable to complete best theory a *mathematically dispensable world.* It is likely that of the worlds in which *different* complete scientific theories are the best ones, some of those worlds are ones in which complete best scientific theory fails to quantify indispensably over mathematical objects: it is likely, that is, that there are mathematically dispensable worlds. That is likely not because we expect contingent scientific theories to posit contingent entities – that need not follow. Rather, the claim is that we have independent reason to expect that in some worlds, mathematical objects *will* be dispensable to best scientific theory, (and in other worlds they will be indispensable to theory) and therefore reason to think them contingent. Colyvan and Field agree that this is the correct dialectic, they merely disagree about whether ours is a mathematically dispensable or indispensable world.

What I call the *original* indispensability argument locates itself squarely within the Quinean framework. Both Quine (1970) and Field are disquotationalists about truth: they think that the predicate 'true' is a device for disquotation that this exhausts all that can be said about truth. For Quine, theories are sets of sentences, and what it is to exist is to be the value of a bound variable in a true sentence. Given this framework, it is relatively straightforward to see why the original indispensability argument yields the conclusion that mathematical objects exist contingently.

Quine's picture is one according to which having correctly regimented a theory into canonical language, we can read off our ontological commitments from the quantifications of that language. A theory, *T,* correctly regimented, is committed to all and only the entities required for it to be true, that is, it is committed to all and only the entities quantified over by the correctly regimented sentences of that theory. And it follows that if *T* is true, those entities exist.

For Quine, mathematical objects are *indispensable* to best theory just in case the canonical regimentation of best scientific theory quantifies over them. Then as long as we think that in some worlds best scientific theory, canonically regimented, will quantify over mathematical objects, and in other worlds best scientific theory, canonically regimented, will not quantify over mathematical objects, we should think that mathematical objects exist contingently. Since the supposition is plausible, so is the contingentist conclusion.

While there are various places to resist the conclusion to the indispensability argument,[2] much of its weight rests on the claim that there is a correct regimentation of a theory from which we can read off the ontological commitments of that theory. For Quine, the theory *T* is itself a set of sentences. We might have thought, then, that if the sentences in *T* are true we should be able to read our ontology from these true sentences. The problem is that the sentences in the un-regimented theory *T* may not be explicit about their quantificational commitments. Thus we regiment those sentences into a form that does wear their commitments on their face. Since there are various ways of regimenting sentences, each of which entails different ontological commitments, the question becomes, which regimentation is the correct one? For Quine, the answer is the canonical notation. Regimenting theories into first order logic is supposed to reveal the tacit commitments of the theory, such that if we know the theory is true, then we know, via the regimentation, which entities exist.

The problem is that it is unclear why we should think that regimenting sentences into first-order logic is a way of determining the ontological commitments of a theory. More generally, the problem is that paraphrases, even paraphrases into 'correct notation,' are cheap. Craig's theorem tells us that in a range of cases that fit the theorem, we can move from the regimentation of theory *T* which quantifies over *E*s, to an alternative regimentation *T** which is equally empirically adequate but does not quantify over *E*s. If there is no unique correct way of regimenting the sentences in *T*, then even knowing that *T* is true will not allow us to read off our ontology from *T*.

In order to navigate around some of these difficulties, Colyvan adopts a different sense of indispensability from Quine. On his view, an entity is dispensable to a theory if there exists a modification of that theory, resulting in a second theory with exactly the same observational consequences as the first, in which the entity in question is neither mentioned nor predicted, and the second theory is preferable to the first (Colyvan 1999). (Henceforth I will refer to this modification as a nominalised version of the theory.) The second theory is preferable to the first if it is more theoretically virtuous than the first.

2.1 The new indispensability argument

For Colyvan, *x* is dispensable from *T* just in case the nominalised version of *T*, *T**, is more virtuous than *T*. This means that *x* is indispensable from *T* just in case *T** is as virtuous or more virtuous than *T*. So *x*s are indispensable just in case of two empirically equivalent (best) theories, the one in which *x* figures is *at least as virtuous* as the one in which it does not. So it is not that *x*s are *indispensable* as such. Rather, they are dispensable, but dispensing with them has associated with it some costs: some other virtue is compromised, which at the very least offsets the additional virtue of ontological parsimony. We might think it is odd to hold that an entity is indispensable to a theory if there is a modification of that theory that does not mention the entity, and where that modified theory is equally virtuous. Since this new account of indispensability is clearly trading on the idea that we should prefer more virtuous theories over less virtuous ones other things being equal, it seems that Colyvan could have adopted a stronger account of indispensability according to which an entity is indispensable to a theory just in case the empirically equivalent nominalised modification of that theory is *less* virtuous than the original theory. Since this way of understanding indispensability is rather easier to work with, and I think more plausible, I will henceforth frame talk of indispensability in this way. But nothing hangs on this. Everything I say could be translated, with appropriate changes, into Colyvan's understanding of indispensability.

The idea behind this account of indispensability is that it will provide what the Quinean account could not: an independent reason to prefer one regimentation to another. (For that reason I will sometimes refer to defenders of the new indispensability argument as neo-Quinean.) That independent reason – the relative theoretical virtues of the regimentations in question – is a good reason only if we also have reason to think that the more virtuous of two empirically equivalent regimentations is more likely to be true.

The new indispensability argument recasts the first premise of the old indispensability argument so it now reads that we should be committed to all and only the entities indispensably quantified over by our best scientific theories. The second premise remains the same – mathematical objects are quantified over indispensably by our best scientific theories, so, in conclusion, we should be committed to the existence of mathematical objects. Moreover, we should think that those objects exist contingently, according to Colyvan, for the same reasons given above, namely that mathematical objects are only indispensable in some possible worlds.

There are various worries about the new indispensability argument. A general worry about the new indispensability argument is that it requires us to be able to compare and weight different virtues. We know that the nominalistic regimentation will be more parsimonious and thus more virtuous in some respects. But frequently the original regimentation, though less parsimonious in terms of entities, will be simpler and more elegant in other respects. It is a further question whether one is more explanatory. Thus there will be different trade-offs with respect to the virtues, and we need to know how to make those trade-offs in order to determine which regimentation is more virtuous. This is notoriously difficult. Even if we focus only on the virtue of simplicity, it is clear that inter-theory (or inter-regimentation) comparisons are difficult because assessment of simplicity is always relative to an inventory of basic kinds or predicates (Lewis 1983, pp. 355–68; Lewis 1986, pp. 123–24; van Fraassen 1989, pp. 41–3, 51–55; Loewer 1996, p. 109). If two theories disagree about the basic kinds, then inter-theoretic comparison of simplicity is not possible. But plausibly, the pairs of original and nominalised regimentations in question are precisely ones that disagree about the basic kinds or predicates. And matters are hardly more straightforward when we consider virtues such as elegance and explanatory power.

Even if these comparisons of virtue are possible, it is not clear that the neo-Quinean can have good grounds to think that the more virtuous of two empirically equivalent theories is more likely to be true. We cannot have evidence for that claim absent there being at least some pairs of empirically equivalent theories, such that we have independent arguments aimed at establishing the truth of one of the pair (and such that the more virtuous of the pair more often turns out to be true). That would mean having *a priori* arguments in favour of one over another of such a pair. But neo-Quineans precisely deny that we can have *a priori* arguments that show that we should be committed to this, rather than that, ontology (or theory). Field and Colyvan both accept that the only argument in favour of the existence of mathematical objects is the indispensability argument. They, like Quine, suppose that our knowledge of ontology is exhausted by empirical investigation, and consideration of the quantifications of our best scientific theories. Given this, they cannot suggest that there might be *a priori* reasons that are distinct from consideration of the theoretical virtues of the theories in question, to think that one of a pair of empirically equivalent theories is true and the other false. But then they have no grounds to claim that the more virtuous of a pair of (empirically equivalent) theories is more likely to be true, and thus no reason to suppose that indispensability is a good guide to ontology.

If one did allow that there are *a priori* reasons to embrace one rather than another of a pair of empirically equivalent theories, this would amount to abandoning much of the Quinean framework in favour of something much more like conventional metaphysics. This new framework would tell us to look to the *totality* of theories about the world to determine our ontological commitments. And that is nothing more than metaphysics as it is usually practiced. Given this, the indispensability argument need not be thought to yield a contingentist conclusion.

Suppose we discovered that in 50% of worlds, the nominalised theory was ever so slightly more virtuous than the original theory, and that in 50% of worlds the nominalised theory was vastly less virtuous than the original theory. Should we conclude that mathematical objects are indispensable in 50% of worlds and dispensable in the other 50% and thus conclude that mathematical objects exist in half of the possible worlds? Not obviously. That will depend both on just how much of a guide to truth we think virtue is, and what our other *a priori* reasons are with respect to the existence of mathematical objects. It is consistent with the discovery just outlined that we conclude that mathematical objects exist and necessarily so (but that in 50% of worlds indispensability is misleading) so long as our credence in the *a priori* claim that mathematical objects exist, if at all, of necessity, is sufficiently high and we think that the correlation between virtue and truth is sufficiently loose. Equally, it is consistent that we conclude that mathematical objects exist contingently. Thus the new indispensability argument need not push us towards one, rather than another, modalised conclusion once we allow that there are independent *a priori* reasons to prefer one theory to another.

There are also other reasons to doubt that the new indispensability argument must yield a contingentist conclusion. Colyvan is pushed towards contingentism because he thinks that it is an empirical, contingent matter what the quantifications of one's best theory are. Thus, presumably, he sees the need to leave room for the possibility that there are worlds where mathematical objects are dispensable. But it is not in any sense an empirical matter which of two empirically equivalent theories is more theoretically virtuous. While it is an open possibility that in some worlds the nominalised theory is more virtuous, and hence mathematical objects are dispensable, and in other worlds the nominalised theory is less virtuous, and hence mathematical objects are indispensable, it seems at least as likely that whatever the verdict of our pair-wise comparisons with respect to their relative virtues in one world, those considerations will carry over to every other world. Further, the process of pair-wise comparison is surely *a priori*. We need not know, for any pair of theories we are considering, which world they are theories *of*. If that is right, then we do not need to know any empirical facts about our world in order to engage in these pair-wise comparisons. And thus we have no strong reason to presume that our conclusions about the existence of mathematical objects will be modally contingent.

2.2 Minimal mathematical objects by indispensability

The original indispensability argument fairly straightforwardly yields the conclusion that mathematical objects exist, and contingently so. But what is the nature of these objects? Quineans are committed to strong naturalism, the claim that the quantificational commitments of (correctly regimented) scientific theories exhaust ontology. Moreover, given Quinean minimalism about truth, the nature of objects indispensably quantified over is exhausted by the scientific theories in which they figure. There can be no hidden metaphysical nature to objects that outstrips what our theories say about them: objects cannot have essential properties, modal properties, or categorical properties that lack causal powers. So too the nature of mathematical objects is exhausted by the true sentences of the scientific theories in which they figure.

Not altogether surprisingly, scientific theories don't have a lot to say about the nature of mathematical objects. One imagines that examination of our scientific theories will show that the number 1 precedes the number 2 in the natural number sequence, that there is a successor function, that there is a range of other functions and so forth. But a great deal about the nature of such objects must remain not just unspecified, but ontologically indeterminate. For instance, questions such as 'is Julius Caesar the number 1?' or, 'could Julius Caesar be the number 1?' are usually taken to be meaningful. But it is not at all obvious that there is any answer to these questions within a Quinean framework, since nothing in scientific theory specifies enough about the nature of number 1 to rule out that Caesar is that number.[3] Indeed, scientific theories do not even say that numbers are not spatio-temporal. To rule out such possibilities, we would need it to be part of scientific theory that the referents of numerical terms are not identical to the referents of any of the other terms mentioned by scientific theory, where that latter set of terms have causal powers and are spatio-temporally located. But as far as I can see, scientific theories will not include any such claim. Thus the original indispensability argument is committed to the existence of *minimal* mathematical objects: objects whose nature is ontologically thin in virtue of there being a whole range of properties of which it is neither true nor false that those objects instantiate those properties.

So if the original indispensability argument is sound, then we should be contingent Platonists. But, we might think, this is a cheap victory both for the Platonist, and for anyone defending contingentism since the objects we end up with are so minimal that, we might think, Platonism (and hence contingent Platonism) has not been vindicated.

Now consider the new indispensability argument. Any defender of this argument must really be a strong naturalist if her view is not to collapse into standard metaphysics. Now, I previously argued that if one is a strong naturalist one can have no reason to think that indispensability is a good guide to ontology. But let us set aside that worry and presuppose strong naturalism. Then the defender of the new indispensability argument who is a minimalist about truth will be straightforwardly committed to the view that mathematical objects are minimal: for the nature of those objects is exhausted by the true sentences of our scientific theories. If she is a maximalist about truth she can think that there could be facts about objects that outstrip what our theories say about them. But the maximalist who is a strong naturalist must give some credence to the view that objects do not have hidden natures, and thus to the view that mathematical objects are minimal. She must also give some credence to the view that objects do not have hidden natures and thus the view that mathematical objects are not minimal. But if they are not minimal, then their hidden properties are ones that we (strong naturalists) could never come to know, and could never have reason to suppose were one way rather than another. We would be radically epistemically impoverished. We might have suppose that Julius Caesar is not the number one. If mathematical objects are not minimal there is a fact of the matter as to whether he is or not, but we could never know this fact. So given the new indispensability argument, either mathematical objects are minimal, or if they are not, then our epistemology is.

3   The neo-Fregean framework: logicist arguments

Hale and Wright work within a Fregean logicist tradition. Roughly, they hold that objects are the referents of singular referring terms. Where a singular term occurs in a true statement we have *prima facie* reason to suppose that term refers, unless we have independent reason, based on the syntax of the sentence, to suppose that it does not refer, as for instance where a sentence has one of a range of grammatical forms that are known to compromise reference. Absent the sentence having such a grammatical form, we should suppose that if it is true, then we have a true extensional context, and hence that the objects referred to by the singular terms of that sentence exist. Hale and Wright argue that there are true extensional statements in which we find numerical singular terms, and hence there are numbers.

More specifically, Hale and Wright endorse three principles, which McBride (2003) calls syntactic decisiveness, referential minimalism and linguistic priority. Syntactic decisiveness is the claim that if an expression exhibits the characteristic syntactic features of a singular term, then that fact decisively determines that the expression in question has the semantic function of a singular term, namely reference. Referential minimalism is the claim that the mere fact that a referring expression figures in a true extensional atomic sentence determines that there is an item in the world to respond to the referential probing of the sentence. Finally, linguistic priority is the claim that linguistic categories are prior to ontological ones. An item belongs to the category of objects if it is possible that a singular term refer to it.

The idea is that given this neo-Fregean background we can introduce new expressions guaranteed to contain singular referring terms – that is, sentences whose syntactic structure is such that the singular terms embedded in that sentence refer if the sentence is true – and, moreover, we can know *a priori* whether these new expressions are true. We do this through so-called abstraction principles. These are stipulations that implicitly introduce some new term or operator through, most often, an equivalence relation holding between the new term and some existing expression. The idea is that the right hand side of the bi-conditional is semantically prior to the left hand side, but that the truth conditions for each side are the same. So, for instance, 'the direction of a = the direction of b iff a is parallel to b,' is an instance of such a bi-conditional which introduces 'directedness.' Since abstraction principles are supposed to guarantee that the terms introduced are singular referring terms, it follows that if the expressions in which they figure are true, then those terms refer. Moreover, we can know when the expressions in which they figure are true, since they are true just in case the right hand side of the biconditional is true (given that each side has the same truth conditions). Since there are cases where a is parallel to b, there are cases where a is the same direction as b. Thus we have successfully introduced the abstract property of having a direction.

On this model, numerical terms are introduced through the HP abstraction principle. HP states that the number of Fs equals the number of Gs iff there is a 1:1 mapping of the Fs to the Gs. Thus, if there is a 1:1 mapping of the Fs onto the Gs, then it follows that 'the number of Fs equals the number of Gs' is true, and hence that there are mathematical objects. From the fact that HP is a necessary truth combined with the fact that the right hand side of the bi-conditional is true in every world (since every world will have some such mapping) it follows that mathematical objects exist of necessity.

There are many objections to the Hale and Wright picture. One central worry is whether it is feasible to suppose that we can tell, on purely syntactic grounds, whether some sentence is of a form such that its singular terms are genuinely referring ones. Even if one could come up with a purely syntactic story about when reference is compromised,[4] it is hard to see how that story would not be the result of considering cases where we have *independent* ontological intuitions about reference failure. It is hard to see how appeal to syntax could get off the ground without at least at some point being grounded in semantics.

Unsurprisingly, other concerns centre on the various claims that form the backdrop to the view. Anyone who rejects one or more of syntactic decisiveness, referential minimalism or linguistic priority, that is, someone who we might broadly think of as a maximalist, ought to find illicit the apparent stipulation of objects into existence via abstraction principles. Whether all three stand up to scrutiny is, therefore a crucial question. Let us, however, put these kinds of worries aside. Instead, I want to consider once again, what we get in the way of mathematical objects if we buy the package we are being offered.

3.1   Minimal mathematical objects by abstraction

Hale and Wright consider themselves to be Platonists. They contend that the ontology of mathematical objects is no less ontologically meaty, as it were, than the ontology of concrete objects.

Interestingly though, abstraction principles share a good deal in common with what Stephen Schiffer (1996, pp. 151–52; 1994, 1996, 2000) calls 'something-from-nothing transformations.' Yet Schiffer accords the products of these transformations a very different ontological status from that which Hale and Wright accord to the products of abstraction principles. Let us first see just how similar the two strategies really are.

An example of a something-from-nothing transformation is that we can move from the expression 'Harry is an apple' to the equivalent expression 'Harry has the property of being an apple.' One expression is true just if the other is, thus we can infer the existence of a property, namely the property of being an apple (Schiffer 1996, p. 149). Or, to consider another more pertinent example, Schiffer suggests we move from the ordinary claim:

(1) Jupiter has four moons

through a trivial transformation to

(2) The number of moons of Jupiter is four

Through that transformation we get a commitment to the existence of the number 4. This transformation has a similar form to Hale and Wright's abstraction principle. In this case, the (rather less general) abstraction principle would be 'the number of moons of Jupiter is four iff Jupiter has four moons.' We can stipulate that the left hand side of the biconditional has the same truth conditions as the right hand side (as is evidenced by the fact that we can trivially move between them). Since the right hand side is true, we can conclude that so it the left hand side, and thus we can conclude that there is a number four.

In both cases the procedure looks very similar. But for Schiffer, the entities we get from this procedure are minimal, where what it means to be minimal in this context is to be in some sense a creation of language. These entities are introduced into our ontology through trivial transformations that take us from a sentence that involves no apparent reference to the entity in question, to a sentence that contains what appears to be a singular referring term. They are therefore language dependent entities that are not metaphysically 'meaty' the way ordinary objects that are the referents of singular referring terms are. The terms referring to minimal entities are guaranteed to have reference, and those objects' properties and nature are exhausted by the language in which they figure. For regardless of whether 'Jupiter has four moons' is true, we can be guaranteed to be able to make the trivial transformation into 'the number of moons of Jupiter is four' where the singular term in the latter seems guaranteed to be a referring singular term: all that is left unknown is whether the right hand side of the biconditional is true, and thus whether the term 'four' refers.

To put it somewhat more loosely, for Schiffer we create minimal entities just by having, as part of our language, the various sentences from which we can derive the more metaphysically loaded sentence via the trivial transformations. The sense in which these minimal entities are creations of our language seems to be analogous to the sense in which, for those like Thomasson (1999, 2003) who defend artefactual views of fiction, fictional characters are considered to be abstract objects created by authors' activities and dependent on the activities of authors and readers for their continued existence. Furthermore, just as the nature of fictional characters is exhausted by what is (or will be) true of them in the fiction as it is created by authors and readers, so too the nature of minimal entities is determined *a priori* by the linguistic practices in which we find those notions. This is very different to the nature and essential properties of ordinary objects in our ontology which seem instead to be discoverable *a posteriori*.

Nevertheless, the features that Schiffer points to as evidence of the minimalistic nature of these entities are also hallmarks of Hale and Wright's view. Given that an abstraction principle is true, it is supposed to guarantee that the terms in the left hand side of the conditional are genuine referring terms, and thus, given that the right hand side of the conditional is true, it is supposed to guarantee that the terms refer. The view that the trivial transformation guarantees that 'the number of moons of Jupiter is four' is an expression containing singular referring terms seems equivalent to Hale and Wright's syntactic decisiveness. The view that 'the number of moons of Jupiter is four' is true just in case 'Jupiter has four moons' is equivalent to referential minimalism.

Where we have biconditionals such as abstraction principles, or more generally biconditionals formed as a result of trivial transformations, there are four options are open to us. On the left-hand side of the biconditional is what appears to be a metaphysically innocent, ontologically non-committing sentence. On the right-hand side is a metaphysically loaded, ontologically committing sentence. Since both sides of the biconditional have the same truth conditions, one option is to say that the left-hand side if not metaphysically innocent. Therefore the trivial transformations are not getting something from nothing, because we didn't start with nothing. This is Hale and Wright's view. The idea is that the left-hand side of the biconditional is a reconceptualization of the right hand side, so that the left-hand side makes explicit the commitments already tacit in the right hand side. As Hale and Wright see it, nothing about the nature of abstraction suggests that the entities introduced on the left-hand side of the biconditional are minimal in the sense of being linguistic creations or mind-dependent entities that are brought into existence via the abstraction. The abstraction principle introduces a new sortal concept and a singular referring term that may be used to pick out instances of that concept. It does not, in itself, guarantee that there are instances: it does not guarantee that the singular referring term succeeds in referring. Whether the terms on the left-hand side refer depends on whether the equivalence relation in question holds with respect to the entities on which the relation is defined, namely the entities on the right-hand side of the biconditional.

The second option is to maintain that we are not getting something from nothing, because we are not getting anything: the left hand side of the biconditional is not metaphysically loaded at all. If the right-hand side of the biconditional successfully paraphrases away the entities on the left-hand side, and if the two sides have the same truth conditions, then this just shows that the left-hand side can be true without being ontologically committing (Moretti 2008).

Third, we might deny that we get something from nothing because we reject the truth of the biconditional. This is Field's view. Field (1989) holds that the HP biconditional should be read as imbedded within a conditional, thus: 'if there are mathematical objects then (the number of Fs = the number of Gs iff there is a 1:1 mapping of the Fs to the Gs).' The un-imbedded biconditional appears to be true because, according to fictionalists, it is true within the fiction of maths. But outside that fiction it is true only if there exist mathematical objects, if there do not, then the left hand side is ontologically committed in a way that the right hand side is not.

The fourth option, Schiffer's view, falls somewhere between the first and second options. On his view we do get something from nothing, but what we get is a modest ontologically minimal something. Put like this, to my mind Schiffer's view is by far the least attractive. Given that the two sides of the biconditional have the same truth conditions, it is hard to see how we could get something, even a little something, from nothing. Perhaps the most charitable interpretation is to say that we don't get something from nothing, rather, we get a minimal something, but it was a minimal something that we always had, because the language of the left-hand metaphysically innocent side of the biconditional was really already committed to the existence of – or responsible for creating – minimal entities.

Put that way, the dispute between Hale and Wright, on the one hand, and Schiffer, on the other, is a debate about how minimal the entities were with which we began *before* the trivial transformation or reconceptualization. This is where we come full circle. For there is a rather different sense from Schiffer's in which it is right to say that the entities we get are minimal. And they are minimal in much the same way that most versions of the indispensability argument yielded minimal entities. HP tells us that there exist numbers just in case there are 1:1 mappings between concepts. There are two obvious responses to HP. One is from someone who starts with a fairly metaphysically robust conception of mathematical abstracta, and then notes that it seems perfectly *epistemically* possible that there are worlds that have 1:1 mappings of concepts, but in which there do not exist mathematical objects. That is, it seems that if mathematical objects failed to exist of necessity, then there would still be 1:1 mappings of concepts. It is these intuitions that would push one towards Field's view that HP is merely conditionally true: it is not a conceptual truth precisely because we can conceive of mathematical objects and 1:1 mappings of concepts *coming apart* in some worlds. If mathematical objects exist of necessity then, of course, they never do come apart in this way. But the fact that we find it epistemically possible that we can have mappings without numbers shows that we are not dealing with a conceptual truth.

Alternatively, one might begin with a less metaphysically robust notion of mathematical objects. Perhaps mathematical objects are just whatever it is in virtue of which our mathematical statements are true. Or, perhaps they are just the *objects* in virtue of which our mathematical statements are true. To be committed to the existence of these objects is just to be committed to the existence of *whatever* it is that makes mathematical statements true: it is not to be committed to anything more substantial than that, with respect to the nature of those objects. One way to express something like this conception is to say that the identity conditions of mathematical objects are given by HP, and therefore that wherever the right hand side of the biconditional is true, mathematical objects exist. But if the identity conditions of mathematical objects are given by HP, then they leave it open just what the nature of those objects is. For instance, it has been notoriously problematic for Hale and Wright to show why, on their account, we cannot identify Julius Caesar with the number 1. For nothing about HP seems to rule out that he could be the number 1. In fact, nothing about HP tells us that mathematical objects are abstracta, or are necessarily abstracta. It tells us only that singular referring mathematical terms refer in every possible world.

In essence, it only makes sense to think of HP as a conceptual truth if one is prepared to think that mathematical objects are minimal in my, rather than Schiffer's sense. For if they are not minimal, then Field's claim that HP is merely conditionally true seems right. That should come as no surprise: HP is supposed to provide the identity conditions of mathematical objects, but HP tells us almost nothing about their nature. So if HP is a conceptual truth, then mathematical objects must be minimal objects.

4   Genuine Platonism or not?

Notice that proponents of the original indispensability argument and the argument from singular referring terms agree about a surprising amount. Quine holds that there is a unique correct regimentation of a theory into canonical notation. Since this regimentation had better not be the result of principles arising from considerations of the quantificational commitments of the different regimentations (i.e., metaphysical principles), it is syntactic features that lead one to regiment a theory one way rather than another. If syntactic features deliver the correct regimentation, then this part of the Quinean picture looks a lot like syntactic decisiveness. The Quinean then holds that ontological commitment can be read off the quantificational commitments of the regimented theory. That is to say, something like referential minimalism is true. If the sentences of the theory are true, then there are items in the world corresponding to each of the quantificational commitments of those true sentences.

In effect, both Fregeans and Quineans introduce mathematical objects by arguing that singular mathematical terms feature in true extensional contexts. One difference between the two views rests on the modal status of the expressions in which mathematical terms figure. The original indispensability argument, located within an empiricist Quinean framework, restricts itself to considering scientific theories and the ontological commitments thereof. Since entities are introduced via these theories, and since these theories will be different in different worlds, it follows that there will be different entities in different worlds (with the exception that different theories in different worlds *might* all quantify over some particular kind of object, despite the fact that each theory is contingently true). In the neo-Fregean framework, mathematical objects are introduced via abstraction principles which are conceptually necessarily true, and where the right hand side of the biconditional is true in every world. Hence mathematical objects will exist of necessity.

Given what each of these accounts have in common, it can hardly be surprising that for both, mathematical objects turn out to be minimal: their nature is exhausted either by the totality of true sentences in which they figure and that jointly make up scientific theory, or by the identity conditions used to stipulatively introduce those objects via an abstraction principle. Nevertheless, the identity conditions used to introduce mathematical objects via HP will afford those objects a different nature from the one afforded the objects introduced by being quantified over by the true sentences of scientific theory. What is striking is that since there is nothing more to their nature than that afforded them in these ways, it turns out that the mathematical objects of the Quinean have a different nature from the mathematical objects of the neo-Fregean.

Those Platonists attracted to a more metaphysically meaty conception of mathematical abstracta might find this hard to swallow. Meaty-style Platonists are likely to think that mathematical objects are non-minimal: they have a fully determinate nature. Then one might think that both HP, and facts about the quantifications of our scientific theories and the entailment thereof give us an imperfect insight into the underlying nature of the very same objects, and that where there is disagreement at most one account can be correct. But this picture is far from the one that the Quinean and neo-Fregean Platonists (as they call themselves) offer. The Quinean and the neo-Fregean posit the existence of distinct kinds of entity, albeit both call these entities mathematical objects. For they each think that the nature of mathematical objects, qua minimal objects, is exhausted by the different identity conditions that each provides.[5]

As I see it, if either the neo-Fregean or the Quinean account succeeds, we are entitled to claim that mathematical objects exist. But this is not to say that Platonism is vindicated, if Platonism is the view that there exist mathematical abstracta that have complete and determinate natures, and which are as ontologically significant as any other entity. Whether minimal mathematical objects are any improvement on no mathematical objects at all is an open question.

The new indispensability argument turns out to have much less in common with the neo-Fregean argument from singular referring terms and the original indispensability argument. It is, in the end, left open what modal conclusion we should draw from the argument. Ultimately I think the argument fails, not because I think any one particular part of the neo-Quinean package is false (though this may well be the case) but more seriously, because parts of the neo-Quinean package themselves are in tension: there is tension between the new definition of indispensability and the thesis of strong naturalism. Depending on how one attempts to resolve these tensions, one will reach different conclusions regarding both the modal status of mathematical objects, and regarding whether they are minimal or non-minimal objects. It is, however, noteworthy that all versions of neo-Quineanism that embrace strong naturalism end up embracing something very like minimalism about mathematical objects. The neo-Quinean who endorses strong naturalism and truth minimalism ends up being committed to minimal mathematical objects, while the neo-Quinean truth maximalist who endorses strong naturalism ends up being committed to it being in principle unknowable whether mathematical objects are minimal or not and to it being unknowable what their non-minimal natures are, if they have one. If Platonists found the Quinean and neo-Fregean conception of minimal mathematical objects problematic then, it seems, they will probably have the very same qualms about the neo-Quinean account.

Notes

1. The claim that we should be committed to *all* entities quantified over by our best theories has been attacked by, among others Maddy (1992, p. 280). She argues that scientific practice does not always accord with this idea.
2. For instance, one might follow Maddy (1992, p 280) in rejecting confirmational holism, thus rejecting the idea that we should be committed to *all* entities quantified over by our best theories. One might, for instance, be committed to all and only the causally efficacious entities quantified over indispensably by suitably well confirmed theories (Azzouni 1997). Alternatively, one might reject the idea that quantificational commitment is ontological commitment (Azzouni 2004, p. 54).
3. If we take 'Julius Caesar' and 'the number one' as both being names that rigidly pick out the same entity in every possible world in which they refer, then the claim that Julius Caesar is the number one could only be true if something like Lewisian contingent identity is true. Since there is presumably a world *w* in where there is a number one, and in which Julius Caesar does not exist, it cannot be that the two names co-refer in every possible world. So those who reject contingent identity have a way to argue that Julius Caesar cannot be the number one. But it is not obvious that this is entailed by scientific theory, but rather, by some views in the philosophy of language and logic.
4. See Dummett (1981) for such a story.
5. For the Quinean, mathematical objects will have different natures in different worlds since their natures are given by the scientific theories in which they figure, and different scientific theories will be true in different worlds.

Bibliography

Azzouni, J. (1997), 'Applied Mathematics, Existential Commitment and the Quine-Putnam Indispensability Thesis,' *Philosophia Mathematica* 3 (5), 193–209.
—— (2004), *Deflating Existential Consequence: A Case for Nominalism* (New York: Oxford University Press).

Colyvan, M. (1998a), 'Is Platonism a Bad Bet?,' *Australasian Journal of Philosophy* 76 (1), 115–19.

—— (1998b), 'In Defence of Indispensability,' *Philosophia Mathematica* 6 (1), 39–62.

—— (1999), 'Contrastive Empiricism and Indispensability,' *Erkenntnis*, 51 (2–3), 323–32.

—— (2000), 'Conceptual Contingency and Abstract Existence,' *Philosophical Quarterly* 50, 87–91.

—— (2001), *The Indispensability of Mathematics* (New York: Oxford University Press).

—— (2008), 'Indispensabilty Arguments in the Philosophy of Maths,' *Stanford Encyclopedia of Philosophy*, <http://plato.stanford.edu/entries/mathphil-indis/>

Dummett, M. (1981), *Frege: Philosophy of Language* (London: Duckworth).

Field, H. (1980), *Science Without Numbers: A Defence of Nominalism* (Oxford: Blackwell).

—— (1985), 'On Conservativeness and Incompleteness,' *The Journal of Philosophy* 82 (5), 239–60.

—— (1993), 'The Conceptual Contingency of Mathematical Objects,' *Mind* 102 (406), 285–99.

Hale, B. (1987), *Abstract Objects* (Oxford: Oxford University Press).

Hale, B., and Wright, C. (1992), 'Nominalism and the Contingency of Abstract Objects,' *The Journal of Philosophy* 89 (3), 111–35.

Lewis, D. (1983), 'New work for a Theory of Universals,' *Australasian Journal of Philosophy* 61, 343–77.

—— (1986), *On the Plurality of Worlds* (Oxford: Basil Blackwell).

Loewer, B. (1996), 'Humean Supervenience,' *Philosophical Topics* 24 (1), 101–27.

Maddy, P. (1990), *Realism in Mathematics* (Oxford: Oxford University Press).

—— (1992), 'Indispensability and Practice,' *Journal of Philosophy*, 89 (6), 275–89.

Mcbride, F. (2003), 'Speaking with Shadows: A Study of Neo-Logicism,' *British Journal for the Philosophy of Science* 54 (1), 103–63.

Moretti, L. (2008), 'The ontological status of minimal entities,' *Philosophical Studies* 141 (1), 97–114.

Quine, W. V. O (1960), *Word and Object* (Cambridge, MA.: MIT Press).

—— (1963), 'Identity, Ostention and Hypostasis,' in his *From a Logical Point of View* (Harper and Row), 65–79.

—— (1970), *Philosophy of Logic* (Englewood Cliffs, NJ: Prentice Hall).

Schiffer, S. (1996), 'Language Created, Language Independent Entities,' *Philosophical Topics* 24, 149–67.

—— (1994), 'A Paradox of Meaning,' *Noûs* 28, 279–324.

—— (2003), *The Things We Mean* (Oxford: Oxford University Press).

Thomasson, A. L. (1999), *Fiction and Metaphysics* (Cambridge: Cambridge University Press).

—— (2003), 'Speaking of Fictional Characters,' *Dialectica* 57 (2), 207–26.

van Fraassen, B. C. (1989), *Laws and Symmetry* (Oxford: Clarendon Press).

Wright, C. (1992), *Truth and Objectivity* (Cambridge, MA: Harvard University Press).

—— (1983), *Frege's Conception of Numbers as Objects* (Aberdeen: Aberdeen University Press).

—— (1988), 'Why Numbers Can Believably Be: A Reply to Hartry Field,' *Revue Internationale de Philosophie* 42, 425–73.

11
Are There Fundamental Intrinsic Properties?

Alyssa Ney

1   Introduction

David Armstrong once said:

> There is a certain picture of the physical world that we all cherish
> in our hearts, although in our philosophical thinking we may con-
> sider ourselves forced to abandon it in a greater or lesser degree.
> According to this picture, the physical world, including our bod-
> ies, consists of a single realm of material objects, and perhaps
> other objects, related in space and enduring and changing in time.
> Material objects have shape and size, they move or are at rest, they
> are hot or cold, hard or soft, rough or smooth, heavy or light, they
> are coloured, they may have a taste, and they may emit sounds or
> smells. These properties of objects are, on occasion, perceived; but
> objects continue to have these properties in a perfectly straight-
> forward way when, as is usually the case, the objects, or particular
> properties of the objects, are not perceived. This is the picture of
> the physical world to which we are all instinctively drawn (even
> Berkeley was). We may think that relatively abstruse evidence gar-
> nered from scientific investigations forces us to modify this pic-
> ture. But it is the picture we have gained through perception, and
> when we are not considering perception as philosophers, we do not
> think that the evidence of ordinary perception tends to overthrow
> it in any way. (1968, pp. 239–40)

This intuitive picture of the physical world tells us that there are material objects located in space and time and possessing properties like
shape, size, motion or rest (what Locke called the 'primary qualities'

and contemporary philosophers call 'intrinsic properties') as well as properties like heat, colour, or smell (what both Locke and many contemporary philosophers call 'secondary qualities'). David Lewis offers a similar picture that adds a tentative commitment to spacetime itself:

> We have geometry: a system of external relations of spatiotemporal distance between points. Maybe points of spacetime itself, maybe point-sized bits of matter or aether or fields, maybe both. And at those points we have local qualities: perfectly natural intrinsic properties which need nothing bigger than a point at which to be instantiated. (1986a, pp. ix–x)

These pictures constitute our way of understanding the physical world, in particular the physical world as it is fundamentally. As Armstrong puts it, these material bodies bearing intrinsic properties and spatial and temporal relations to each other are of what the physical world, including our bodies *consists*.

This is no doubt an intuitive picture of the physical world at its most fundamental, a picture we can make sense of, to a large extent can visualize, and one which many of us as metaphysicians indeed do cherish due to our ability to understand it. But is it accurate? Do our best fundamental physical theories confirm this picture? In particular, do our best, fundamental physical theories reveal a physical world consisting of material bodies with intrinsic properties?

Several philosophers have suggested that the answer to these questions is 'no.' When we consider the picture of fundamental reality given to us by physics, we find only extrinsic properties, relations. We do not find fundamental intrinsic properties. Here is Armstrong again:

> [I]f we look at the properties of physical objects that physicists are prepared to allow them, such as mass, electric charge, or momentum, these show a distressing tendency to dissolve into relations that one object has to another. What, then, are the things that have these relations to each other? Must they not have a non-relational nature if they are to sustain relations? But what is this nature? Physics does not tell us. (1968, p. 282)

In a more recent book, James Ladyman and Don Ross argue for a similar conclusion:

> Both [quantum mechanics] and relativity theory teach us that the nature of space, time, and matter raises profound challenges for a metaphysics that describes the world as composed of self-subsistent

individuals. In so far as quantum particles and spacetime points are individuals, facts about their identity and diversity are not intrinsic to them but rather are determined by the relational structures into which they enter.…. [A]ll the properties of fundamental physics seem to be extrinsic to individual objects. (2007, p. 151)[1]

Such claims then often lead to worries about whether or not a picture of a world fundamentally consisting of relations, with no fundamental intrinsic properties can even be made coherent. Although some philosophers are willing to accept such a conclusion and happily endorse such a metaphysical structuralism (Ladyman and Ross are a clear example; John Hawthorne (2001) also takes the idea seriously), many cling to the intuitive picture. These philosophers reluctantly end up endorsing a kind of Kantian position: material bodies have fundamental intrinsic properties, but since fundamental physical science only reveals the relations these bodies bear to each other, we can never know how things fundamentally are in themselves, what their fundamental intrinsic properties are.[2]

Our task here will be to evaluate the truth of this claim: that all of the properties of fundamental physics are extrinsic properties. As I will argue, although certainly a lot of what we might have previously thought were cases of intrinsic properties are revealed by physics to be extrinsic, this does not entail that no properties of fundamental physics are intrinsic. Mass, charge, momentum: these may all be extrinsic properties. However, this does not entail the non-existence of fundamental physical properties that are intrinsic. Indeed current, fundamental physical theories do posit intrinsic properties, and in doing so are able to support another picture of fundamental reality that we may cherish.

We will begin by making more precise the distinction between intrinsic and extrinsic properties that this debate presupposes. The next sections will investigate the status of fundamental intrinsic properties in quantum mechanics. To make the discussion somewhat manageable and compact, I have put off the question of intrinsic properties in relativity theory and our theories of fundamental interactions to another day, though certainly there are more places to look if one wants to know if there exist fundamental intrinsic properties.[3]

2 Intrinsic/extrinsic

No better synopsis of the intrinsic/extrinsic distinction could be provided than this one from David Lewis:

We distinguish *intrinsic* properties, which things have in virtue of the way they themselves are, from *extrinsic* properties, which they have in virtue of their relations or lack of relations to other things. (1986b, p. 61)

This, I take it, is the basic sense of intrinsic property with which most philosophers work. It is the historical descendent of Locke's notion of a primary quality (1690, II.viii. 9–24) and the central notion of intrinsic-ness with which this chapter is concerned. Intrinsic properties are ways things are in themselves, not ways they are with respect to other things. As Lloyd Humberstone puts it, 'an intrinsic property is one whose pos-session just depends on the possessor itself' (1993, p. 239).

When a property is intrinsic, this is a feature of the property itself; it is not a feature of the way we think about the property. Sometimes it is argued that all of the properties of science fail to be intrinsic because we only come to know or think about them by way of their structural or causal profiles. In particular, in science we learn about properties by learning about the patterns in which they are instanti-ated, and how these instantiations affect our senses and the instan-tiations of other properties. So, it is argued, the properties of science are relational.[4]

It is worth emphasizing that there is another distinction lurking in this argument, however it is not the distinction between intrinsic and extrinsic properties with which we are concerned. And so, such general arguments about 'science' cannot give us good reason to think that no fundamental physical property is intrinsic. What arguments like this one rely on is a distinction not between two kinds of properties (intrin-sic and extrinsic), but rather a distinction between two ways of think-ing about properties (relationally and non-relationally). In particular, the argument's suggestion is that in science, all properties are thought of under relational descriptions. Note though that this does not entail that the properties of science are not intrinsic. Frank Jackson makes the point well:

When physicists tell us about the properties they take to be fun-damental, they tell us about what these properties *do.* This is no accident. We know about what things are like essentially through the way they impinge on us and on our measuring instruments. It does not follow from this that the fundamental properties of current physics...are causal cum relational ones. It may be that our terms for the fundamental properties pick out the properties they do via the causal relations the properties enter into, but that at least some of the properties so picked out are intrinsic. (1997, p. 23)

Jackson moves from here to worry that still we might not know these intrinsic properties' 'intrinsic nature' (p. 24). The worry it seems is that we can only come to know these properties under relational descriptions and never under a non-relational description. The discussion below will likely give us reason to doubt this claim. However, even if this is right, the point remains that the properties of science are not thereby extrinsic. To see this, suppose for a moment that shapes are intrinsic. The planet Mercury has a particular shape. This is an intrinsic property of Mercury. However, we may think about this property in a relational way. We may think about it relationally under the description 'the shape of the first planet from the Sun.' Even if we only thought of the shape of Mercury under this relational description, this would not entail that the shape was extrinsic, that it was a property that Mercury had in virtue of its relations to other things. The shape's intrinsicness or extrinsicness is a fact independent of how we think about it.

To reiterate, just because we may think about a property in terms of its relations to other things (us, the Sun, etc.), this does not entail that the property itself is extrinsic. So an argument that all of the properties of fundamental physics are extrinsic starting from a premise about how we learn about those properties will be a *non-sequitur*. The fact that we often come to learn about these properties by virtue of their relations to us or patterns of instantiation is not enough to establish the extrinsicness of these properties. To see whether the properties of fundamental physics are all extrinsic properties, one must instead consider whether these properties tell us how those objects are in themselves, or just merely how they are with respect to other things.

3 Intrinsic properties in quantum mechanics

There are several interesting aspects of quantum mechanics that have been thought to pose a threat to the existence of fundamental intrinsic properties. In this section, we will examine just one kind of argument philosophers seem to have in mind when it is suggested that quantum mechanics commits us to the denial of fundamental intrinsic properties.[5] To my knowledge, such an argument has never been carefully formulated, so the first task will be to spell out an argument that appears to have some plausible validity starting from premises about important consequences of quantum mechanics. The argument we will consider is motivated by the fact that quantum mechanics permits systems to evolve into what, following Schrödinger (1935), are known as *entangled states*. Let's begin by getting clear on this central notion of entanglement.

3.1 Entanglement

The quantum state of a system is the system's wavefunction (Ψ). Here, we will use standard bracket (or Dirac) notation to express quantum states. For example, the quantum state of a system of just one particle that is at location (4, 0, 0) will be represented by:

$$\Psi_1 = |(4, 0, 0)>$$

And the quantum state of a system of just one particle that has spin up in the x direction will be represented by:

$$\Psi_2 = |\text{x-spin up}>$$

We can also use the Dirac notation to represent states of multi-particle systems. Subscripts will then be used to indicate which part represents the state of which particle. For example, if we want to represent the state of a two particle system in which particle 1 is at location (4, 0, 0) and particle 2 is at location (7, 0, 0), we will write:

$$\Psi_3 = |(4, 0, 0)>_1 |(7, 0, 0)>_2$$

And the state of a two particle system in which particle 1 has x-spin in the up direction and particle 2 has x-spin in the down direction will be represented by:

$$\Psi_4 = |\text{x-spin up}>_1 |\text{x-spin down}>_2$$

Using this notation, we can represent the states of systems of any number of particles.

However, let us briefly return to discuss single particle states. The most interesting thing about quantum mechanics is that it allows for systems to evolve into states that are superpositions; for example, the state in which there is a single particle in a superposition of being at location (4, 0, 0) and being at location (7, 0, 0). This state will be represented in the following way:

$$\Psi_5 = \sqrt{\tfrac{1}{2}}\ |(4, 0, 0)> + \sqrt{\tfrac{1}{2}}\ |(7, 0, 0)>$$

It is also possible for a system to be in a superposition of spin states. For example, an electron coming out of a z-spin detector will often be said to be in a superposition of having x-spin up and x-spin down:

$$\Psi_6 = \sqrt{\tfrac{1}{2}} \,|\text{x-spin up}\rangle + \sqrt{\tfrac{1}{2}} \,|\text{x-spin down}\rangle$$

How to understand superpositions like these is one of the central controversies in the philosophy of quantum mechanics. However, there are several things one can say about states like these that are almost entirely uncontentious.

Let us focus on this last case. To say that a system is in this quantum state is not to say that the particle has x-spin up, nor is it to say that it has x-spin down. It is also not to say that particle has both x-spin up and x-spin down; nor, is it to say that the particle has neither x-spin up nor x-spin down. One thing that is true of a particle that is in this quantum state is that if the particle's x-spin is measured, then there is a 0.5 chance that it will be found to have x-spin up. And if the particle's x-spin is measured, there is a 0.5 chance that it will be found to have x-spin down. The probability is 0 that the particle will be found to have any other x-spin. These probabilities are given by the square of the coefficients in the representation of the quantum state. When a system is not in a superposition of x-spin, but rather the system's quantum state does entail that it has one or the other of x-spin up or x-spin down, then one says that it is in an *eigenstate* of x-spin, and similarly for other properties of quantum systems. Ψ_2 is an eigenstate of x-spin. Ψ_1 is an eigenstate of position.

So, for the general case, if a system of one particle is in a superposition of being in state A and state B such that its quantum state may be represented in the following way:

$$\Psi = a\,|A\rangle + b\,|B\rangle$$

Then although it is false that this quantum state represents the particle as being in state A, and false that it represents the particle as being in state B, or both state A and state B, or neither state A nor state B, this quantum state does represent the following fact. If one measures the system to determine whether it is in state A or state B, there is a chance of a^2 that the particle will be found in state A, and there is a chance of b^2 that the particle will be found in state B.

All of this so far has been uncontentious. There is one last thing however that must be mentioned that is a matter of controversy. A nearly universal view is that a system's wavefunction encodes complete information about it with respect to the property in question. For example, if a system is correctly described as being in Ψ_5, there is nothing more that can truly be said about its position. The particle has a 0.5 chance that it will be found at (4, 0, 0) and a 0.5 chance that it will be found at (7, 0, 0), and that is all. And if a system is correctly described as being in Ψ_6, there is nothing more that can be said about its x-spin. Perhaps systems may evolve out of superpositions, into states that are eigenstates of position or x-spin, but when they are in these superpositions, their positions or x-spin as the case may be, are not determinately here or there, up or down. To adopt the terminology of Tim Maudlin (2007), this is to say that the quantum state is *ontologically complete*. This is the case according to most contemporary, realist[6] approaches to quantum mechanics, but not all. In particular, we will talk a bit about the Bohmian approach to quantum mechanics below. Bohmians say that in the case of position, the quantum state is not a complete representation of the state of the particles. According to this view, particles always have determinate positions, even if the system's quantum state is a superposition of position.[7] Set this aside for now. For most approaches to quantum mechanics, the quantum state is a complete characterization of the system at a time. It is an ontologically complete characterization of the particles' position, x-spin, or what have you.

Entangled states are superpositions involving multi-particle systems. For example, we might consider a system of two particles that are entangled with respect to their position:

$$\Psi_7 = \sqrt{1/2}\ |(4, 0, 0)\rangle_1 |(7, 0, 0)\rangle_2 + \sqrt{1/2}|(7, 0, 0)\rangle_1 |(4, 0, 0)\rangle_2$$

What is true of particles in such a state? On the assumption that the quantum state is ontologically complete, it is not true that either particle has a determinate location, either of being at (4, 0, 0) or of being at (7, 0, 0). However, it is true that if one were to successfully measure the positions of the particles, they would be found in one of the following two states. There is a 0.5 chance that particle 1 would be found at (4, 0, 0) and particle 2 would be found at (7, 0, 0). And there is a 0.5 chance that particle 1 would be found at (7, 0, 0) and particle 2 would be found at (4, 0, 0). And these are the only possibilities. It is natural to conclude from this fact that although neither particle in Ψ_7 has a determinate position, the relation between the positions of the two particles is determinate. For, there is a probability 1 that the particles will be found at a distance of 3 from each other.

Particles can be in entangled states of position, momentum, spin, and so on. Many philosophers have tried to parlay these facts about entangled systems into a case against the existence of fundamental intrinsic properties. To see how this goes, we will use the example of the singlet state, to be explained momentarily. The reason we will use this state for the discussion is the following. As I've said, there exist entangled states of particle positions. However, most philosophers do not think of positions as intrinsic properties. If anything, they are relations objects bear to spacetime, or if one is a relationalist about spacetime, then relations objects bear to other objects. So, considering entanglements of position will not show us that objects fail to have intrinsic properties of the kind we thought they had. The singlet state on the other hand involves the spin properties of particles. These are the kind of properties that philosophers often take to be intrinsic. So, if we can show that quantum mechanics reveals that all of the spin properties of objects are extrinsic, this will be useful for formulating an argument against the existence of intrinsic properties in quantum mechanics.

The singlet state can be represented in the following way:

$$\Psi_{singlet} = \sqrt{\tfrac{1}{2}} \; |\text{x-spin up}\rangle_1 |\text{x-spin down}\rangle_2 - \sqrt{\tfrac{1}{2}} |\text{x-spin down}\rangle_1 |\text{x-spin up}\rangle_2$$

When two particles are in the singlet state, neither can individually be said to have a determinate x-spin. So even if spin properties like x-spin up or x-spin down are intrinsic, they are not the sort of properties that particles in states like the singlet state possess. It is rather only the case (given the ontological completeness of the quantum state) for particle 1 that it has the extrinsic property of having the opposite x-spin of particle 2, and for particle 2 that it has the extrinsic property of having the opposite x-spin of particle 1. At best, the spin properties attributed to particles by virtue of their entering into entangled spin states are extrinsic spin properties.[8]

3.2 From entanglement to the denial of intrinsic properties

The argument from the existence of entangled states to the universal denial of intrinsic properties in quantum mechanics has three parts. First, one establishes that there exist certain entangled states, and that such states characterize systems merely in terms of extrinsic properties. Second, one argues that the initial quantum state of all the particles in the universe is an entangled state. Finally, one argues that systems never evolve out of entangled states – once entangled, always entangled.

We have already seen examples of entangled states. The existence of such states has been confirmed repeatedly by experiment since they were initially predicted to be a consequence of quantum mechanics. On those approaches that take the quantum state of a system to be complete, systems in entanglements of x-spin will only have extrinsic x-spin properties, those in entanglements of momentum will only have extrinsic momenta, and so on. We noted above that most approaches to quantum mechanics do take the quantum state of a system to be complete. So, according to these views, systems that are entangled with respect to all of their quantum mechanical properties will fail to have any such intrinsic properties. An exception to the completeness view we noted above was the Bohmian approach. Here by contrast, the quantum state of a system is not ontologically complete because on this view, particles always have determinate positions, even if the system is entangled with respect to position. Nevertheless, even the Bohmian approach can allow that quantum mechanics only allows entangled particles extrinsic properties since positions are not intrinsic properties.

It is common to argue for the next step, that the initial quantum state of all the particles in the universe is an entangled state, by appealing to the Big Bang as the initial state of the universe.[9] This initial state was one so enormously entangled that it is correctly described as one that is a superposition of particle cardinality. The initial quantum state is one in which particles are entangled with respect to all of their properties, indeed even their properties of identity and diversity.[10] Combining the first and second steps, we are led to the conclusion that quantum mechanics does not ascribe intrinsic properties in the initial quantum state of the universe.

The question is then whether systems ever evolve out of entangled states into eigenstates of spin, momentum, or what have you so that they may be accurately described as instantiating fundamental intrinsic properties. If we just consult the Schrödinger equation, the central dynamical law of quantum mechanics, the answer would appear to be 'no.' There is nothing about the law analytically ruling out the evolution of systems from entangled states into states that are separable with respect to position, x-spin, etc.[11] Nevertheless, given the universe's initial state, the actual likelihood that a system will ever evolve via the Schrödinger equation into anything like separable state is (on any reasonable probability distribution) zero.[12] Several approaches to quantum mechanics take the Schrödinger equation to be a dynamical law that is never violated. This is true of both the Everett or many worlds approach to quantum mechanics as well as Bohmian mechanics.

However, there exist other approaches to quantum mechanics according to which the Schrödinger equation is at times violated. And this may allow particles to evolve out of entangled states of one or another property, into eigenstates of that property. According to the traditional (sometimes called the 'orthodox') approach to quantum mechanics advocated by von Neumann (1955), systems evolve linearly according to the Schrödinger equation until a measurement on the system takes place at which point systems in a superposition will collapse onto one or another eigenstate. The Schrödinger equation is also at times violated according to the approach to quantum mechanics advocated by Ghirardi et al. (1986). According to Ghirardi et al., systems evolve out of superpositions spontaneously with a probability proportional to the complexity of the system. So, it looks like on what are often called 'collapse approaches' to quantum mechanics, systems can evolve into eigenstates in which particles are correctly described as individually instantiating intrinsic properties like spin.

Now, it is often pointed out (for example, in Schaffer forthcoming) that even if systems do sometimes evolve out of entanglements of one or another property, quantum mechanics entails that they will very quickly evolve right back into them, and so even if particles do seem to have fundamental intrinsic properties, these instantiations never last for very long. This is true, however, this response does not seem satisfactory if we are interested in giving an argument for the claim that quantum mechanics *never* ascribes intrinsic properties to particles.

What instead needs to be noted is that even on a plausible collapse approach, systems never quite evolve completely out of entanglements.[13] Rather, what happens in collapse is that systems evolve into states which are very nearly eigenstates, but only very nearly. To see why, let's return back to consider the simple entangled state of position:

$$\Psi_7 = \sqrt{\tfrac{1}{2}} \,|\, (4, 0, 0)>_1 |\, (7, 0, 0)>_2 + \sqrt{\tfrac{1}{2}}|\, (7, 0, 0)>_1 |\, (4, 0, 0)>_2$$

Now, if it were the case that such a state could evolve into an eigenstate of position, then this would mean it could collapse into one or the other of Ψ_8 or Ψ_9:

$$\Psi_8 = \,|\,(4, 0, 0)>_1 |\,(7, 0, 0)>_2$$
$$\Psi_9 = \,|\,(7, 0, 0)>_1 |\,(4, 0, 0)>_2$$

And if this were the case then we could know for sure where the particles were; because they would each have a determinate position. However, this cannot be what happens in a collapse, for if it were then this would entail a very high momentum and hence energy for the particles that would wildly violate conservation principles. Instead, upon collapse, the system evolves into one or the other of Ψ_{10} or Ψ_{11}:

$$\Psi_{10} = \sqrt{p}\ |(4, 0, 0)>_1|(7, 0, 0)>_2 + \sqrt{(1-p)}|(7, 0, 0)>_1|(4, 0, 0)>_2$$
$$\Psi_{11} = \sqrt{(1-p)}\ |(4, 0, 0)>_1|(7, 0, 0)>_2 + \sqrt{p}|(7, 0, 0)>_1|(4, 0, 0)>_2,$$

where p is very close to, but not equal to 1.

Why would the system's collapsing completely onto an eigenstate for position entail an objectionably high energy? Consider Heisenberg's uncertainty principle. This entails that the determinateness of a system's position and energy states are related in such a way that as the indeterminateness of the position gets very small, the indeterminateness of the system's energy gets very large. If the system were in an eigenstate of position (i.e., a state in which the indeterminateness with respect to position of the particles is zero), then the indeterminateness in its energy would be infinite. This then would make it extremely likely that the system's energy is extremely high, as there are far more ways for it to be very high than low. So, the collapse of systems completely into eigenstates of position would entail enormous violations of energy conservation.[14]

What all of this entails is that entangled systems stay entangled. This is true whether we are considering a view according to which quantum states collapse or one according to which they do not. And now we can conclude the argument of this section. Since the universe began in a state in which all particles were entangled, and does not evolve out of entanglement, and since quantum mechanics does not attribute intrinsic properties to systems in entangled states, quantum mechanics does not attribute intrinsic properties to systems in our universe.

3.3   Realism about the wavefunction

Although this argument appears compelling, I want to show here that its conclusion should not be accepted. Indeed despite the availability of such an argument, all mainstream, realist approaches to quantum mechanics do take it that quantum mechanics attributes intrinsic properties to systems in our universe, and so the argument of the previous section is unsound.

The problem with the argument is not in its claims regarding the pervasiveness of entanglement, but rather with its first step. It is not correct to say that quantum mechanics characterizes systems in entangled states completely in terms of extrinsic properties. We have seen good reason to accept that quantum mechanics will not attribute intrinsic properties to particles in entangled states, but on any mainstream, realist approach, quantum mechanics will attribute intrinsic properties to something else: the wavefunction.

Up to now, I have been speaking as if the wavefunction is some linguistic or mathematical entity used merely to describe the state of a system in quantum mechanics. However, what the phenomenon of entanglement shows us is that we must take the wavefunction to be more than this; indeed, we must accept it as a real element in our ontology. The initial case for wavefunction realism is stated well by Peter Lewis:

> The wavefunction figures in quantum mechanics in much the same way that particle configurations figure in classical mechanics; its evolution over time successfully explains our observations. So absent some compelling argument to the contrary, the prima facie conclusion is that the wavefunction should be accorded the same status that we used to accord to particle configurations. (2004, p. 714)

There is also an argument for taking the wavefunction with ontological seriousness that is relatively simple. It can be summarized in the following way:

1. There exist entangled states.
2. These states cannot be adequately characterized as states of something inhabiting a three-dimensional space, but rather must be characterized as spread out in a higher-dimensional configuration space.
3. So, (from 1 and 2) there is something of the kind that must be characterized as spread out in a higher-dimensional configuration space: call this the 'wavefunction.'
4. So, the wavefunction exists.[15]

The crucial premise is the second one. To see why, let us return to the example of the entangled state of position:

$$\Psi_7 = \sqrt{\tfrac{1}{2}} \ |(4, 0, 0)\rangle_1 |(7, 0, 0)\rangle_2 + \sqrt{\tfrac{1}{2}} |(7, 0, 0)\rangle_1 |(4, 0, 0)\rangle_2$$

Could this be the state of something existing in a three-dimensional space? One thing you might think is that this is a state that is had by an object spread out in three-dimensional space in virtue of instantiating certain intensities at various locations. Then we can capture what is represented by Ψ_7 by taking there to be two peaks of intensity 0.5 at each of the two locations, (4, 0, 0) and (7, 0, 0), in three-dimensional space. In Figure 1, this is illustrated using grey peaks for the intensities of particle 1, and white peaks for those of particle 2.

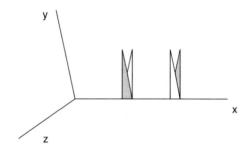

Figure 1   Representation of Ψ7 in three-dimensional space.

The trouble with trying to view quantum states in this way, as states of something spread out in three-dimensional space, can be seen by considering an empirically distinguishable state that we may call 'Ψ_{12}':

$$\Psi_{12} = \sqrt{\tfrac{1}{2}} \,|(4, 0, 0)>_1|(4, 0, 0)>_2 + \sqrt{\tfrac{1}{2}} \,|(7, 0, 0)>_1|(7, 0, 0)>_2$$

Ψ_{12} is clearly a distinct quantum state from Ψ_7. Unlike Ψ_7, if we try to test whether this state obtains, we will find particles not at distinct locations three units apart, but instead two particles at the same location. However, try to understand Ψ_{12} as the state of something spread out in a three-dimensional space and we wind up being unable to distinguish it from Ψ_7.[16] And this is in general the case. Empirically distinct entangled states cannot be adequately distinguished unless they are understood to be states of something spread out in a higher-dimensional, what is called 'configuration space.' Once we modify our ontology and consider the quantum state to be the state of something in this configuration space, Ψ_7 and Ψ_{12} can be seen clearly to be distinct.

The configuration space that is used to represent quantum states is standardly introduced as having 3N dimensions, where N is the number of particles in the system. The first three coordinates in the configuration space may be taken to correspond to x, y, and z coordinates for particle 1, the second three coordinates in the configuration space correspond to x, y, and z coordinates for particle 2, and so on. Now, Ψ_7 can be taken as describing intensities at locations (4, 0, 0, 7, 0, 0) and

(7, 0, 0, 4, 0, 0) in the six-dimensional configuration space. Figure 2 illustrates this.

In configuration space, Ψ_{12} constitutes a completely different state that can be represented this way (see Figure 3).

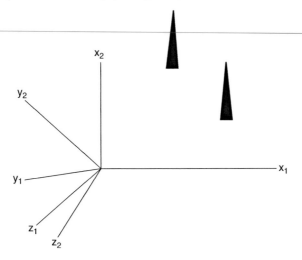

Figure 2 Representation of Ψ7 in configuration space.

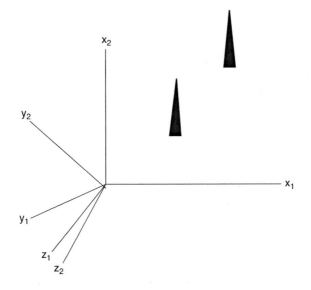

Figure 3 Representation of Ψ12 in configuration space.

For a system in Ψ_{12}, non-zero intensities in the configuration space occur only at locations (4, 0, 0, 4, 0, 0) and (7, 0, 0, 7, 0, 0).

So, entangled states can only be distinguished if we assume they are states of something with intensities in a higher-than-three-dimensional configuration space. This is the quantum wavefunction.

As David Albert puts it, criticizing the anti-realism and confusion pervasive in early attempts to understand quantum mechanics:

> [I]t has consequently been essential to the project of digging one's way *out* of those sorts of confusion, it has been essential (that is) to the project of quantum-mechanical *realism* (in *whatever* particular form it takes – Bohm's theory, or modal theories, or Everettian theories, or theories of spontaneous localization [GRW]), to learn to think of wave functions as physical objects *in and of themselves.* (1996, p. 277)

But what kind of entity is the wavefunction? The wavefunction is understood by most authors (including Albert) as a field. John Bell is extremely clear on this point, saying:

> No one can understand this theory until he is willing to think of Ψ [the wavefunction] as a real objective field rather than just a 'probability amplitude.' Even though it propagates not in 3-space but in 3N-space. (1987, p. 128)

What it means to characterize the wavefunction as a field is simply to take it to be an entity that pervades all of space and has amplitude and phase at each point in this space (in this case, configuration space). These amplitudes were represented by peaks on the last two diagrams, and they are intrinsic properties of a quantum mechanical entity whose instantiations are located at points.[17]

The phenomenon of quantum entanglement shows us that we cannot represent quantum systems as systems of particles instantiating intrinsic properties. But this is only half of the story. For recognition of quantum entanglement shows us that in order to capture the complete facts of entanglement we must accept a wavefunction ontology. Once we do so, we see that quantum systems do instantiate intrinsic properties. However these are not intrinsic properties of the particles, but intrinsic properties of the wavefunction – its phase and amplitude at points. So, it is wrong to think that quantum mechanics shows us that there are no fundamental intrinsic properties.

One might be dissatisfied with this response to the argument of the previous section and think that it misses the point of the argument against fundamental intrinsics. The thought is that even if it is the case that quantum mechanics allows for the instantiation of some intrinsic properties, those instantiated by the wavefunction, still there is an important sense in which we learn from quantum mechanics that the fundamental properties of *our* world, those that are instantiated by those things that most fundamentally constitute us, are all of them extrinsic. For, the wavefunction is something external to us and the physical world we inhabit. Indeed it is something altogether external to our shared, three-dimensional physical world, occupying its own 3N-dimensional configuration space. Therefore, it is consistent with the above points about wavefunction realism, that the fundamental properties of our world, those that constitute things like people, tables, chairs, and planets, are all extrinsic properties. And so we do indeed have to revise our intuitive picture of the world as one that involves fundamentally the instantiation of intrinsic properties.

This is a tempting way of viewing the lessons of quantum mechanics for fundamental ontology. Indeed this seems to be the most straightforward way to understand the ontology of the Bohmian approach to quantum mechanics. What the theory posits is two distinct kinds of entities inhabiting two separate spaces. There is the wavefunction inhabiting a 3N-dimensional space, instantiating its own intrinsic properties of phase and amplitude, and there are particles inhabiting a distinct three-dimensional space that are fundamentally attributed nothing but positions in that space.

There are a couple of things that need to be noted about this view, and its putative consequences for the constitution of people, tables, chairs, and the other inhabitants of what we think of as our physical world. First, Bohmian mechanics is only one of several promising approaches to quantum mechanics. Although it is does seem plausible to take it to motivate this kind of two-world, two-kind-of-entity ontology, on nearly all other realist approaches to quantum mechanics, particles are typically regarded as non-fundamental and reducible to elements of the wavefunction, not separate entities in a separate space. This kind of one-world picture of quantum mechanics is elaborated by David Albert (1996) and Peter Lewis (2004) with respect to collapse approaches for quantum mechanics, and David Wallace (2003) who endorses an Everettian no-collapse view. If one thinks everything reduces to the wavefunction, then the physical world is the world of the wavefunction. There is no separate three-dimensional space. The only space that exists is 3N-dimensional and does contain instantiations of fundamental intrinsic properties. So in particular, people like you and I, tables, chairs, and planets are all constituted fundamentally by an entity (the wavefunction) instantiating intrinsic properties.

There are many reasons to prefer this latter picture, as opposed to the 'two-world' picture in which the wavefunction is a separate, wholly distinct entity from the particles that make up physical objects. There is, as always in matters of ontology, the pull from Ockham's razor to reduce, in this case reduce the particle ontology to the wavefunction. However, a more relevant consideration for our purposes arises from the fact that even on a two-world picture like the one that seems implied by Bohmian mechanics, the properties of physical objects like people, tables, and chairs, those properties that seem to make these objects what they are, are all ultimately grounded in the properties of the wavefunction, not the properties of the particles in the three-dimensional space. Even on a picture in which particles are separate from the wavefunction, it is states of the wavefunction that determine their behaviour over time.[18] The particles only have positions; they have no other causally relevant features. So, all causal features you or I have constituting our ability to affect the world, that is, do what it is that we do, are ultimately grounded in features of the wavefunction, not in any basic features of the particles, that is, their positions. As a result, there does not seem to be any legitimate sense in which one can accept the wavefunction ontology of quantum mechanics and yet still maintain that the physical world of which you and I are members is a world lacking in fundamental intrinsic properties. Even if what we perceive as the physical world is not ultimately constituted (in a mereological sense of 'constituted') by the instantiation of intrinsic properties, its entire character results from the instantiation of intrinsic properties. So, it is false that quantum mechanics gives us reason to reject that intuitive picture according to which the physical world fundamentally involves the instantiation of intrinsic properties.

4 Conclusion

In this chapter, I have tried to show that despite an interesting argument to the contrary, at least some properties of fundamental physics are intrinsic. And these are indeed the properties that ground the causal powers of material objects in our world. Thus, we have no reason at this time to fear that we cannot know the intrinsic natures of things, how they are in themselves.

Notes

Thanks to David Albert, Allan Hazlett, Barry Loewer, and Ted Sider for enormously helpful discussion and/or comments on earlier drafts.

1. Similarly negative verdicts regarding the status of intrinsic properties in fundamental physics are discussed by Blackburn (1990), Jackson (1998), Langton (1998), Stoljar (2001), and Lewis (2009).
2. Discussion of such sceptical arguments can be found in my (2007).
3. My own view is that the metrical and topological properties attributed to spacetime by relativity theory are exemplary cases of fundamental intrinsic properties. Our theories of the fundamental interactions, the gauge theories of e.g., electromagnetism and quantum chromodynamics, also posit intrinsic properties.
4. This is partly how David Lewis reasons in his (2009).
5. There is at least one other kind of argument challenging the existence of intrinsic properties in quantum mechanics that I will not discuss. Arguments of this kind appeal to the alleged existence in quantum mechanics of 'identical particles,' and attempt to deny the existence of particles' intrinsic natures. French and Krause (2007) is a recent book discussing such arguments.
6. By a realist approach, I mean one that takes the theory (in this case, quantum mechanics) to be providing a true description of the world independent of us as observers. There are other approaches to quantum mechanics that would plausibly be considered mainstream (in that they are endorsed by many physicists) that aren't realist. For example, many physicists prefer an information-theoretic understanding of quantum mechanics according to which the theory doesn't describe the world independent of us as observers, but rather the evolution of our states of knowledge as we perform experiments. As this is an essay about the ontology of our fundamental physical theories, I will ignore these sorts of approaches.
7. To foreshadow the conclusion that will be reached below, this is because the quantum state Ψ on the Bohmian approach does not describe the state of the particle(s) at all, but the state of something else.
8. Some readers will be aware that particles in superpositions of x-spin are often said to simultaneously be in eigenstates of z-spin. At this point, I am only trying to motivate the claim that entities entangled with respect to one kind of property (here, x-spin) lack intrinsic properties of that kind. In the next section, we will consider reasons to doubt the claim that entities are ever in eigenstates of any properties.
9. A similar premise is used by Jonathan Schaffer (forthcoming) in defence of his view that the universe as a whole, as opposed to its individual particle parts, is what is fundamental. We will discuss a position that is similar in some ways to Schaffer's.
10. Some take this to indicate that this is an initial state in which the number of particles is zero.
11. David Albert (p.c.) mentions the possibility, consistent with Schrödinger evolution, of the time-reverse of a process in which a system enters an entangled state from an initial state that is unentangled (separable).

12. Given the fact that the Schrödinger equation is deterministic, what is being described here is a subjective likelihood.
13. This is what leads to what is often called 'the tails problem' for collapse theories.
14. Analogous considerations lead to the conclusion that particles in superpositions of spin (x-spin or z-spin, etc.) will never completely collapse into their respective eigenstates.
15. A similar kind of argument is given by Peter Lewis (2004). David Albert (1996) also endorses the conclusion, following John Bell (1987).
16. The reader can check this against Figure 1.
17. See also Barry Loewer (1996) for discussion of this point, that these amplitudes are intrinsic properties of the wavefunction.
18. In Bohmian mechanics, there are two fundamental laws: the Schrödinger equation that describes the evolution of wavefunction as a function of its prior state, and the guidance equation that describes the evolution of the particle positions as a function of the prior state of the wavefunction. There is no fundamental law describing the evolution of anything as a function of earlier states of the particles (Goldstein 2006).

Bibliography

Albert, D. Z. (1996), 'Elementary Quantum Metaphysics,' in Cushing, Fine, and Goldstein (eds.), *Bohmian Mechanics and Quantum Theory: An Appraisal* (Dordrecht, The Netherlands: Kluwer).

Armstrong, D. M. (1968), *A Materialist Theory of the Mind* (London: Routledge and Kegan Paul).

Bell, J. (1987), *Speakable and Unspeakable in Quantum Mechanics* (Cambridge: Cambridge University Press).

Blackburn, S. (1990), 'Filling in Space,' *Analysis* 50, 62–5.

French, S. and Decio K. (2007), *Identity in Physics: A Historical, Philosophical, and Formal Analysis* (Oxford: Oxford University Press).

Ghirardi, G., Rimini, A., and Weber, T. (1986), 'Unified Dynamics for Microscopic and Macroscopic Systems,' *Physical Review D* 34, 470–91.

Goldstein, S. (2006), 'Bohmian Mechanics,' *Stanford Encyclopedia of Philosophy,* http://plato.stanford.edu/entries/qm-bohm/.

Hawthorne, J. (2001), 'Causal Structuralism,' *Philosophical Perspectives* 15, 361–78.

Humberstone, I. L. (1996), 'Intrinsic/Extrinsic,' *Synthese* 108, 205–67.

Jackson, F. (1998), *From Metaphysics to Ethics: A Defence of Conceptual Analysis* (Oxford: Oxford University Press).

Ladyman, J. and Ross, D. (2007), *Every Thing Must Go: Metaphysics Naturalized* (Oxford: Oxford University Press).

Langton, R. (1998), *Kantian Humility: Our Ignorance of Things in Themselves* (Oxford: Oxford University Press).

Lewis, D. (1986a), *Philosophical Papers Volume II* (Oxford: Oxford University Press).

—— (1986b), *On the Plurality of Worlds* (Oxford: Blackwell).

—— (2009), 'Ramseyan Humility,' in Braddon-Mitchell and Nola (eds.), *Conceptual Analysis and Philosophical Naturalism* (Cambridge, MA: MIT Press), pp. 203–22.

Lewis, P. (2004), 'Life in Configuration Space,' *British Journal for the Philosophy of Science* 55, 713–29.

Locke, J. (1690), *An Essay Concerning Human Understanding*. Online at http://www.earlymoderntexts.com/loess.html.

Loewer, B. (1996), 'Humean Supervenience,' *Philosophical Topics* 24, 101–27.

Maudlin, T. (2007), 'Completeness, Supervenience, and Ontology,' *Journal of Physics A: Mathematical and Theoretical* 40, 3151–171.

Ney, A. (2007), 'Physicalism and Our Knowledge of Intrinsic Properties,' *Australasian Journal of Philosophy* 85, 41–60.

Schaffer, J. (forthcoming), 'Monism: The Priority of the Whole,' *Philosophical Review*.

Schrödinger, E. (1935), 'The Present Situation in Quantum Mechanics,' *Proceedings of the American Philosophical Society* 124, 323–38.

Stoljar, D. (2001), 'Two Conceptions of the Physical,' *Philosophy and Phenomenological Research* 62, 253–81.

Von Neumann, J. (1955), *Mathematical Foundations of Quantum Mechanics* (Princeton, NJ: Princeton University Press).

Wallace, D. (2003), 'Everett and Structure,' *Studies in History and Philosophy of Modern Physics* 34, 87–105.

12
On the Very Idea of an Ecosystem
Jay Odenbaugh

1 Introduction

In this chapter, I consider several different issues. First, I examine how token ecosystems are individuated by ecologists. Second, I examine whether ecosystems, or more specifically their components, can have functions. Philosophers have offered two accounts of functions, a *selected effect function account* and a *systemic capacity account*. On the former, functions are understood in terms of evolutionary history and on the latter in terms of nested dispositions. Here I side with systemic capacity functions as providing the more reasonable account of functional ascriptions in ecosystem ecology. However, this has downstream implications with regard to the next topic. Thirdly, many ecologists and conservationists have taken to talking of 'ecosystem health.' Some treat this as mere metaphor but others construe it literally. The notion of ecosystem health is intimately tied to the notion of ecosystemic functions. However, the notion of a 'healthy' or 'diseased' state requires norms of performance, which are noticeably absent on a systemic functions view. In summary, I offer an extended argument there are mind-independently existing ecosystems, which have functions, but which are neither healthy nor diseased.

2 Token ecosystems

In the 1970s, the environmental writer Barry Commoner claimed that the science of ecology demonstrates that 'everything is connected to everything else' – what he termed 'ecology's first law' (1971). This mantra is often heard in environmental circles.[1] However, it is unclear what this even means. If everything is intimately connected to everything else why is there not simply one thing, the universe? Similarly, one might argue, given these intimate connections, that there are no objects, since there is nothing to differentiate 'it' from everything else. Every object has an 'inside' and 'outside,' but the universe would not. For those mystically inclined, this might be satisfying but philosophically we must do better.

For clarity, let's circumscribe our discussion. First, in the beginning of this section, I will be considering objects qua *concrete particulars*. A concrete particular is anything that exists in space-time.[2] Second, I will suppose that if two or more objects are *connected,* then they are *causally connected.*[3] Third, since the sorts of objects under consideration are *ecological ones,* the type of causal relation must be an *ecological relation.*[4] If someone claimed that all spatiotemporal objects are causally connected through gravitational attraction, then this might be true, but irrelevant for our purposes. As examples of ecological causal relations, here are a few. Populations of organisms are those organisms that are causally connected through the relation of interbreeding, which may be an evolutionary relation.[5] However, they are also connected through competition for shared resources such as food, light, and habitat. Likewise, ecological communities are those populations of species that are causally connected through predator-prey, interspecific competition, mutualism, amensalism, commensalism, and so on, relations.[6] In this essay, we will be concerned primarily with the natural kind *ecosystem* and its associated ontology, so let's begin there with some history.

The history of ecosystem ecology is rich and we certainly cannot do it justice.[7] Still, we can consider high points. In the 1920s, British ecologist Charles Elton noted that organisms living in the same place are linked through their feeding relationships. This he termed a 'food chain,' or what we now more generally call a 'food web.' For example, plants are eaten by animals, which are eaten by other animals and so on. In effect, Elton notes that populations of species occupy *functional roles* including *autotroph, carnivore, herbivore,* and *detrivore.* An *autotroph* is any organism that produces organic compounds from inorganic molecules (i.e., photosynthesizes), a *carnivore* is any organism that consumes animals and only animals, a *herbivore* is any organism that consumes plants and only plants, and a *detrivore* is any organism that consumes dead animals and only dead animals. Elton was explicit about ecological niches being functional roles when he wrote: 'When an ecologist says "there goes a badger" he should include in his thoughts some definite idea of the animal's place in the community

to which it belongs, just as if he had said "there goes the vicar." '
(1927, p. 64).

In 1935, the British ecologist A. G. Tansley explicitly articulated the
concept of an *ecosystem*. Tansley rejects the concept of an ecological
community, in favour of the concept of the total biological (biotic) and
physical (abiotic) system, as he believes the former is incomplete:

> But the more fundamental conception is, as it seems to me, the whole
> *system* (in the sense of physics), including not only the organism-
> complex, but also the whole complex of physical factors forming
> what we call the environment of the biome – the habitat factors
> in the widest sense. Though the organisms may claim our primary
> interest, when we are trying to think fundamentally we cannot sep-
> arate them from their special environment, with which they form
> one physical system...These *ecosystems,* as we may call them, are
> of the most various kinds and sizes. They form one category of the
> multitudinous physical systems of the universe, which range from
> the universe as a whole down to the atom. (1935)

Tansley's overzealousness is evident, since ecosystems are objects composed by causal relations between biotic and abiotic components qua
those types of components, and this would apparently rule out the universe and atoms respectively.[8] Nevertheless, he is suggesting that we
cannot understand or predict the changes in suites of species without
taking into account their physical environment. For example, suppose
a plant species is being consumed by a predator species. If prey abundances are largely affected by nutrient availability, then one may not be
able to predict or explain prey abundances simply in terms of predator
abundances and their rate of consumption.

Thereafter ecologists began playing close to attention to several recog-
nized facts. Plants transform light energy into chemical potential energy
through photosynthesis. The accumulation of energy through photosynthesis is *primary production*. Of course, plants use some of the energy
for their own maintenance and hence only part of primary production
is available for herbivores. The total amount of production in an ecosystem is *gross primary production*. Gross primary production subtracting the
energy used by plants is *net primary production*. Alfred J. Lotka continued developing the notion of an ecosystem by viewing it as an 'energy-
transforming machine.' He suggested that one could describe a set of
biotic and abiotic components by equations representing exchanges of
energy between them, subject to principles of thermodynamics.

In 1942, Raymond Lindeman united Lotka's and Tansley's work, suggesting that the ecosystem is the fundamental unit of ecology and that energy is transferred through links in the food web where each link is a trophic level. On the basis of this account of ecosystems, he famously conducted research, which allowed him to describe how energy flows through trophic levels and how inefficiencies invariably occur.[9]

By the 1950s, Lindeman's 'trophic-dynamic' account of ecosystems, which considers kinds of organisms and studies the flow of energy between them, was the basis of much research. However, Eugene Odum argued that ecologists should also study various biogeochemical cycles, which include the cycling of water, nitrogen, and carbon. He noted that though the flow of energy and the cycling of nutrients were very different, since energy enters an ecosystem as light and is degraded as heat, while nutrients can cycle indefinitely while they are converted from inorganic to organic molecules. Still, the cycling of nutrients can provide an index to the flow of energy since they can be tightly linked. Here organisms simply 'drop out' and we have compartments through which flows and cycling occur. These compartments include atmospheric, mineral, and organic groups. Thus, the history of ecosystem ecology provides us with interesting different and nuanced ecosystem concepts: *Lindeman-Elton ecosystems, Lotka ecosystems, Odum ecosystems,* and so forth (Odenbaugh 2007).

It is interesting to note that some have been sceptical that ecosystem ecology is part of the life sciences, since Odum ecosystems are concerned with the flows of energy and nutrients like phosphorus, carbon, nitrogen, and so on. For example, philosopher Greg Cooper has suggested that ecosystem ecology is not part of ecology, narrowly construed, but only broadly construed (2004). Thus, ecosystem ecology is simply a part of physics, chemistry, or possibly geology. Having said this, a worry of this sort is not applicable to the notion of Lindeman-Elton ecosystems because these are composed of biotic and abiotic parts. By the late twentieth century, though, the concept of *ecosystem* is usually defined as 'a spatially explicit unit of the Earth that includes all of the organisms, along with all of components of the abiotic environment within its boundaries' (Likens 1992).

There has been genuine scepticism concerning the existence of ecosystems, in part due to the sort of boundaries Likens mentions. Philosopher Dale Jamieson articulates the worry in the following way,

Skeptics say that talking about an ecosystem is simply a way of conceptualizing a collection of individual organisms and features of their environment. On this view, ecosystems are like constellations, while organisms and features of their environment are like stars. Talking about ecosystems (like talking about constellations) is a way of talking about other things. It may be useful to do so, but we shouldn't think that the world responds to every useful turn of phrase by manufacturing an entity (2008, p.149).[10]

To make the point Jamieson is pushing vivid, consider what I call the '(n + 1)th problem' (Odenbaugh 2007). Imagine a group of n biotic and abiotic components at a particular place and time, and suppose for the sake of argument they compose a token ecosystem. Now, if the group of n factors are an ecosystem, then why not some $(n + 1)$th component as well? If everything is ecologically connected, why are the n components on the 'inside' but the $(n + 1)$th component is not? There are two possible answers: either the n components compose an ecosystem because of some mind-independent relation that holds between them and only them, or they compose an ecosystem because of some mind-dependent relation that holds between them and only them. (These two answers may not be mutually exclusive, see below.) Jamieson's concern is that there are no mind-independent ecosystemic causal relations that hold between just those components qua those components. Jamieson is not alone in his worries. Here is philosopher Katie McShane expressing similar thoughts.

The worry is this: as we saw above, ecosystems are not natural kinds. What constitutes the ecosystem, where its boundaries are, and so on, are matters of decision and not simply discovery. The delineation of ecosystems is underdetermined by nature itself; so this isn't just in fact a matter of decision, it's necessarily and inescapably so. (McShane 2004).

Finally, it is not just philosophers who are sceptical about ecosystems. The Department of the Interior's Fuel Coordinator Allan Fitzsimmons has in fact written an entire book criticizing the ecosystem concept and ecosystem management (1999). He writes,

The problem starts with the idea of an ecosystem itself. The term was coined by Arthur Tansley in 1935, who described them as physical systems encompassing living and nonliving things and their interactions. Ask the Forest Service, the Environmental Protection Agency, the Fish and Wildlife Service, and the Sierra Club to show you their maps of the ecosystems of the United States. They differ

greatly. The so-called Greater Yellowstone Ecosystem can cover anywhere from 5 to 19 million acres, depending on who is defining it.
These discrepancies occur because the human mind fabricates ecosystems. Nature does not put ecosystems on the land for researchers
to discover. Ecosystems are only mental constructs, not real, discrete,
or living things on the landscape. (Fitzsimmons 1999, p. 3)

Jamieson is quite correct that ecosystems might be conventional
(that is, mind-dependent) as the sceptics suggest. However, there are
several problems with the arguments of McShane and Fitzsimmons.
First, ecosystems are concrete particulars, as I suggested in beginning
of this section. They are spatiotemporal objects that have beginnings
and endings. Hence, they themselves are not natural kinds, though
I will argue the category *ecosystem* is. Second, the supposition that
there is one and only one ecosystem present in a given region is false;
ecosystems can exist at different scales and may be embedded in one
another as parts to wholes. Third, different groups of mapmakers need
not map the same token ecosystem in the same way. For any collection
of objects, we can map them in a variety of different ways, and this
says nothing about the existence of the object in question. If one is
in doubt, just consider some artifactual object like the London Tube
(Kitcher 2001).

To answer this $(n + 1)$th problem, we must specify what type or types
of causal relations must hold between biotic and abiotic components
to compose an ecosystem. These are energy flows and biogeochemical
cycles between biotic and abiotic components. Let us say that an ecosystem exists just in case biotic and abiotic members of a set are closed
under these ecosystemic causal relations. More generally, if we specify a
causal relation R of interest, then an *interactive boundary* exists between
the objects in a set S relative to a set S^* just in case the members of S bear
R to each other and not to members of S^*.[11]

As an illustration, consider the relation *feeds on,* which is essential to
the notion of a trophic level. Suppose that S_1 feeds on S_2, S_2 feeds on S_3,
S_3 feeds on S_3, S_4 feeds on no species in the set, and no species feeds on
S_4 as depicted by Figure 1.[12]

Figure 1 Populations of species causally closed under the relation feeds on.

Hence, the set of species {S_1, S_2, and S_3} is causally closed under the causal relation *feeds on*, and there is an interactive boundary between the members of that set and S_4. Unfortunately, this proposal is simply too strong. The biotic and abiotic components in sets of interest may be causally closed under certain ecosystemic relations, but will not be where nutrient cycling and energy flows are concerned. Consider again Figure 1, but now let the S_i be atmospheric, mineral, or organic sub-systems or compartments, the ecosystemic relation *exchanging CO_2 with,* and the 'weight' of the dashed line represent the strength of the interaction between the S_i. This is represented in Figure 2.

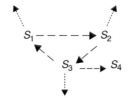

Figure 2   Ecosystemic sub-systems or sub-compartments not closed under the relation exchanging CO_2.

Clearly, the set {S_1, S_2, S_3, S_4} is not closed under the relation *exchanges CO2* since its members exchange CO_2 with sub-subsystems outside the set. Ecosystem ecologists' implicit response to this sort of case is that S_4 is not part of the ecosystem composed of S_1, S_2, and S_3, because S_3 and S_4 only 'weakly interact,' and similarly for sub-systems outside of the set {S_1, S_2, S_3, S_4} where the strength of interaction is even weaker. The 'strength' of these causal relations or interactions may seem mysterious, but need not. Ecologists have long been interested in the interaction strength or average interaction strength between species in a food web. Typically, they characterize it as follows. The strength of interaction between species N_i and N_j is equal to how a change in N_j leads to a change in N_i other things being equal.[13] More generally, the strength of an causal interaction between variables X_i and X_j (where $i \neq j$), relative to constant background variables X_k (where $k \neq i, j$), is how a change in X_j results in a change in X_i, against that constant background.

Provided that we can make metaphysical sense of the notion of causal or interaction strength along the lines mentioned above, how should this fit into our account of ecosystems? One might offer the following account:

> An ecosystem exists just in case biotic and abiotic members of a set are such that the minimal (or average interaction strength) is greater than or equal to *n*.

Now, this approach raises a variety of issues. First, if all that is required is minimal or average interaction strength $n > 0$, then weakly interacting biotic and abiotic components compose an ecosystem. Thus, we might find that the only ecosystem is all of planet Earth, or all of Earth and the Sun, and so on. We might suppose that there is some other value $n \gg 0$ which determines ecosystem composition, but it would seem arbitrary at best. Analogously, some philosophers argue that there is some number of hairs n such that one with hairs $m \geq n$ is hirsute and if $m < n$ then they are bald. Apart from the number of hairs being greater than zero, there is no non-arbitrary reason for choosing that value and not some other one.[14] That is, for any $m \neq n > 0$, there is no reason to be given for m which cannot also be given for n. Technically then, a set of biotic and abiotic components are an ecosystem insofar as they instance an ecosystemic causal relation and the minimal or average interaction strength is greater than or equal to n and where $n > 0$. *However,* ecosystem ecologists proceed in a more specific manner. Typically, they will reason in the following way. Informally, they specify two sets S and S^*, which is a proper subset of S', where S' is the complement of S. They then claim that S is an ecosystem relative to S^*, given some ecosystem causal relation R of interest, since the average interaction strength between the members of S is greater than that between $S \cup S^*$.

Let's consider a concrete case. Here is an informal account of the concept of *ecosystem* that serves our purposes.

> An *ecosystem* is group of abiotic and biotic components that interact through the nutrients and energy that cycle or flow through them and which interact more strongly with respect to each other than with regard to a comparison group of abiotic and biotic components.

Here the issues of precision mentioned above fade away since one is concerned with making sure that the members of a set interact more strongly with each other than the with members of some other set. One way in which ecosystems are bounded interactively is through *watersheds*. A watershed is an area of land that drains water, sediment and dissolved materials to a common receiving body or outlet. The boundaries of a watershed follow major ridgelines around channels and meet at the bottom, where water flows out of the watershed into streams, rivers, or lakes. In this case, there are geomorphologic boundaries and these geomorphologic boundaries ensure that nutrient cycling and energetic flows have differential rates inside and outside the drainage basin. Thus, the biotic and abiotic components in a watershed causally interact qua ecosystem more strongly than those biotic and abiotic components outside the watershed.

Recognizing watersheds as token ecosystems is not only an instance of 'ontology made concrete,' but this makes sense of the commitments of ecosystem ecologists in several ways. First, watersheds are multiscalar; that is, within a watershed, there are sub-watersheds, and sub-sub-watersheds, and so on. Ecologists have long thought that ecosystems can be parts to wholes of each other as was mentioned above. Second, ecosystem ecologists have used watersheds to conduct experimental research with great success, the most famous example being the Hubbard Brook Experiment Forest. The Hubbard Brook ecosystem is in the White Mountains national forest in New Hampshire, with nine sub-watersheds that drain into Hubbard Brook and eventually the Atlantic Ocean. Gene Likens and Herbert Boorman (along with many others) have manipulated these sub-watersheds, examining the effects of clear cutting, acid rain, and many other factors on ecosystem processes. Likens himself writes,

> F. Herbert Boorman, Robert S. Pierce and I recognized that watershed-ecosystems within the Hubbard Brook Experimental Forest with watertight basins, well-defined watershed boundaries, reasonably homogeneous geologic formations, uniform distribution of soil, vegetation and climate, year-round precipitation and streamflow and several clusters of three or more similar-sized watersheds provided ideal considerations where entire watersheds could be experimentally tested and compared to gain a clearer understanding about the ecology of forested landscapes.

There are several caveats and issues to pursue here. First different ecosystemic causal relations may specify distinct ecosystems (cycling of H_2O, C, P, and N for example). Second, causal relations are time-lagged and episodic and the degree of interaction strength is imprecise, and this takes us deep into the waters of vagueness. Insofar as one is a realist about ecosystems, this presuppose that ecosystem sub-systems or compartments have interactive boundaries, in sense defined earlier; if these boundaries do not exist then we must be anti-realists about ecosystems.[15]

3　Ecosystem functions

Consider the following claims made by ecosystem ecologists. A large amount of woody material falls to the floor of forests. This material is composed of cellulose and lignin, which are indigestible by most animals. Fungi serve the important function of decomposing this plant material, thereby releasing nutrients into the soil for uptake by plants. Fungi consist of a network, or mycelium, of hyphae, which are thread-like elements composed of cells connected end to end. Fungal hyphae are able to penetrate woody cells of plant litter that bacteria cannot reach. They secrete enzymes into the litter or wood and absorb the simple sugar and amino acid breakdown products of this extracellular digestion. Carbon accumulates in wood. Microorganisms and fungi break down wood and return carbon to the global cycles. If these organisms were absent, carbon would accumulate in the wood, where it could not be recycled into the environment. Ecologists thus claim that fungi decomposing woody products contributes to the cycling of carbon. So, we can summarize this functional claim as follows:

> (F_1) A function of fungi is to decompose woody products, contributing to the carbon cycle.

The nitrogen cycle involves the movement of nitrogen and nitrogen-containing compounds through the biosphere. Our atmosphere is a reservoir of nitrogen in a gaseous form (N_2). N_2 is converted from its gaseous state to ammonia or nitrate by the process of nitrogen fixation, which can result from physical or biological processes. Let's consider biological processes, since 90% of nitrogen fixation results from them. Nitrogen fixation occurs biologically through free-living organisms such as *Azotobacter, Clostridium,* and cyanobacteria found in soil or water, or by organisms such as *Rhizobium* bacteria, which live in specialized root structures of some plants. In the case of *Rhizobium,* once nitrogen is converted to ammonia or nitrate, it can be assimilated in plant roots and ultimately the organic matter of consumers. Ecologists claim that *Rhizobium* bacteria fix nitrogen, which contributes to the cycling of nitrogen. Let's summarize this functional claim as well:

> (F_2) A function of *Rhizobium* is to fix nitrogen, contributing to the nitrogen cycle.

Philosophers have spilt much ink attempting to make sense of functional claims. One of the most important proposals comes from Larry Wright (1973). On Wright's view,
The function of *x* is to *z* means

> a. *x* is there because it *z*s, and
> b. *z* is a consequence of *x* being there.[16]

A customary example is this: to say that the function of the human heart is to circulate blood means the heart is there because it circulates blood, and circulating blood is a consequence of human hearts' being there. This account was rejected due to many criticisms; here is one popular one proposed by Christopher Boorse (1976). Suppose in a scientist's lab there is a gas leak rendering the scientist unconscious; it appears that this case satisfies both (a) and (b). To say that the function of the gas is to render the scientist unconscious means the gas leak is there because it renders the scientist unconscious and the scientist's unconscious state is a consequence of the gas leak. Surely, the gas leak has no function or at least not this function.

The most common response to Wright's etiological account has been to couch it in the context of evolution by natural selection. The function of a trait *T* is that for which *T* evolved by natural selection in the recent past.[17] A trait *T* evolves by natural selection if, and only if, *T* is heritable, entities with *T* have greater reproductive success relative to alternatives due to possessing *T*, and there is variation with respect to *T*. Thus, the human heart has the function of circulating blood if, and only if, having a human heart is heritable, having a human heart contributed to the reproductive success of those who possessed it in the recent past by circulating blood, relative to the alternatives, and there was variation in the recent past with respect to humans' hearts concerning the circulation of blood. This *selected effect account* avoids Boorse's counterexample, since *T* is a token of a 'reproductive family'; that is, *T* is a copy of other tokens of the same kind. The gas leak is not a member of a reproductive family.

If we apply the selected effect account to (F_1) and (F_2), then we should find the following to be true:

1. Decomposing woody products is a heritable trait amongst fungi, and fixing nitrogen is a heritable trait amongst *Rhizobium*.
2. Decomposing woody products contributed to the reproductive success of fungi relative to alternative traits in the recent past, and fixing nitrogen contributed to the reproduced success of *Rhizobium* relative to alternative traits in the recent past.
3. There was variation in decomposing woody products amongst fungi, and there was variation in fixing nitrogen amongst *Rhizobium*.

Now we haven't examined the empirical details to substantiate these functional claims; however, it very well may be the case that they are true. If so, then fungi have the selected effects function of decomposing woody plants, and *Rhizobium* have the selected effects function of fixing nitrogen. However, it is important to note that these are not the only functional claims made in (F_1) and (F_2). Specifically, they claim that fungi decompose woody products, which contributes to the carbon cycle, and *Rhizobium* fixes nitrogen, which contributes to the nitrogen cycle. Even if it is plausible to suppose that (1)–(3) are satisfied, it is extremely unlikely to suppose that contributing to the carbon cycle was selected for in fungi and that contributing to the nitrogen cycle was selected for in *Rhizobium*. First, both of these traits benefit organisms other than just fungi and *Rhizobium*, and thus would require large scale altruism, which can occur but only under relatively stringent circumstances. Rather, these dispositions appear to be 'side effects' or 'by products' of those activities (Cahen 1988). Second, and more importantly, ecosystem ecologists also attribute functions to *abiotic components*. For example, though 90% of nitrogen fixation is accomplished by living things, 10% is accomplished by non-living things. For example, lightning and volcanoes can fix nitrogen as well. Thus, an ecosystem ecologist could have made the following functional claim: a function of volcanoes is that they fix nitrogen contributing to the nitrogen cycle. Clearly, volcanoes do not reproduce and are not targets of natural selection. Hence, they do not evolve by natural selection. Therefore, they do not have selected effects functions. Thus, if we are to make sense of at least some of the functional claims in ecosystem ecology, then we need an alternative account. Fortunately, there is such an account on the books, the *systemic capacity account*.

Robert Cummins (1975) has articulated and defended what is termed the 'systemic capacity account' of functions. Suppose that x is some part of a system S, has a disposition F, and S itself has some disposition C. Roughly then, the *systemic capacity function* of x in a system S is to F if, and only if, x is capable of F-ing and x's capacity to F in part accounts for S's capacity to C. Let's apply this account to (F_1) and (F_2).

> Fungi have the function of decomposing woody products in an ecosystem if, and only if, fungi are capable of decomposing woody products and fungi's capacity to decompose woody products in part accounts for an ecosystem's capacity to contribute to the carbon cycle.

> *Rhizobium* has the function of fixing nitrogen in an ecosystem if, and only if, *Rhizobium* are capable of fixing nitrogen and *Rhizobium*'s

capacity to fix nitrogen in part accounts for an ecosystem's capacity to contribute to the nitrogen cycle.

The systemic capacity function account understands the function of x to F in terms of how the capacity or disposition to F contributes to a system S's capacity or disposition to C. One disposition realizes – along with other dispositions possibly – some more general systemic disposition. This account applies very nicely in ecosystem ecology. Moreover, it applies as well when we consider abiotic components, too.

> Volcanoes have the function of fixing nitrogen in an ecosystem if, and only if, volcanoes have the capacity to fix nitrogen and volcanoes capacity to fix nitrogen in part accounts for an ecosystems capacity to contribute to the nitrogen cycle.

This functional claim fits the systemic capacity account, though it does not satisfy the selected effects account. If my arguments are sound, then selected effects functions cannot render the functional claims of ecosystem ecology sensible though the systemic capacity account can.

4   Ecosystem health

Many ecologists and conservationists argue that we should promote the health of ecosystems. However, it is very unclear what it means for an ecosystem to be 'healthy.' Though much has been written attributing states of health and disease to ecosystems, philosopher Katie McShane has provided the most thoughtful and philosophically rigorous account of ecosystem health. Most biologists and conservationists who accept that attributions of health and disease to ecosystems are sensible simply assume what the healthy states of an ecosystem are, and spend their time attempting to operationalize them. This is to put the empirical cart before the conceptual horse. Thus, it is useful to consider McShane's account.

Considering something which is healthy, McShane writes,

> When it is in a state of perfect health, all of its essential parts are in good working order, and its vital processes are running smoothly or capable of running smoothly when called upon. Furthermore, when something is healthy, it is, in this regard, better off than it would be if it were unhealthy (2004, p. 230).[18]

She suggests that health ascriptions involve the following: An object must have (a) a structure, (b) parts with functions, and (c) the ability to be better/worse off (2004, p. 230). Let me say something briefly about each of these.

First, an object must maintain some structure to be healthy. McShane notes that every object has some structure or other; it would not be an object otherwise.[19] Thus, we can say that 'healthy things are those that maintain the structure that they are *supposed* to have – the structure that is appropriate for them in their particular circumstances (age, environment, etc.).' (2004, p. 230) With respect to ecosystems, it is not clear how this normative language is to be grounded in the science, so we might provide an alternative. 'We mean that they're healthy in virtue of maintaining a certain kind of structure' (2004, p. 231).

Second, in light of this, we need an account of this *normativity,* or *proper function*. McShane uses Larry Wright's etiological account of functions we explored above. As we saw, Wright's account is subject to counterexamples. McShane accepts that Boore's gas leak has a function of rendering the scientist unconscious, and suggests that on Wright's view there are *lots* and *lots* of functions in the world.[20] One implication of this is that there will be functions that do not maintain health. So, there must be some criteria to detect those functions that are and are those that are not related to health, which leads to the next component.

Third, the notion of health is a normative one. It concerns the 'goodness' of a characteristic for an *x*. However, how do we unpack this? There are at least three ways of doing so – *moral* goodness, good of a *kind,* and good *for* (2004, p. 233–6). McShane suggests that the relevant notion of *good* is that of *good for*. Note also that we say that *F* is *good for x* we mean to say that *F* is *pro tanto* good for *x;* there may be other considerations that may outweigh the fact that *F* is good for *x* (2004, p. 233). Clearly, we need some account or other for 'well-being' of *x*. McShane suggests Stephen Darwall's account of rational care (2004, p. 234–5):

> Something is good for you if it would make sense for someone who cared for you to want it for you for your sake.

One could replace this account of well-being with others. Thus, by way of summary:

> *x*'s health consists in those functions of the structure of *x* such that are *pro tanto* good for *x;* they contribute to the well being of *x*.

Finally, her account of ecosystem health consists in the following,

> An ecosystem is good for its own sake if it would make sense for someone who cared for it to want it to function properly for its own sake.

There are several serious problems with this account of ecosystem health, and any which makes similar sorts of assumptions. First, consider the incorporation of Wright's plausibly false etiological account of functions. Second, the notion of health presupposes a notion of *proper function.* That is, if some x has a function F, then x *ought to F;* there would thereby be *norms of performance.* One can plausibly argue that the selected effects account provides us with norms of performance since x has the selected function F in virtue of past xs F-ing even when x as a matter of fact cannot F. For example, a defective heart ought to circulate blood because past hearts were selected to do just circulate blood. However, the systemic capacity account ascribes functions even when no previous x F-ed. That is, we cannot ground norms of performance in terms of past xs F-ing. Thus, if ecosystem functions are systemic capacity functions and systemic capacity functions do not supply norms of performance, then ecosystem functions are not proper functions. However, the notion of ecosystem health requires ecosystem functions be proper functions. Therefore, the notion of ecosystem health is a nonstarter.

To summarize the arguments of this section, I have suggested that it would make sense to talk about ecosystem health, if the selected effects account were correct. But this account does not work for ecosystems; the best account for ecosystems is the systemic capacities account. But there is no normativity in the system capacities account, that would tell us what capacities are healthy and which are unhealthy. Thus, we should reject the notion of ecosystem health.

5   Conclusion

In this chapter, I have offered an extended argument for moderate realism about ecosystems. Likewise, I have provided an account of ecosystem functions that derives from the systemic capacity account used more generally. Finally, I attempted to show that the popular notion of ecosystem health cannot be made sense of in terms of systemic capacity functions, since they do not provide norms of performance which are required for any notion of health.

Notes

1. For example, self-proclaimed 'deep ecologists' (not to be confused with scientific ecologists) suggest that the fundamental norm of their favoured environmental ethic is 'Self-realization.' Put less cryptically, there is but one thing. If we further add that one ought to promote one's self-interest, then one ought to promote the interest of the Self. Needless to say I suppose, there are several problems with this argument.

2. If one believes for example that properties exist only if they are exemplified or instanced in space-time (e.g., David Armstrong), then one might add that a concrete particular is anything that exists in space-time that cannot be exemplified or instanced.

3. Some philosophers hold that events are causally connected to another and not objects per se. Nothing hangs on talking about objects being causally related since one could rewrite this essay using the more cumbersome locution of event causation. Likewise, as an aside, one can substitute their preferred metaphysics of persistence – objects are 'wholly present' whenever they exist, or have temporal parts, and so on. One could rewrite this essay as a perdurantist or endurantist and the content not be substantially affected.

4. It is doubtful that Commoner was attending to such niceties, though if ecology teaches us that everything is connected to everything else, then surely this is because everything is *ecologically connected.*

5. *Potential interbreeding* is a concept that deserves metaphysical scrutiny. If organisms compose a population, then they must be *able* to interbreed. Clearly, we must 'fix' certain properties of the organisms for this to make sense. For example, for some set of organisms, asexual organisms could interbreed with provided they might have been sexual, have the right breeding season, and so on. By the same token we cannot construe populations in terms of actual interbreeding because some members/parts may never interbreed.

6. This notion of an ecological community needs further refinement as well. I have provided a disjunction of causal relations that are 'community-level' causal relations. However, what makes them community causal relations? One might define a community-level causal relation as any causal relation that holds between two or more species. This criterion provides the right answer when we consider competition between conspecifics for shared resources; however, this is insufficient since gravitational attraction could hold between two or more species as well. So, we should say that a community-level causal relation is any causal relation that holds between two or more species *qua species.*

7. See Golley 1993.

8. When one considers causal relations between objects, we should distinguish between different types of causal relations. That is, objects can causally interact in different ways – gravitationally, chemically, ecologically, and so on. Thus, one of way of putting this point is that x causally interacts with y *qua K* where K is some kind of causal relation. For example, the same set of populations can exhibit gravitational forces on one another and interact ecologically.

9. Energy cannot be created or destroyed, only transformed from one state to another. However, energy transformations are inefficient. Thus, when one

organism consumes another, some of the energy in the consumed organism will be lost as heat. The efficiency of these trophic transitions is extremely important in ecology because they constrain the way energy moves in ecosystems and ultimately its structure. For example, the number of 'steps' in a food chain is dependent on the efficiency of the trophic transformations in the web and many believe this explains why there are so few links in food chains. As a rule of thumb, on 5–20% of energy is transferred from a trophic level to the very next level.

10. One view of material composition – mereological universalism – states that any group of objects compose another object. If this view is correct, then Jamieson's worry can be answered, but it has the very odd implication that for example the Eiffel Tower, my dog Evie, and Banff, Alberta compose an object.

11. It should be noted that boundaries between objects can be vague; vagueness need not signal the absence of boundaries. For example, David Lewis has suggested that the Outback exists but has a vague boundary. There are many ways to make sense of such vague boundaries.

12. This is an unusual topology for a food web. Generally one does not observe food cycles, but that is immaterial to the points being made here.

13. Thus, they represent the interaction strength between N_i and N_j as $\partial N_i/\partial N_j$.

14. Epistemicists about vagueness such as Timothy Williamson hold that for predicates such as 'is thin' or 'is bald' there is some number of hairs such that one is bald whether we know what that number is. One can argue that for any number it is unjustified. Therefore, there is no number that is justified. However, this argument would be fallacious – the only justifiable number is where the number is greater than zero.

15. Some like Fitzsimmons might run the following argument: One can protect something only if it mind-independently exists. However, ecosystems by and large do not mind-independently exist. Hence, one cannot protect them. There are two problems with this argument. First, even if ecosystems do not mind-independently exist, abiotic and biotic entities do and we can protect them even if the 'ecosystem' of which they are a part is largely conventional (e.g., Greater Yellowstone Ecosystem). Second, even where ecosystems exist mind-independently, we can protect we can protect proper subsets of them which are defined in a mind-independent or conventional manner.

16. Wright viewed his project as explicating the meaning of functional claims. Philosophers thereafter have not been so concerned whether they were explicating functional claims as much as making sense of scientific practice. Thus, it is possible that theories of functions would be inconsistent with ordinary usage. As an example, many of the folk still talk of living things as being designed. However, this claim many would argue has a false presupposition.

17. This may appear circular given the phrase 'for which'. However, here is a more complicated version of the account due to Peter Godfrey-Smith (1994). The function of m is to F iff: (1) m is a member of family T, (2) members of family T are components of biologically real systems of type

S, (3) among the properties copied between members of *T* is property or property cluster *C*, which can do *F*, (4) one reason members of *T* such as *m* exist now is the fact that past members of *T* were successful under selection in the recent past, through positively contributing to the fitness of systems of type *S*, and (5) members of *T* were selected because they did *F*, through having *C*.

18. When something is in perfect health, of course all of its essential properties are in good working order since without them the thing would not exist; however, I would also suggest that many accidental properties are important as well. For example, it is an accidental property of me that I have the heart that I do. If my heart did not function properly, I would be unhealthy though I would continue to exist after I received a transplant.

19. I suppose one might argue that simples – objects with no proper parts – do not have any structure. Presumably though they have properties in virtue of which they can causally interact with other objects. They have brute dispositions with which they interact with other simples. As an example, suppose electrons and protons are not composed of other objects (contrary to our best particle physics). One might suppose that the negative charge of an electron and positive charge of a proton are brute dispositions about how these objects behave with respect to one another.

20. We might mitigate the force of this objection by noting that Wright distinguishes between *a* and *the* function of *X* as McShane suggests. However, this seems to do nothing in dealing with the gas leak case.

Bibliography

Boorse, C. (1976), 'What a Theory of Mental Health Should be,' *Journal for the Theory of Social Behavior* 6, 61–84.

Cahen H. (1988), 'Against the Moral Considerability of Ecosystems,' *Environmental Ethics* 10, 195–215.

Commoner, B. (1971), *The Closing Circle: Nature, Man, and Technology* (New York: Knopf).

Cooper, G. (2003), *The Science of the Struggle for Existence: On the Foundations of Ecology.* (Cambridge: Cambridge University Press).

Cummins, R. (1975), 'Functional Analysis,' *Journal of Philosophy* 72, 741–65.

Elton, C. (1927), *Animal Ecology* (London: Sidgwick and Jackson).

Fitzsimmons, A. (1999), 'Ecosystem Management: An Illusions?' *Perc Reports* 17, 3–5.

Godfrey-Smith, P. (1994), 'A Modern History Theory of Functions,' *Noûs* 28, 344–62.

Jamieson, D. (2008), *Ethics and the Environment: An Introduction* (Cambridge: Cambridge University Press).

Kitcher, P. (1989) 'Some Puzzles about Species,' in Michael Ruse (ed.), *What the Philosophy of Biology Is: Essays for David Hull* (Dordrecht: Springer), pp. 183–208.

—— (2001), *Science, Truth, and Democracy* (Oxford: Oxford University Press).

Likens, G. (1992), *An Ecosystem Approach: Its Use and Abuse,* Excellence in Ecology, Book 3 (Oldendorf/Luhe: Ecology Institute).

McShane, K. (2004), 'Ecosystem Health,' *Environmental Ethics* 26, 227–45.

Odenbaugh, J. (2007) 'Seeing the Forest *and* the Trees: Realism about Communities and Ecosystems,' *Philosophy of Science* 74, 628–41.

Tansley, A. (1935), 'The Use and Abuse of Vegetational Concepts and Terms,' *Ecology* 16, 284–307.

Wright, L. (1973), 'Functions,' *Philosophical Review* 82, 139–68.

13
The Prince of Wales Problem for Counterfactual Theories of Causation

Carolina Sartorio

1 Introduction

In 1992, as part of a larger charitable campaign, the Prince of Wales (Prince Charles, Queen Elizabeth's older son and heir) launched a line of organic food products called 'Prince's Duchy Originals' (http://www. duchyoriginals.com). The first product that went on sale was an oat cookie: 'the oaten biscuit.' Since then the oaten biscuit has been joined by hundreds of other products and Duchy Originals has become one of the leading organic food brands in the United Kingdom. Presumably, the Prince of Wales is very proud of his Duchy Originals products, and of the oaten biscuits in particular. Let's imagine that he is so proud of the biscuits that he eats them regularly. Also, let's imagine that one day Queen Elizabeth asks the prince to water her plant. As she explains to him, she'll be gone for the day and the plant needs to be watered every afternoon. But the prince decides not to water the plant. Instead of watering it, he spends his afternoon savouring some oaten biscuits, and the plant dies.

What caused the plant's death? If you were to ask the queen, she would presumably say: the prince, plus some 'natural causes' (including the fact that the plant was particularly delicate and needed intensive watering). Now, in virtue of what could the prince be a cause of the plant's death? When we say that an agent caused some event in the world, we typically mean to say that there is something that the agent did, or something that the agent failed to do, which caused the outcome. There are several things that the prince did and failed to do that afternoon: he ate some oaten biscuits, he read the newspaper, he scratched his nose, he didn't phone a friend, he didn't watch TV, he didn't water the queen's plant, and so on. Among these, we clearly want to say that his not watering the plant is relevant to the plant's death: the plant died because he didn't water it. Under slightly different circumstances, some of the things he *did* would also be relevant. Imagine, for instance, that the oaten biscuits are so amazingly good that they induce some kind of psychological trance that makes you forget any obligations that you might have. So maybe the prince was determined to water the plant until he ate the biscuits, at which time he forgot all about it. In that scenario his eating the biscuits would also be a cause of the plant's death. But note that, even in that case, the prince's contribution to the plant's death is ultimately 'negative' in nature. For his eating the biscuits causes the plant's death *by means of* causing the prince's subsequent failure to water the plant. At the end of the day, the plant still dies because of something that the prince *doesn't* do: it dies because he doesn't water it.

Scenarios of this kind suggest that omissions, and absences in general, can be causes, and that our reconstructions of the causal histories of the outcomes are somehow flawed if they don't include the omissions of agents or the absences of certain events but instead include only 'positive' causes. For, again, in these cases, the outcomes seem to happen, at least partly, because of something that someone doesn't do, or because of something that doesn't happen, not (just) because of something that someone does, or because of something that actually happens. I will call the apparent failure of positive causes to adequately account for the outcome's occurrence in these cases 'the inadequacy fact about positive causes.' The inadequacy fact about positive causes is an important motivation for accepting negative causes.

Now, assuming that we want to make room for negative causes, how could we make sense of omissions and absences being causes? A natural thought is to appeal to the notion of *counterfactual dependence.* We can say that the prince's not watering the plant is a cause of the plant's death because the plant's death counterfactually depends on the prince's failure to water it: had his failure to water the plant not occurred (i.e., had he watered the plant), the plant wouldn't have died. In other words: in the closest possible world(s) where the prince waters the plant, the plant doesn't die. Counterfactual theories of causation claim that the causal facts are grounded in facts about counterfactual dependence. On these views, causes are 'difference-makers' with respect to their effects in that effects (at least typically) counterfactually depend on their causes (Lewis 1986a).

Now, this idea has to be refined in two kinds of ways.[1] First, as cases of 'pre-emption' suggest, sometimes effects don't counterfactually depend on their causes. For example, an assassin can cause his victim's death even if the death would still have happened if he hadn't shot him, given that a backup assassin would then have shot the victim himself. This suggests that counterfactual dependence is not necessary for causation. At least originally, Lewis thought that we can sidestep this problem by taking causation to be, not simple counterfactual dependence, but the ancestral of counterfactual dependence. Second, counterfactual dependence also doesn't seem to be sufficient for causation: some counterfactual dependencies track 'tighter,' non-causal connections, such as logical and mereological relations. For example, my writing the word 'cat' counterfactually depends on my writing the letter 'c' but my writing 'c' isn't a cause of my writing 'cat' (Kim 1973). So the relevant concept of counterfactual dependence would have to be circumscribed accordingly. Lewis does this by setting constraints on potential causes and effects. On Lewis's view, a necessary condition for C to cause E is that C and E be fully 'distinct,' where C and E are not fully distinct if, for example, one is part of the other. Also, some counterfactual conditionals express counterfactual relations that aren't causal because they are *backtracking* – as when I say 'If my friend had invited me to his birthday party today, then we wouldn't have had a fight yesterday.' Lewis's suggestion is that we should restrict our focus to ordinary or standard contexts, in which backtracking counterfactuals aren't true.

In spite of these problems, the claim that counterfactual views have at least identified a *sufficient* condition for causation once counterfactual dependence has been restricted in these ways has seemed quite plausible to people. In particular, at least in recent times, it has seemed much more plausible than the converse claim that counterfactual dependence, or something close to it, is *necessary* for causation (the consensus seems to be that counterfactual theories have a really hard time addressing the pre-emption problem). From now on I will focus on the sufficiency claim only. I'll call it 'the counterfactual criterion':

(CC) If there is counterfactual dependence of the ordinary (non-backtracking) kind between C and E, and if C and E are fully 'distinct' (e.g., they are not logically or mereologically related), then C is a cause of E.

CC seems to be initially plausible: if E counterfactually depends on C, then C is a difference-maker with respect to E – it makes the difference between E's occurring and E's not occurring – and so (if the counterfactual dependence is of the ordinary kind and if C and E are fully distinct) it is plausible to think that C is one of the things (among potentially multiple things) that causally contributed to E's occurrence.[2]

Given CC's initial plausibility, an advantage of counterfactual theories seems to be that they have the basic resources to accommodate causation by omission, which many other theories lack.[3] For example, theories according to which a causal relation requires the transfer of some physical quantity, like energy or momentum (Salmon 1994), or any other kind of physical interaction, don't have the resources to do this. For there is no physical interaction between the prince and the plant in virtue of which he caused the plant's death. Counterfactual dependence, by contrast, doesn't require the existence of physical interaction: on the basis of CC, we can say that the prince caused the plant's death even if he never physically interacted with it. So the ability to accommodate causation by omission appears to be at least a prima facie advantage of counterfactual theories over theories that don't allow for this type of causation.[4]

I will argue that this is a misconception. I will argue that, despite appearances to the contrary, the ability to accommodate causation by omission is not a prima facie advantage of counterfactual views, at least to the extent that we take the main motivation for believing in causation by omission to be the inadequacy fact about positive causes (as I am assuming we do). For I will argue that, even if omissions are causes, and even if counterfactual views can accommodate causation by omission, those views still fail to respect the inadequacy fact about positive causes. Although my main focus will be counterfactual theories of *causation,* in the final section I will suggest that the arguments of this chapter apply, more generally, to theories that attempt to account for the contribution of agents' omissions in counterfactual terms, regardless of whether this is a causal contribution or not.

2   The problem of unwanted positive causes

Let's start by drawing attention to a familiar problem that arises for counterfactual views of causation by omission. As several people have pointed out, the ability that counterfactual theories have to account for causation by omission seems to backfire (Schaffer 2000; Thomson 2003; Beebee 2004; McGrath 2005). Consider the plant in my backyard, which also just died from lack of water. Had I watered it, it would have survived; so, given that I didn't, CC entails that I caused it to die by failing to water it (note that the counterfactual dependence that exists between my not watering the plant and the plant's death is not backtracking, logical, mereological, etc.). But if, say, the *Queen of England* had watered it, it *also* would have survived (and, again, the counterfactual dependence between the queen's not watering my plant and the plant's death is of the right kind). So it follows from CC that the queen also caused it to die, by failing to water it! But it seems wrong to say that the queen caused my plant to die. In other words, the problem is that, in accounting for causation by omission in counterfactual terms, we go from *too few* causes to *too many* causes. Let's call this apparent problem for counterfactual theories of causation 'the Queen of England problem.'[5]

Now, although this is a surprising result, I don't consider the Queen of England problem to be a genuine problem. For, on reflection, there seems to be no metaphysically relevant difference between the queen and me in virtue of which we can say that I'm a cause of my plant's death but the queen isn't. Even if the plant is mine and not the queen's, even if I regularly water it and the queen doesn't, and so on, these don't seem to be grounds for a genuine *causal* difference, but only for a difference in what it is reasonable to expect each one of us will do. So perhaps CC is right and I am a cause of the plant's death and so is the queen. Still, I am a much more *salient* cause than the queen, given that I was expected to water it. This might be sufficient to explain our initial reluctance to regard the queen as a cause.

At any rate, I will assume that this is a satisfactory answer to the Queen of England problem. But I will argue that there is another problem that arises for CC concerning omissions and that is, unlike the Queen of England problem, a genuine and serious problem. I will also give it a royal name, *the Prince of Wales problem,* for it can be seen as a close relative of the Queen of England's problem, in fact, as its 'successor.' The problem is, again, that by embracing CC we go from too few causes to too many causes. But, in this case, by contrast with the Queen of England problem, there is no good reason to think that those things that CC entails are causes are really causes. Moreover, in this case the unwanted causes that CC lets in are of both kinds: negative and positive. So the counterfactual strategy *truly* backfires, and it does so *doubly.* In what follows, I discuss the problem of unwanted positive causes (I discuss the opposite problem – the problem of unwanted negative causes – in the next section).

Let's draw a basic but helpful distinction between different ways in which agents can causally contribute to outcomes in the world. As we have mentioned, on the face of it agents can causally contribute to outcomes either by acting in certain ways or by failing to act in certain ways. Let's say that an agent's contribution is *positive* when the agent causes the outcome in virtue of having acted in a certain way. For example, an agent's contribution is positive when the agent does something that is part of a physical process leading to the outcome (as when some-one poisons a plant and the plant dies as a result). On the other hand, let's say that an agent's contribution is *negative* when the agent causes the outcome in virtue of having failed to act in a certain way. For exam-ple, an agent's contribution is negative when the agent fails to interfere with an existing physical process that eventually leads to the outcome (as when someone fails to water a plant and the plant dies). Finally, let's say that an agent's contribution is *mixed* when it's both positive and negative. Some contributions are mixed in that they contain successive positive and negative components (as in the amnesia-inducing-biscuits scenario imagined in the previous section: the prince's eating the bis-cuits results in the plant's death by means of resulting in the prince's failure to water the plant). Other causal contributions are mixed in that they contain simultaneous or overlapping positive and negative compo-nents (if I push a boulder over your head and I fail to warn you about it, I am responsible for the fact that the boulder is falling over your head and also for not warning you about the falling boulder; in this case I cause your death by pushing the boulder, and I also cause your death by failing to warn you about the falling boulder).

Now return to the example of the queen and the prince. Imagine, again, that the queen asks the prince to water her plant. Imagine that the prince decides to spend the afternoon savouring some oaten biscuits on his lounge chair instead of watering the plant. Imagine, moreover, that his eating the biscuits doesn't *result in* his failing to water the plant (as it does in the amnesia-inducing biscuit scenario described above): he simply eats the biscuits *instead of* watering the plant. Now consider two different scenarios of this sort:

1. Had the prince not eaten the biscuits, he still wouldn't have watered the queen's plant: he would have attended a theatre performance instead.
2. Had the prince not eaten the biscuits, he would have watered the queen's plant.

Imagine, for example, that the prince keeps a list of possible things to do at different times on a given day, ranked by order of preference. In the second scenario watering the queen's plant is second on that list. So, had he not eaten the biscuits, he would have watered the plant. In the first scenario, by contrast, watering the plant is ranked lower, perhaps third, or fourth, or at the very bottom of the list. So, in that scenario, had he not eaten the biscuits, he still wouldn't have watered the plant.

Now, on the face of it, the causal relation between the prince and the queen's plant is of the same kind in both scenarios: it is purely *negative*. It seems clear that, in both cases, the prince causes the plant to die by failing to water it, that is, by failing to interfere with the natural processes that led to the plant's drying up and dying. And it seems clear that this is the only way in which he contributes to the plant's death: he contributes to the plant's death by failing to act in a certain way, and not by acting in a certain way. Or, at least, this is true of the prince's contribution to the plant's death *at the relevant time, on that particular afternoon:* nothing he did *then* contributed to the plant's death.[6]

However, CC entails otherwise. Consider the counterfactual:

> Had the prince not eaten the biscuits, the plant's death wouldn't have occurred.

This counterfactual is false in the first scenario, but true in the second scenario. Moreover, the counterfactual dependence that exists between the prince's eating the biscuits and the plant's death in the second scenario is an ordinary dependence between fully distinct events (it is not backtracking, logical, mereological, etc.).[7] So CC entails that the prince's eating the biscuits is a cause of the plant's death in the first scenario (whereas it doesn't entail this about the first scenario). Thus, according to CC, whereas the prince's contribution to the plant's death (at the relevant time) is purely negative in the first scenario, it is *mixed* in the second: in the second scenario, CC entails that the prince caused the plant's death by failing to water the plant, and also by eating the biscuits. This is the wrong result; again, the prince's contribution to the plant's death (at the relevant time) is of the same type in both cases: it is a purely negative contribution.

As I explained earlier, it is possible to imagine a scenario of a different kind where the prince's eating the biscuits does cause the plant's death. The scenario where the biscuits cause the prince to forget to water the plant is a scenario of that kind. But, in the more ordinary type of scenario I'm imagining, his eating the biscuits doesn't cause his failure to water the plant. And so neither does it cause the plant's death.

The problem generalizes. Many times we make 'simple choices': we choose between doing one thing and doing some alternative thing. When we choose in favour of, say, A and against B, and then act accordingly, there's something we do and something we omit to do: we do A and we omit to do B. Accordingly, there are certain upshots that we cause in virtue of doing A and certain upshots that we cause in virtue of omitting to do B. Although there can be overlap between these two sets of effects, the overlap is not perfect, and it is usually only very minimal. In particular, not every upshot that we cause in virtue of omitting to do B is an upshot that we cause in virtue of doing A; in fact, very few upshots that we cause in virtue of omitting to do B are upshots that we also cause in virtue of doing A.[8] Now, in circumstances of this type, where we would have done B if we had failed to do A, it is likely that, if an upshot U counterfactually depends on our *omitting to do B*, U will also counterfactually depend on our *doing A*. As a result, if we embrace CC, we end up with numerous unwanted positive causes. And thus we are committed to saying that, when an agent makes a simple choice and his contribution (at the relevant time) is purely negative, it is actually mixed.

This is bad because it clashes with the natural classification of types of causal contribution that we introduced above. But, more importantly for our purposes, it is bad because it conflicts with the initial motivation for accepting omissions as causes: *the inadequacy fact about positive causes*. We wanted to say that omissions can be causes partly because the positive events in the offing don't seem to do the job themselves. In particular, it seemed wrong to say that, if the prince just ate some biscuits instead of watering the plant, then something he *did* that afternoon (eating the biscuits) caused the plant's death. We want to be able to say, instead, that the prince's failure to water the plant caused the plant's death. By appeal to CC, we can say that. But the problem is that we *also* have to say (in simple choice scenarios) that something the prince did (his eating the biscuits) caused the plant's death. So the counterfactual strategy truly backfires, for it lets in the wanted negative causes at the price of also letting in the inadequate positive causes, whose inadequacy was the reason we wanted the negative causes in the first place.

3   The problem of unwanted negative causes

In the preceding section we saw that CC is subject to the following objection: sometimes an upshot is caused by what an agent fails to do and not by what he does, but the upshot counterfactually depends both on what he fails to do and on what he does. In this section we will see that CC is also subject to the opposite objection: sometimes an upshot is caused by what the agent does and not by what he fails to do, but the upshot counterfactually depends both on what he does and on what he fails to do. So, again, CC entails that the agent's contribution to the outcome (at the relevant time) is mixed, when it isn't. As we will see, if the problem of unwanted positive causes was quite common, the opposite problem – the problem of unwanted negative causes – is even *more* widespread.

Imagine, again, that the prince decided to not water the plant and to eat some oaten biscuits on his lounge chair instead. Imagine, also, that the high content of fat and sugar in the biscuits made him feel sick to his stomach. Finally, imagine that, had he not eaten the biscuits, he wouldn't have had a stomach ache (for example, nothing else he ate that day would have made him sick), so the stomach ache counterfactually depends on his eating the biscuits. Since the counterfactual dependence in question is of the right kind (not backtracking, logical, mereological, etc.), CC entails that his eating the biscuits caused his stomach ache. This is the right result. However, CC also entails that *the prince's failure to water the plant* caused the stomach ache. For, had the prince watered the plant, he also wouldn't have had a stomach ache (since he wouldn't have eaten the biscuits); and, again, the counterfactual dependence in question is not backtracking, logical, mereological, and so on. But the prince's failure to water the plant didn't cause his stomach ache. If the prince's contribution to the outcome of the plant's death (at the relevant time) was purely negative, his contribution to the outcome of his own stomach ache (at the relevant time) was mainly *positive:* he caused it mainly by doing something (eating the biscuits) that resulted in his having a stomach ache. I say 'mainly' instead of 'only' because, although the more salient cause of his stomach ache was his eating the biscuits, there are other less salient causes of his stomach ache, including, presumably, things he failed to do that afternoon, such as his not taking a powerful drug that would have prevented the stomach ache.[9] But, even if the stomach ache had some (non-salient) negative causes consisting in the prince's failure to do certain things that afternoon, it seems clear that his failure to water the plant *isn't* one of them. If the prince's contribution to his own stomach ache is mixed, it is not mixed by virtue of including the failure to water the plant as a negative cause.

A special kind of scenario in which it would be right to say that the prince's failure to water the plant caused his stomach ache is one where the prince's failure to water the plant resulted in his eating the biscuits. For, if his failure to water the plant resulted in his eating the biscuits, then it would be plausible to say that the prince's stomach ache was caused (albeit indirectly) by his failure to water the plant. Imagine, for example, that his not watering the plant made him feel guilty, which triggered his hunger, which caused him to eat the biscuits. In that case his failure to water the plant would also be a cause of the stomach ache. But, in the original case, where he simply eats the biscuits *instead of* watering the plant, not *because* he didn't water the plant, his failing to water the plant is not similarly a cause of the stomach ache.

The problem of unwanted negative causes generalizes to many omissions by the prince at the time, namely, the omissions of (most of) those acts that eating the biscuits on his lounge chair *precludes:* his not attending a theatre performance, his not riding a horse, his not going on a hunting trip, and so on. CC is likely to entail that each of these omissions also caused his stomach ache because, if the prince had engaged in any of those activities, he wouldn't have had a stomach ache (because he wouldn't have eaten the biscuits). In other words, CC gets the wrong result for (most) omissions of acts that are incompatible (physically incompatible, or incompatible as a matter of physical necessity) with the act that the prince actually performed and that caused his stomach ache.[10] Thus, besides entailing that the prince's contribution to the stomach ache is mixed in a certain way, CC entails that there exist, in addition to the relevant positive causal relation, *countless* negative causal relations that aren't really there.

In this respect, the problem of unwanted negative causes is more general and widespread than the problem of unwanted positive causes from the previous section. As we have seen, the problem of unwanted positive causes is the problem that arises when there is counterfactual dependence between actions and the upshots of omissions. In contrast, the problem of unwanted negative causes is the problem that arises when there is counterfactual dependence between omissions and the upshots of actions. But the number of things we fail to do at any given time is usually, if not always, much larger than the number of things we do at that time. As a result, there are many more 'fake' counterfactual dependencies between *omissions* and upshots than between *actions* and upshots. In other words, there are many more unwanted *negative* causes than unwanted *positive* causes.

There is a second respect in which the problem of unwanted negative causes is more general than the problem of unwanted positive causes. As we have seen, the problem of unwanted positive causes arises when certain dependencies obtain 'accidentally.' It is, in a sense, an accident that the prince was deciding between only two alternatives, and thus, that, if he hadn't eaten the biscuits, he would have watered the plant. As a result, this problem doesn't generalize to all acts and omissions of physically incompatible acts, only to those where an agent makes what I have called a 'simple choice.' By contrast, the problem of unwanted negative causes arises for *any* act and *any* omission of a physically incompatible act. For, arguably, it is always true that, when doing

A and doing B physically exclude each other, if the agent had done B, he wouldn't have done A.

I conclude that, just as there is a problem of unwanted positive causes for counterfactual theories of causation, there is also a problem of unwanted negative causes. In addition, the latter problem is more general than the former problem, in two respects. First, there are *always* unwanted negative causes (not so for unwanted positive causes: there are unwanted positive causes only sometimes). And, second, there are always *several* unwanted negative causes (not so for positive causes: even when there are some unwanted positive causes, there aren't always several of them).

The problem of unwanted negative causes is a serious problem because it shows that counterfactual views commit us to many more negative causes than we want to be committed to. But, more importantly for our purposes, it is a serious problem because it shows that, although counterfactual views can accommodate causation by omission, they do this by failing to respect the motivation for accepting that kind of causation: the inadequacy fact about positive causes. We wanted to say that omissions are causes when positive causes were inadequate to account for the occurrence of certain outcomes. But we *don't* want to say that omissions are causes when the positive causes are perfectly adequate to account for those outcomes! However, this is what we would have to say, if we were to endorse CC.

4 Commensuration

Briefly, the Prince of Wales problem for counterfactual theories of causation (and, in particular, for CC) is this. As we have seen, there seems to be an important distinction between the outcomes that we cause by *doing* certain things and the outcomes that we cause by *failing* to do certain things. More generally, there seems to be an important distinction between what results from how things *are* and what results from how things are *not;* these sets of outcomes are usually not the same. However, there can easily be counterfactual dependence between how things *are* and the outcomes of how things are *not;* conversely, there can easily be counterfactual dependence between how things are *not* and the outcomes of how things *are*. Hence counterfactual dependencies can, quite ordinarily, be 'fake' in that they can fail to reveal genuinely causal connections in the world.

The Prince of Wales problem is particularly puzzling because it initially seemed as if a counterfactual theory, armed with CC, was in an optimal position to account for the possibility of causation by omission. For, on the face of it, outcomes can counterfactually depend on omissions and other absences just like they can counterfactually depend on (positive) events, and it is quite plausible to think that counterfactual dependence is all it takes for causation by omission to take place. Now, this initial advantage of counterfactual theories appears to be lost (or at least significantly reduced) once we realize that CC commits us to numerous unwanted causes, both of the positive and the negative kind, including many of those unwanted positive causes whose 'inadequacy' motivated the search for negative causes in the first place and, also, many unwanted negative causes operating in those cases where the positive causes seemed perfectly adequate.

How could a counterfactual theorist try to address the Prince of Wales problem? In this section I discuss one main attempt to address it. The proposed solution I have in mind consists in abandoning CC, while at the same time trying to preserve the 'spirit' of a counterfactual view.

One natural way to try to do this would be to appeal to Yablo's idea that causes are 'commensurate with' or 'proportionate to' their effects, where the relevant notion of commensurability or proportionality is itself spelled out in counterfactual terms (Yablo 1992). The proposal is complicated, but the rough idea is that a cause is something that has just the right kind of 'essence' for its effect: nothing with a poorer essence would have been sufficient for the effect to happen, and nothing with a richer essence was necessary for the effect to happen. For example, imagine that, when Socrates drank the hemlock, he guzzled it. Arguably, Socrates' *guzzling* the hemlock didn't cause his death because he would still have died if he hadn't guzzled it, but if he had drunk it more slowly. Something with a poorer essence than his guzzling the hemlock (his simply drinking it) would have been sufficient for his death; thus the guzzling isn't a cause of the death. This is so, Yablo says, even if, as a matter of fact, Socrates wouldn't have drunk the hemlock without guzzling it (for example, if he was a sloppy eater); even in this case, it was the drinking and not the guzzling that caused the death. Also, let's imagine that a bridge collapsed after one of its bolts suddenly snapped. The bridge is built in such a way that, given time to respond, it can shift its weight away from any failing bolts; so, if the bolt had snapped less abruptly, the bridge wouldn't have collapsed. Arguably, the bolt's simply snapping didn't cause the bridge's collapse; its *suddenly* snapping did. This is so because something with a richer essence than its simply snapping was needed for the bridge to collapse. And, again, Yablo claims, we would still want to say that the sudden snapping, not the snapping, caused the collapse, even if the circumstances are such that the bolt wouldn't have snapped at all if it hadn't done so suddenly (for example, if the temperature was low enough that bolts snap suddenly if at all). So, Yablo concludes, causes are commensurate with their effects in that they have the right amount of specificity built into their essences: nothing less specific would have done and nothing more specific was needed.

Note that, if Yablo is right, there are reasons to reject CC that are independent from those discussed in this essay (in the sense that they are provided by positive causes alone). For, on Yablo's view, Socrates' guzzling the hemlock wouldn't cause Socrates' death even if the death counterfactually depended on the guzzling (e.g., if Socrates was a sloppy eater and thus he wouldn't have drunk the hemlock unless he guzzled it). Also, on Yablo's view, the bolt's simply snapping wouldn't cause the bridge's collapse even if the collapse counterfactually depended on the snapping (e.g., if the bolt wouldn't have snapped at all unless it snapped suddenly). Of course, all of this rests on a fine-grained conception of events according to which different events can occupy the same spatio-temporal location, as long as they differ in their modal properties, which is something that friends of more coarse-grained views of events would not accept.[11] But I am not interested in assessing the prospects of the commensuration view as an objection to CC here. Instead, I'm interested in examining the prospects of that view as a way of *improving on* CC.

How could the commensuration view be used to improve on CC? Take, first, the fact that the prince's eating the biscuits didn't cause the queen's plant's death. On the basis of the commensuration view, we could say that this is because something with a 'poorer essence,' namely, the prince's failure to water the plant, would have been sufficient for the plant's death. (The prince's eating the biscuits has a 'richer essence' than his failing to water the plant in the sense that it takes more for him to eat the biscuits than it does for him to fail to water the plant: if he was eating the biscuits on his lounge chair, he was at the very least not watering the plant, but there are other requirements on what he was doing.) So his eating the biscuits isn't commensurate with the plant's death, even if the plant's death counterfactually depends on his eating the biscuits. Also, we could say that the prince's failure to water the plant didn't cause his stomach ache because something with a richer essence, namely, his eating the biscuits, was needed for his stomach ache to obtain. Again, his failure to water the plant isn't commensurate with the stomach ache, even if the stomach ache counterfactually depends on his failure to water the plant.

Importantly, following Yablo, one could try to cash out all of these claims in purely counterfactual terms, thus preserving the spirit of a counterfactual view. For example, we could say that the eating of the biscuits didn't cause the plant's death because something less specific than the eating of the biscuits was sufficient, and that this is true in virtue of the truth of the following counterfactual:

> If the prince's failure to water the plant had obtained *without his eating the biscuits,* then the plant's death would still have occurred.

Also, we could say that the failure to water the plant didn't cause the stomachache because something more specific was needed, and that this is true in virtue of the truth of the following counterfactual:

> If the prince's failure to water the plant had obtained *without his eating the biscuits,* then the stomachache wouldn't have occurred.

With this in mind, we could revise CC as follows:

(CC*)   If there is (ordinary) counterfactual dependence between C and E (where C and E are fully distinct), *and if nothing less specific than C is sufficient for E and nothing more specific than C is needed for E,* then C is a cause of E.

where the locutions 'less/more specific,' 'sufficient,' and 'needed' have to be understood as explained earlier. To be clear: CC* is not Yablo's own preferred approach. Whereas CC* states a sufficient condition on causation, Yablo regarded commensuration more as a necessary condition on causation than as a sufficient condition.[12] Also, he never tried to apply the proposal to negative causes. Still, I think that Yablo's ideas about commensuration can be naturally applied to our problem at hand, and this is what CC* attempts to capture.

Now, is retreating to CC* a satisfactory solution to the Prince of Wales problem? I will offer two main reasons to be sceptical.

First, it's important to realize that, on this picture, counterfactual dependence is no longer sufficient for causation (if anything, it's *commensuration* that's sufficient for causation). This can still be within the spirit of a counterfactual view if, as Yablo suggests, commensuration itself can be spelled out in counterfactual terms. But the resulting view no longer has the neatness and simplicity of the counterfactual criterion that might have seemed attractive in the first place (or what was left of such neatness and simplicity after the necessary refinements discussed when we first introduced CC).

Second, retreating to CC* introduces new problems of its own for the idea that we can give sufficient conditions for causation in counterfactual terms. Interestingly, these are *pre-emption* problems.

Let me explain. Consider, again, the relation between the prince's failure to water the plant and his stomachache. Let 'C' be the non-watering and 'E' the stomach ache. E counterfactually depends on C: had the prince watered the plant, he wouldn't have had a stomach ache (because he wouldn't have eaten the biscuits). CC* attempts to avoid the implication that the non-watering caused the stomach ache by claiming that the non-watering isn't commensurate with the stomach ache. The non-watering isn't commensurate with the stomach ache because something more specific (the eating of the biscuits; call it 'D') was needed for the stomach ache to occur. And this is supposed to be captured by the fact that, had the prince not watered the plant *while failing to eat the biscuits,* the stomach ache wouldn't have occurred (had C occurred without D, E would not have occurred). But we may imagine a slightly different scenario where, had C occurred without D, E would still have occurred. For example, imagine that, had the prince failed to water the plant and failed to eat the biscuits, he would have gone for a walk outside, when it was bitterly cold, and this would equally have resulted in a stomach ache. In that scenario D wasn't needed for E to occur (although of course it still causes E). So, presumably, in that case CC* would entail that the non-watering causes the stomach ache.[13] But, again, this is the wrong result.

In other words, once we move from CC to CC*, the counterfactual criterion faces problems that used to be just problems for the claim that counterfactual dependence is necessary for causation. Pre-emption becomes a problem, not just for the idea that counterfactual dependence (or something close to it) is necessary for causation, but also for the idea that counterfactual dependence (or something close to it) is sufficient for causation. This is not a promising result.

5 Conclusion

I have argued that counterfactual views of causation cannot accommodate causation by omission while remaining faithful to the motivation for accepting that kind of causation. In this final section I attempt to generalize this result.

Some philosophers reject the possibility of causation by omission. Still, some of these philosophers feel the need to provide an account of the relation that omissions can bear to outcomes, in virtue of which agents can be morally responsible for those outcomes. Notably, Dowe has offered an account of a relation of this kind, which he called 'quasi-causation' (Dowe 2000, 2001, 2004). According to Dowe, omissions can quasi-cause outcomes, and it is in virtue of this relation of quasi-causation that agents can be morally responsible by omission. Quasi-causation is a counterfactual relation. Basically, whereas for a counterfactual theorist of causation who believes in causation by omission counterfactual dependence between an omission and an outcome is the mark of a causal relation between the omission and the outcome, for Dowe it is the mark of a quasi-causal relation. As far as I can see, everything I've said about the prospects of a counterfactual theory of causation can be said, *mutatis mutandis,* about a counterfactual theory of quasi-causation like Dowe's.

Briefly, for someone like Dowe, the problem arises as follows. We think that agents can be responsible for outcomes in the world in different ways. Sometimes they are responsible in virtue of having caused those outcomes. Other times they are responsible without causing those outcomes. So we need to find a new way to account for the agents' responsibility in these scenarios. Let's call this fact 'the inadequacy fact about *causes.*' The inadequacy fact about causes motivates the search for a new theory, a theory of 'quasi-causation.' It is natural to try to give such a theory in counterfactual terms. But a counterfactual theory of quasi-causation would face the Prince of Wales problem. For similar arguments to those offered here would show that there are 'fake' counterfactual dependencies between genuine causes and the upshots of quasi-causes as well as between quasi-causes and the upshots of genuine causes. As a result, a counterfactual theory of quasi-causation would fail to respect the initial motivation for giving a theory of that kind, i.e. the inadequacy fact about causes.

To conclude: the Prince of Wales problem is not just a problem for counterfactual theories of causation. It is a more general problem that arises for any theory that attempts to understand the contribution of omissions in counterfactual terms.

Notes

For helpful comments, thanks to Juan Comesaña, Dan Hausman, Allan Hazlett, Patrick Monaghan, Elliott Sober, and audiences at the University of Iowa and the 2009 Pacific APA.

1. For a more extensive discussion of these problems, see Lewis 1986a, 1986b, and 1986c.
2. A few people would reject CC. Thomson would reject it on the grounds that it entails, for example, that a person's birth always causes that person's death

(Thomson 2003, section 11). Lewis responds to an objection of this kind in his 2002, p. 101. Hall (2004) also rejects CC, but only for one concept of causation (he thinks there are two concepts of causation: the 'productive' concept and the 'dependence' concept). Yablo (1992) also rejects CC. Yablo's view is particularly relevant for our purposes; I discuss it in Section 4.

3. To say that counterfactual theories have the basic resources to account for causation by omission is not to say that there aren't problems arising from the intangibility and elusive nature of omissions. Lewis, in particular, had trouble fitting causation by omission into his general picture of causation and events (see Lewis 1986a, postscript D). He takes on the topic of causation by omission again in Lewis 2004.

4. Of course, this is consistent with there being good overall reasons for rejecting counterfactual theories (as well as for rejecting the possibility of causation by omission). For a recent debate about the legitimacy of causation by omission, see Dowe 2004 and Schaffer 2004 (Schaffer is in favour, and Dowe is opposed).

5. I gave the problem this label in Sartorio 2004.

6. Maybe something he did *earlier* contributed to the plant's death. This would be the case if, for example, he had poisoned the queen's plant earlier that day and, as a result, the plant needs to be watered now in order to survive.

7. Why isn't it backtracking? Someone could argue that it is backtracking by pointing out that, by the time the prince started eating the biscuits, he had already made up his mind to not water the plant. So the counterfactual 'Had the prince not eaten the biscuits, the plant wouldn't have died' comes out true only if we assume that the prince's antecedent process of deliberation resulted in a different outcome, in other words, only if we assume that the past is different in a certain way. However, this reasoning is not really backtracking, at least not in Lewis' sense. According to Lewis, we must allow for a 'transition period' and imagine that the *immediate* past is different in some (non-fully specified) ways; otherwise there would be abrupt discontinuities in the facts and thus major violations of the laws (Lewis 1986c, pp. 39–40). So, unless the prince made up his mind well in advance, the counterfactual dependence between the prince's eating the biscuits and the plant's death would be of the ordinary type. Lewis's view aside, note that, if the counterfactual about the prince is backtracking, so is *any* counterfactual stating that an agent would have intentionally done Y if he hadn't intentionally done X, when the agent is deciding between X and Y. But we assert counterfactual claims of this kind all the time.

8. I draw attention to this fact in a different context in Sartorio (2009).

9. Even if it is unreasonable to expect that the prince would do any of those things (as we have seen, it is unreasonable to expect that the queen would water my plant, but this doesn't prevent her from being a cause of its death in virtue of not watering it).

10. *Most* of them, but not *all* of them, because eating a dozen burgers would also have resulted in a stomach ache.

11. E.g., Davidson 1967. The distinction between actions and omissions on which this paper rests is, I think, much more basic and established than the distinction between, say, the event of Socrates' guzzling the hemlock and the event of his simply drinking it.

12. I think this is because he took the consensus to be that the problems for the sufficiency of counterfactual dependence for causation are more serious than those for its necessity. This might be right of the time when he wrote his article. As I have pointed out, the consensus now appears to be that the opposite is true.

13. CC* would only entail this if nothing more specific was needed (and if no event with a poorer essence was sufficient). Of course, I haven't shown this. But I take it that Yablo's idea is that the event that plays the role of D is the event that is actually the cause. And that event is, in this case too, the eating of the biscuits.

Bibliography

Beebee, H. (2004), 'Causing and Nothingness,' in Collins, Hall, and Paul (eds.), *Causation and Counterfactuals* (Cambridge, MA: MIT Press), pp. 291–308.

Davidson, D. (1967), 'Causal Relations,' *Journal of Philosophy* 64.

Dowe, P. (2000), *Physical Causation* (Cambridge: Cambridge University Press).

—— (2001), 'A Counterfactual Theory of Prevention and "Causation" by Omission,' *Australasian Journal of Philosophy* 79 (2), 216–26.

—— (2004) 'Causes Are Physically Connected to Their Effects: Why Preventers and Omissions Are Not Causes,' in Hitchcock (ed.) *Contemporary Debates in Philosophy of Science* (Oxford: Blackwell), ch. 9.

Hall, N. (2004), 'Two Concepts of Causation,' in Collins, Hall, and Paul (eds.), *Causation and Counterfactuals* (Cambridge, MA: MIT Press), pp. 225–76.

Kim, J. (1973), 'Causes and Counterfactuals,' *The Journal of Philosophy* 70 (17), 570–2.

Lewis, D. (1986a), 'Causation,' in his *Philosophical Papers II* (New York: Oxford University Press), pp. 159–213.

—— (1986b), 'Events,' in his *Philosophical Papers II* (New York: Oxford University Press), pp. 241–269.

—— (1986c) 'Counterfactual Dependence and Time's Arrow,' in his *Philosophical Papers II* (New York: Oxford University Press), pp. 32–66.

—— (2002), 'Causation as Influence,' reprinted Collins, Hall, and Paul (eds.), *Causation and Counterfactuals* (Cambridge, MA: MIT Press, 2004), pp. 75–106.

Lewis, D. (2004), 'Void and Object,' in Collins, Hall, and Paul (eds.), *Causation and Counterfactuals* (Cambridge, MA: MIT Press), 277–90.

McGrath, S. (2005), 'Causation by Omission: A Dilemma,' *Philosophical Studies* 123, 125–48.

Sartorio, C. (2004), 'How to Be Responsible for Something Without Causing It,' *Philosophical Perspectives* 18, 315–36.

Sartorio, C. (2009), 'Omissions and Causalism,' *Noûs* 43(3), 513–30.

Schaffer, J. (2000), 'Causation by Disconnection,' *Philosophy of Science* 67, 285–300.

Schaffer, J. (2004), 'Causes Need Not Be Physically Connected to Their Effects: The Case for Negative Causation,' in Hitchcock (ed.), *Contemporary Debates in Philosophy of Science*, (Oxford: Blackwell), ch. 10.

Thomson, J. (2003), 'Causation: Omissions,' *Philosophy and Phenomenological Research* 66 (1), 81–103.

Yablo, S. (1992), 'Cause and Essence,' *Synthese* 93, 403–49.

Index